A GOVERNMENT OF LAWS

A GOVERNMENT OF LAWS Political

Theory, Religion, and the

American Founding

Ellis Sandoz

Louisiana State University Press *Baton Rouge and London*

Designer: Pat Crowder
Typeface: Linotron 202 Sabon
Typesetter: G & S Typesetters, Inc.

LIBRARY OF CONGRESS CATALOGING-IN-PUBLICATION DATA
Sandoz, Ellis, 1931–
    A government of laws : political theory, religion, and the
American founding / Ellis Sandoz.
        p.   cm.
    Essays originally published in various publications between
1971–1988.
    Bibliography: p.
    Includes index.
    ISBN 0-8071-1551-7 (cloth)
    ISBN 0-8071-1711-0 (paper)
    1. Political science—United States—History.   2. Civil rights—
United States—History.   I. Title.
JA84.U5S26   1989
320.5'0973—dc20   89-33787
                                                        CIP

Louisiana Paperback Edition, 1991
00 99 98 97 96 95   5 4 3 2

To the memory of Eric Voegelin

And the rule of law, it is argued, is preferable to that of any individual. . . . For he who bids the law rule may be deemed to bid God and Reason alone rule, but he who bids man rule adds an element of the beast; for desire is a wild beast, and passion perverts the minds of rulers, even when they are the best of men. The law is reason unaffected by desire.

—ARISTOTLE

All good government is republican; . . . the only valuable part of the British constitution is so; for the true idea of a republic is an empire of laws, and not of men; and, therefore, as a republic is the best of governments, so that particular combination of power which is best contrived for a faithful execution of the law, is the best of republics.

—JOHN ADAMS (1776)

Contents

Preface and Acknowledgments

A Government of Laws is a book I have been thinking about and writing for many years. Its subject never was far from my mind and steadily commanded deep interest, even when my research was directed to other apparently unrelated subjects.

The thread of abiding interest lay in a sense that much of the usual fare relating to the American political order obscured as much as it clarified by not exploring the intellectual, spiritual, and institutional roots of American experience. There is more to America than many academicians have dreamt of and certainly a great deal more to it than most are prepared to write about. The chief flaws lay in stopping too soon historically and failing to pursue the philosophical issues to the point where American experience converged with the universal and perennial theories of humankind. The profundities tended to be eclipsed by the superficialities, leading to a disquieting tacit assumption that there were no profundities, or at least, none worth discussing.

Exactly when and how I first arrived at such views is obscure to me now, but they were certainly present during undergraduate days in college. During that same time, I was struck by the coincidence of concerns and insights of chief spokesmen of the American order and of the great classical philosophers of antiquity. This intuition matured, as I silently tested it over time, into the kind of conviction characteristic of knowledge. A component of that conviction, for example (and not the least important component of it), was that the In God We Trust imprinted on the coins in our pockets represented in laconic American fashion the report of a cultural consensus. A vision of comprehensive reality lies at the center of American experience that, to considerable extent, is unintelligible without it. Yet that contextual and existential dimension is routinely ignored in typical secularizing accounts of the American mind and culture, once the Puritan epoch of the seventeenth century is left behind.

After refining and revising my persistent intuition on the basis of a study of the relevant materials and years of discussion, I offer the results herein as something of a corrective to the various deficiencies just hinted and more fully investigated in the course of the work before you. The core of the book is an attempt to relate the political consensus of the American founding, as the focal point of the study, to the heritage of politics, philosophy, and religion that consciously informs it. The several elements in this illustrative analysis are held together by the common theme of relating the novelties of the American founding to the great tradition of Western political theory and praxis.

For this purpose, not only the American colonial or even the merely English experiences but also a broad canvass of adapted experience and theoretical insight drawn from Renaissance, medieval, and ancient sources receive consideration. Since neither political archaeology nor complacent antiquarianism but the roots of the American order is the subject, however, I would stress at the outset the thesis here argued: the American founders consciously, explicitly, and shrewdly sought within the limits of the practicable to establish a just political order, one fully attentive to the demands of human nature and its differentiated ontological structure. Hence, the American founding as limned herein is concerned with both justice and truth beyond evident pragmatic concerns that are familiar to us and are better understood. Moreover, as the terms *justice* and *truth* themselves imply, the founding is immediately directed to both action and knowledge in the respective spheres of politics and theory. The comprehensive reality contemplated by the founders, in other words, demanded of them a reflective assessment of their own efforts as participants fully aware of the whole hierarchy of being and their humanly creative role in it, as we shall presently see.

The unique and parochial in the founding are quite consciously embedded, at least in the minds of leading lights of the period such as Adams, Jefferson, and Madison, in the philosophers' quest for a just order. This means the founding as intended conduces to the fostering and, perchance, attainment of liberty and happiness in the spectrum of meaning evoked by those symbols in classical, biblical, and modern sources. These existential insights are amplified and institutionalized in the American founding as both presupposition and fruition of *novus ordo seclorum.* Finally, it is the argument of the study that the skein of truth then uncovered and symbolized in language and social vessels as the cogent basis of concord, public order, and well-being at the time retains its validity and vitality into the present. It continues to serve as the pulse and standard of American reality in the contemporary world and, equally, to be experienced by the affected community as a particular historical embodiment of the enduring truth of universal reality.

Acknowledgment of support and for permission to reprint materials previously published in different form are appreciatively given to the following organizations and entities. Support for research at various times and in various ways or other direct assistance was provided by Louisiana State University, Earhart Foundation, John M. Olin Foundation, Liberty Fund, Inc., Henry E. Huntington Library, Texas Education Association, Exxon Education Foundation, Marguerite Eyer Wilbur Foundation, White Burkett Miller Center of Public Affairs of the University of Virginia, American Antiquarian Society, Lynde and Harry Bradley Foundation, and the Doheny Library of the University of Southern California. I am grateful to all of them and hope none is disappointed with the result of my efforts.

While the Introduction was first delivered as a lecture and published in Spanish translation as "Reflexiones sobre Naturaleza Humana, Politica y Democracia" (with a commentary by Mario Gongora), in *Revista de Ciencia Politica,* V (1983), 95–116, the English original is published herein for the first time. Chapter One was published originally in *Review of Politics,* XXXIII (1971), 95–121. Chapter Two was published originally in *Journal of Politics,* XXXIV (1972), 2–36. Chapter Three was published originally in *Modern Age,* XXV (1981), 14–25. Chapter Four was published originally in Francis P. Canavan (ed.), *Ethical Dimensions of Political Life: Essays in Honor of John H. Hallowell* (Durham, N.C.: 1982), 200–15, 267–70. Chapter 6 was published originally in briefer form as "The Constitution and Civil Rights in the Founding," in *To Secure The Blessings of Liberty: First Principles of the Constitution,* ed. Sara Baumgartner Thurow (Lanham, Md., 1988), 172–88, Vol. I of *Constitutionalism in America,* ed. Thurow, 5 vols. projected. Chapter 7 was published originally in *Social Science Quarterly,* LXVIII (1987), 723–44 (© University of Texas Press). I am grateful to each of these journals and respective copyright holders for permission to republish here. All of these materials have been revised for inclusion in the book.

Lastly, a word of affectionate appreciation goes to my wife Alverne and my younger daughter Erica, who took time out from wedding preparations to proofread the final typescript with all the tender, loving care that accompanies everything they do to help me personally and professionally. Musicians, it turns out (or at least these two), make astonishingly good proofreaders.

A GOVERNMENT OF LAWS

INTRODUCTION Human Nature,

Politics, and Democracy

I wish to begin by reflecting on the question of man: "Human Nature, Politics, and Democracy." We have in the contemporary crisis of Western civilization *two* great crises. One relates to the social and economic organization that is most conducive to human well-being and prosperity. This is age old. In the Gospel we are told, "The poor you have with you always" (Matt. 26:11). This is not to say that we need to rejoice in that sad fact, of course, but there is another crisis that we must consider, too. This is the contemporary crisis of the spirit. It is the crisis of the intellectual integrity of human existence. And I wish to reflect upon that because, after all, whatever the political order may be, the fundamental requirement is that the political order be a fit habitation for human beings.

I stress this criterion: *a fit habitation for human beings.* This, then, goes to the heart of the question, which is certainly not a new one (in fact, all of the good questions are very old): *What is man?* We remember Job in the midst of his tribulations and the extraordinary attention he was receiving from on high asking this fundamental question. Job cries out: "What is man, that you should magnify him? and that you should set your heart upon him? and that you should visit him every morning, and try him every moment?"[1] And the psalmist somewhat more cheerfully, one would say, again repeats the great

---

1. Job 7:17.

question: "What is man, that you are mindful of him and the son of man that you visit him? For you have made him a little lower than the angels, and have crowned him with glory and honor. You made him to have dominion over the works of your hands; you have put all things under his feet."[2]

Now from the horizon of revelation, of which we are reminded by these familiar passages, we may turn to the horizon of the philosophers. Information about man and his ultimate place in reality comes to us from two principal sources in our Western civilization, namely, from the prophets and apostles of our biblical heritage that we find in Judaism and Christianity, and from the inventors of philosophy in antiquity, the Hellenic pre-Socratic philosophers as well as from Socrates, Plato, and Aristotle, who perfected philosophy. If we glance at the very first treatise in political science, we find Aristotle, who was Plato's pupil for twenty years, beginning with the question of man. After all, if we are to devise an optimal, or at least a moderately satisfactory order for men, we must understand *who* it is that will occupy this habitation so as to be able to judge its fitness for human occupancy. In the whole history of political theory, right down to the most urgent contemporary debates about social and political order, are on the surface, or very near to it, fundamental questions about the nature of human beings and human existence itself. And we must notice that the question is not about some *other* reality. It is not about *them;* rather it is about *us.* Who are we? Ask him who he is, Socrates urges in the *Protagoras.*[3] This is the abiding question of being. We begin with an understanding developed in classical antiquity, not least of all because the anthropology (or the theory of man) that is developed in antiquity is, with modification, adopted in the Middle Ages as the keystone of Christian anthropology. First of all, this applies to a degree in Augustine already, but then it certainly continues in Thomas Aquinas when Aristotle becomes *the* Philosopher.

My discussion has two facets. One facet is to remind us of our birthright and to recollect it. We live in a house that we did not make—a house called our civilization, our language, our forms of thought, and our conceptions of reality, a house that composes the

2. Ps. 8:4–6.
3. Plato *Protagoras* 311.

reality that *is* preeminently human reality. The second facet is this: I am not interested in providing definitions, engaging in a polemic, talking in terms of propositions, dealing with this or that doctrine, or teaching. Rather, I wish to speak in a common sense and persuasive way that goes to our common experience of our humanity. Ultimately, the question that underlies any philosophical discussion is always Socrates' question: Look and see if this is not the case.[4] This question does not mean ring doorbells and knock on doors to take a public opinion poll as a validation test. Instead, Socrates means for us to consult the content of our own personal experience; consider the matter with our reason; consult with those whose opinions are worthy of consultation; and honestly ascertain, as far as we can, whether or not what is asserted truly conforms with the realities. These, then, compose the facts of our own experience, and to that we can give a rather strong name and speak of *existential truth*. This designates the truth of human existence as empirically ascertained, *i.e.*, as sifted and winnowed through the process of a person's reflective powers and honestly confronting experienced reality.

This, then, will indicate the reflective and persuasive spirit of the present introduction. I shall briefly and in broad strokes first discuss the classical and the Judaeo-Christian conceptions of man and then turn to two very different modern traditions: to *radical* man, as found especially in Mikhail Bakunin, Karl Marx, Auguste Comte, and Friedrich Nietzsche; and to the liberal tradition of democracy and *liberal* man, which is represented especially by John Locke in the seventeenth century and by the American founders in the eighteenth century. Finally, I shall make general remarks about the nature of politics and why the notion of saving mankind through politics is, indeed, not only mistaken but ultimately disastrous.

I

First, a little about Aristotle. Plato advances in the *Republic* a fundamental proposition—a fundamental insight—about politics, and he has Socrates do it in a sly and unobtrusive way. The nub of it is that the *polis* is man written large. This conveys the insight that the sub-

4. E.g., Plato *Crito* 49; *Gorgias* 495; *Republic* 349.

stance of the *polis,* of the political, social, and economic order, is *man;* and the substance of man is *psyche* or soul. Eric Voegelin called this insight the anthropological principle.[5] Further, Socrates argues that we cannot attain a true anthropology unless we first have a true theology. He elaborates a basic theology and then continues with the explanation of man (of personal no less than of social reality, interchangeably) and the question of Justice (*Dike*), which is the ostensible theme of the *Republic* (379–92.) This points up a basic question for us no less than for Aristotle. If we ask ourselves *what* is the political order, how do we define it? Is it a territory or a set of institutions that can be identified and studied as phenomena? Is it this or that particular characteristic? Ultimately, Plato gives the answer: the substance of politics is *psyche,* or soul. We would say, not to be thought old-fashioned, that the substance of politics is *consciousness.* What does this mean? It means that the order and disorders of politics are orders and disorders in the souls of the men and women who constitute society.

Here is the fundamental starting point for the understanding of politics as we have it from the hands of the philosophers of antiquity.[6] It gives rise to the discussion of health and disease in the soul in language adapted from Hypocratic medicine and intended to clarify the fundamental matter at issue, which is, in dealing with justice and injustice, good and evil, right and wrong, and questions of what is conducive to human well-being, the philosophers are concerned not merely with external behavior but with the order and disorders of consciousness present in the society under scrutiny. Thus, if we have a diseased leadership or a ruler who is a tyrant, to recall the great analysis of tyranny and other declining forms in Books VIII and IX of the *Republic* (543–76), then we can understand that the sort of maladies represented can more generally be imputed to the society itself. Society has no existence apart from the human beings who compose it.

Aristotle takes over all of this from Plato and critically elaborates his own theory of man and politics. At the beginning of the *Ethics,* he

5. Plato *Republic* 368–69; Eric Voegelin, *Plato and Aristotle* (Baton Rouge, 1957), 68–70. Vol. III of Voegelin, *Order and History.*

6. *Cf.* Aristotle *Nicomachean Ethics* I. 2. 8. 1094b10, ed. and trans. Martin Ostwald (Indianapolis, 1962).

gives the familiar analysis that man's nature is indeed complex. There are three aspects: synthetic, essential, and political nature. Man, he says (and he asks us to think with him and to see if this is not the case), has a physical being that is both inorganic and organic. He has a vegetative nature; he has an animal nature, which he shares with the beasts of the field. His *psyche,* or soul, which is specifically human, is divided between the passions and reason, and reason itself is divided between the part that is calculative or instrumental (which can be represented by the participle as that part of mind which engages in *reasoning*), and the noetic reason of intuition, whereby human beings arrive at first principles. Aristotle gives this, it is vital to notice, not simply as a content inventory of man but as an experienced reality that is empirically verifiable (so we can ask whether this accurately represents our being) and calls it the composite or the synthetic nature of man. More than this, however, he also describes it as having another importance, insofar as man *participates* in all strata of being. The language of *participation* was invented by Plato and applied and elaborated by Aristotle out of the cognitive awareness that man participates in all levels of reality, from the merely physical reality of the stone to the divine reality of the God whose activity is a thinking on thinking. Understood in this way, "human" reason (or Aristotle's *nous*), including intuitive intellect, is in some sense the same as the mind of the divine, and *man* is the epitome of being (*Metaphysics* XII.9.4).

While man participates in all of these levels, his uniqueness lies in reason, the *differentia specifica* of man *qua* man, and his highest faculty. The hierarchical structure analyzed by Aristotle has, then, twin aspects of foundation and formation. There is an order of *foundation* in that man is founded in the world. He is founded in a physical reality. Human "nature" does not exist apart from a presence in concrete human beings. Every human being is founded in this structured or hierarchical series of grades from the bottom (so to speak) up to the point where he participates in the divine being as his own true self. Noetic participation in divine being distinguishes man from all other beings, insofar as man thereby has something of the divine in him. This is the order of foundation. The order of *formation* is from the "top" down. We are *founded* physically, but we are *formed* by highest reality. It is participation in highest reality that distinguishes men from other beings and makes them uniquely what they are. Aristotle calls this divine reality *Reason*. Standards of order for men are imposed by reason.

In addition, a tensional relationship must be understood. Aristotle always defines from the best case, from the end. The nature of the acorn is the oak tree; the nature of man is displayed in the man who fulfills his potential as a human being and lives as a mature man (*spoudaios*), or optimally, the best case. This discloses the horizon for human endeavor and human actualization. All of the language of potential and actual that the Scholastic philosophers, including Thomas Aquinas, later utilize arises from this biological metaphor, which is then woven into the account of ethics and politics contained in the *Nicomachean* and *Eudemian Ethics* and the *Politics*. Virtues or various excellences become the means to actualization. Moral and intellectual virtues are enumerated, followed by others that are not specifically called excellences. Yet the space given to *friendship* and *prudence,* the discussion of *immortalizing* toward the end of the *Nicomachean Ethics* suggest a further class of existential virtues. Love, faith, and hope were coined, we should recall, not by the Apostle Paul, who made them the chief Christian virtues, but by Heraclitus. At least they are present in Heraclitus' fragments.[7]

These symbols designate fundamental *tensions* of human reality. Thus, the existential virtue of love, the affection that we bear toward one another, and the relationships that are basic to any kind of free community can be called an existential virtue. This is what makes life worth living. Aristotle terms it *philia* and discusses it marvelously for two books (Books VIII and IX) in the *Ethics*. Near the end of Book X is a powerful discussion of the paradox that reason is the specific essence of man. Reason above all else—reason as Aristotle understands it and tries to elaborate it as a symbol—distinguishes man. Yet there is a paradox, for the reason that apparently is uniquely human is not *solely* man's, because man, through reason, participates in divine Reason. In a remarkable passage Aristotle exhorts: "Do not follow those

7. *Cf.* Hermann Diels and Walter Kranz, *Die Fragmente der Vorsokratiker* (7th ed.; Berlin, 1954), Heraclitus frags. B 18, 27, 34, 86, 107, 123.

who advise us to have merely human thoughts since we are [only] men and mortal thoughts as mortals should, [but] on the contrary we should try [to] become immortal as far as that is possible and [to] do our utmost to live in accordance with what is highest in us. For though this is small in bulk, it far surpasses everything else in power and value. One might even regard it as each man's true self, since it is the controlling and better part. It would, therefore, be strange if a man chose not to live his own life but someone else's."[8]

A further attribute is to be recalled, namely, the insight that man is naturally a political being. Aristotle gives this relational factor at the beginning of the *Politics* as being the basis of man's association, and he identifies man as a *politikon zoon* (as a political living being). He says this is to be more than merely gregarious.[9] The bees are gregarious; the cattle are gregarious; wolves are gregarious and run in packs; but man is political. What distinguishes them? What is the specific distinction of being political? In a word, men associate on the basis of their capacity for rational speech, and they alone have a moral sense. A capacity for reasoned speech is unique to humans. Other animals have voices, make sounds, and can express pain and pleasure, but man alone has the capacity for reasoned speech. Only human beings discern what is just and what is unjust, what is good and evil. Indeed, before the constitution of a community can become the basis of a political order, it depends upon a shared understanding of (or like-mindness about [*homonoia*]) justice and injustice. This is central—to the constitution of man as a political being and to concord in a society of free men.

II

In manifold ways, present to man's consciousness *is* this tensional dimension of participatory reality. Existentially, we are drawn to someone we love and are repelled by someone we dislike or hate. Similarly, we are drawn *naturally* to what is good, according to Plato's and

8. Aristotle *Nicomachean Ethics* X. 7. 8. 1177b32–1178a3; for context cf. *ibid*. I. 9. 3. and X. 8. 7. and 13.
9. Aristotle *Politics* I. 1. 10. 1253a3, trans. T. A. Sinclair (Harmondsworth, England, 1981).

Aristotle's analysis, which, of course, coincides with the Christian experience.[10] Yet we might not know the good we seek, and even if we know it, we might not find and enjoy it. This experience gives rise, then, to the core understanding in Christianity of sin as making an error or mistake about the good we seek; sin is a missing of the mark.[11] This understanding is rooted in Aristotelian psychology as generally augmented by the Gospels, the Judaic tradition, and Christianity. Of this seeking of the good, each of us can ask, Is this statement true? Do I, in fact, seek the good? Indeed, I do seek it. I seek what is beautiful, what is true, what is ennobling to me, and what is worth having. The opposite I would like to avoid—I wish to spurn it. The argument holds even in perversity, or so Bernard of Clairvaux maintains. This principle then applies to the whole hierarchial structure of man, including his material well-being as well as his emotional, intellectual, and spiritual spheres. The whole of man, *all* of man, is involved in this reaching out toward what is good, with the understanding that the highest good attainable by human action, according to Aristotle, is called happiness (*eudaimonia*) or blessedness (*makarios*) if it is emphatically the result of participation in divine being. The latter then becomes the wonderful understanding of union with God or beatitude that we get from Christianity as that is greatly elaborated by mystics in subsequent centuries. In principle, however, it is there already in the old Greek philosophers, which is the reason why Augustine does his best to baptize Plato. It is also why Aristotle comes so readily to hand in the work and mind of Thomas in the middle of the thirteenth century.

The tensional movement in consciousness develops as a striving for attunement: we seek attunement with truth as far as we can. If we do not attain it with some degree of satisfaction, then there is discord and misery in our own being. We become what is variously represented as evil, unjust, and unhappy men. The higher capacities do not master the lower. Such men may be a walking civil war, as was H. G. Wells' Mr. Polly. The revolt of the passions can overwhelm reason and bring existential disorientation. Such a malady can strike in personal life or be institutionalized in political reality, such as the lust for

---

10. *Cf.* Rom. 7:7–25; Thomas Aquinas *Summa Theologica* I–II. q. 109. a. 3.
11. The New Testament term for sin is *Hamartia* (*e.g.*, Rom. 3:23; I John 2:1–17).

power of the tyrant exemplified in Plato's *eros tyrannos*.[12] This ancient theory of politics and of man remains fundamental to our understanding of human existence.

The technical name for the human reality explored by the classical
philosophers is the *In-Between*. Man exists in the in-between reality.
Plato calls it the *Metaxy*. In the *Symposium* (202A) and *Philebus*
(16D–E) are found principal reflections on the metaxy, whose significance for present purposes can be summarized this way: man is neither brute nor is he God; he is something in-between. Ours is the in-
between reality of human existence and participation. The language
of participation is carried over into the Scholastic philosophers, but
the In-Between symbol will not be so familiar as a technical term for
man's existence. This fact has importance for contemporary political
science as well. Man's existence is *not* primarily an external or phenomenal reality but rather the In-Between existence of participation.
He is strung between mortality and immortality. He is capable of virtue and faith but inclined to vice and sin. He aspires to divinity but
knows that he is indeed lower than the angels. He is a "mixed bag,"
we might say. Man is capable of nobility but, as Soren Kierkegaard
remarks, he (who can live almost at the level of the angels) more often
than not lives like his dog. This pungent statement expresses an understanding of the human condition as the In-Between reality, *i.e.*, as the
permanent state of man seeking immortality but not finding perfection *in* this world.

There emerges, then, a horizon of reality symbolized with the spatial
indices *immanent* and *transcendent*. Because we have no discursive
transcendental language, we have to speak figuratively. Only Mozart
and other great artists overcome the poverty of the philosophers'
three-dimensional language. Yet we, however poorly we express it,
exist in a comprehensive reality which we know (and constantly tell
one another) is not merely the reality of the here and now. Rather, it is
reality that is divine and infinite as well as three-dimensional and
finite. *Somehow* we participate and *must* participate in both the temporal and the spiritual, *if* we are to live lives esteemed to be fit for
human beings. We get this entire ontological analysis from the classic
philosophers without any help from Hebrew prophets or Christian

12. Plato *Republic* 576–80.

apostles and saints. Of course, the biblical spokesmen augment and wonderfully enrich it.

The experience of what human existence is, as just adumbrated and symbolized in the metaxy as participatory existence in the in-between, can objectively be studied only on its own terms. This means not through the kind of science associated with the study of biology and chemistry and physics as phenomenal and mathematizing sciences, but only as a historical and philosophical science whose essentially meditative methods permit the arrival at a clearer grasp of the kinds of realities vital to men *qua* human beings. After all, goodness does not appear. It is not a phenomenon or a thing. Yet no one would say it is nothing. Similarly, justice does not appear nor can it be studied as an external something, except through indirection. And so on with love and the other indispensable goods that crown human existence. Thus, to explore consciousness and its structure, and the order and disorders of consciousness that exist in a particular personal, political, and social order, a different mode of analysis is requisite. That different mode of analysis constitutes historically what we are now reminding ourselves of, namely, the classical and Christian science of man as it has persisted in philosophy into the present.

A complicating factor must be reckoned with at this juncture. It arises in the discovery of transcendence, that there is a reality *beyond* visible reality (*epekeina; Republic* 509C). This is represented in Plato, for example, in the Allegory of the Cave and symbolized there in the Vision of the *Agathon*, or Good (*Republic* 514–21). Yet in a book-length dialogue Plato does not give one word about what the Good is. Why is that? The problem of ineffability. We can name the reality, thereby indicating its *thatness*, but we cannot give a blueprint of its *whatness*, the complete specifications of the furnishings and floor plan of the ultimate reality that human beings somehow touch—and emphatically (and not a little paradoxically) regard as more real than palpable reality.

The experiences of transcendence occur not only in the horizon of philosophy but, obviously, also in the horizon of revelation much before the philosophers, as with Moses and Abraham. In fact, such experiences are so characteristic of human thought that Karl Jaspers spoke of the Axis-time of history as being that period between 800 and 200 B.C. when human beings (without any cultural diffusion) in China, India, Israel, and ancient Greece all arrived at a wonderful common inference based upon equivalent but highly diverse spiritual experiences, namely, in Aristotle's term, that human existence is *not* merely mortal. Somehow it participates in the immortal and the divine, a decisive trait of universal mankind which was affirmed in this period, with Confucius, Laotse, the Buddha, Heraclitus, Pythagoras, and Deutero-Isaiah remarkably all being members of a single generation when the irruption of transcendence occurred most universally around the year 500 B.C. While there are difficulties in detail with the Axis-time conception, it is important for this point: man's existence, as he has interpreted it over the millennia, is open to transcendence.[13] And, of course, this is all we have. The only reality we have is the reality present to human consciousness, an elementary verity to be stressed. This is fortunately not just my consciousness or the contemporary generation's consciousness (which may be in very bad condition or at least not representative of the whole of mankind) but that of human beings of stature such as those I have mentioned, the true masterpieces of mankind.

Human existence for philosophers and for prophets, and certainly for saints as well as for the sages of other traditions, has been experienced-symbolized as structured by the kind of reach called transcendent and immanent. Thus, reality is not exhausted by the reality of the world, which would be the immanent side. The militant assertion that the reality of man *is* exhausted by immanent reality is a mark of the modern revolt, although Israel's tribulations with idolatries of one sort or another and Plato's struggle with the sophists tell us this is nothing new in principle. One consequence of the great differentiation of reality is to *de*-divinize the world and history. The gods are not *in* the world, or at least they are not *of* the world. This insight works the effective end of polytheism and the beginning of monotheism for a bench mark, especially in the West. The world is good as a creation but is not itself divine. This definition has consequences other than theological ones, of course. Obviously, God is transcen-

---

13. Karl Jaspers, *Vom Ursprung und Ziel der Geschichte* (Frankfurt-am-Main, 1955), 14–31; cf. Ellis Sandoz, *Voegelinian Revolution: A Biographical Introduction* (Baton Rouge, 1981), 103–104, 227–90.

dent. No man has seen God. Graven images are not to be carved to this God, for example, to recall the first commandments (Exod. 20:1–5). It is a Creator-creature relationship as symbolized in Genesis I. This means, however, that there is a *world* and no longer only a partly divine cosmos. The world that differentiates, then, is the world of nature, a world of nature and of a human existence in the in-between reality called *history*. It is that world over which man has dominion. It is not itself divine, even though it is good as coming from the hand of a good God.

This fundamental understanding is found not only in Genesis I, where it is expressed succinctly as well as elsewhere in the Bible, but also in the philosophers, *e.g.*, in the *Republic* (379–92). There, God is good and the author of only good things, Socrates says (380C-D). This is the first proposition he advances as his minimum theology or creed that everyone must accept if there is to be a true basis for understanding divine being. Reality itself is good, and the reality of the world is good but not divine. A consequence of this differentiation of reality, then, is the de-divinization of the world, which results in something we easily call nature; and nature can then be explored by science. When this break is not radical, as it is in the West, then there is trouble in having a natural science. Joseph Needham has spent over thirty years writing a huge and still unfinished "reconnaissance" of the history of science in China. He has struggled to find any modern science in China, one reason being that the break was not radical there. The divine and the non-divine have remained mixed up in the cosmos of the earlier experience. Differentiation was not full enough to generate a radically transcendent divine ground of being and a de-divinized world of nature and history as in the West, heir of Israel and Hellas. As a peculiarity and even something of a mystery, we have the fact that modern science and technology originate and mature preeminently in the West because, among other reasons, of the de-divinization of the world and nature, which then constitutes a presupposition for *natural* science and rational inquiry into nature and history.[14]

14. *Cf.* Joseph Needham, *Science and Civilization in China* (Cambridge, Eng., 1954–75), V, Pt. 3, xxii–xxxi and literature cited therein, for example. The term *de-divinization* is taken from Eric Voegelin, *New Science of Politics: An Introduction* (Chicago, 1952), 100–106.

III

With the triumph of Christianity in the West (in the fourth century A.D.) comes the paradigmatic figure of Christ as God Incarnate, the overwhelming emblem for 1,500 years of participatory reality whereby the radical otherness of transcendent divine Being is reconciled with the world and mankind in the mystery of the Atonement and salvation. Christian personalism, the understanding inherited from Judaism that every human being is created in the image and likeness of God and that this nature and personality are the foundation of the dignity of every single human being (not a general sort of oversoul or something that is merely a biological term), sharpens and deepens the understanding glimpsed in discussing Greek antiquity. The heightening of love as the cardinal virtue occurs through the experience of God as essentially love, as the tensional center of divine being whose goodness maintains constant communion with men and all creation.[15] Not only, then, is there human *equality* in the Classical and Stoic sense that all human beings possess a common nature but also in the Judaic and Christian sense that there is human equality in so far as there is a brotherhood of man, which comes from the hand of the loving Father and Creator of mankind. We are not our own creation, we are reminded. There is also an understanding of fundamental *liberty* as a structure present in the being of every man along with *reason*. Thus, the free will of man drawn to God in the turning from love of self to the *amor Dei* perfects both volition and reason through the embrace of truth. The creature then enjoys the true liberty symbolized in Anselm as *fides quaerens intellectum*, faith in search of understanding.

The Christian anthropology just summarized somehow gets short shrift in recent political discussions, but it constitutes the deepest basis for ever asserting that there ought to be democracy or self-rule by the people. *Democracy* is a rule *of, by,* and *for* the people, and rule *of, by,* and *for* the people in its modern version partakes heavily of something that it has not necessarily had in many Christian countries and did not widely have antiquity. In the modern period, rather

15. 1 Cor. 13; 1 John 4:7–21.

ironically, is a notion that insofar as there *is* this ineradicable natural integrity that inheres in every single human being, then there is also the claim buttressed in a variety of ways that democracy is *the* natural political order.

This conclusion is reached by several avenues and has more than one meaning, to be sure. To generalize (as we must), the assumption remains that a mature polity or political order will in some sense be an order in which all the population of the society not only is ruled but also has some share in ruling. The accent shifts to *man*—indeed, to *men*—as the center of politics. Their consent is essential to legitimize rule, and their well-being must be served if a regime is to be acceptable. These conceptions are as old as the Greek philosophers and the suffering servant of Deutero-Isaiah in certain respects. Yet they gain general ascendancy to become the hallmarks of actual governance, or reasonable aspirations to governance, only in the wake of the collapse of absolutism in the West and the coming of the Age of Democratic Revolution in the eighteenth century. At the very center of this development is a magnification of the dignity and worth of the individual human being, which is profoundly indebted to the philosophical and meditative traditions of the Christian West and, indeed, quite incomprehensible apart from them.

Numerous other influential factors merit attention, but at the center stands the conviction that institutions exist for men and not the reverse. This is most especially true for English and American societies. I argue, therefore, that the *foundation* for the sorts of assertions that are found in the first third of the American Declaration of Independence achieves its firmness and "self-evidence" primarily from *pre*-modern experiences. *All men are created equal and endowed by their Creator with certain unalienable rights,* including the rights to life, liberty, and the pursuit of Happiness. Happiness, happiness—*eudaimonia* and *makarios,* or *beatitudo,* or felicity, or what was it? It was happiness. Jefferson did not define the symbol, which was intended to cover the range of experience evoked by the rich ambiguity of the *summum bonum.*

The persistent tradition I have sketched constitutes the fundamentals of our conception of human existence and of its dignity, with happiness being the highest good attainable by human action, in Jefferson no less than in Aristotle. The difference lies in this: to Jefferson and his American contemporaries, "free government" and representative democracy are instituted as the overt means of fostering that happiness. This is a major innovation in politics, whatever the debt to Athenian democracy, the ancient Roman republic, and the Old Testament's primordial republic of Israel, from Moses and Joshua down to Samuel, last of the Judges.[16]

IV

We also have in the modern period, and especially since the Enlightenment, a revolt, indeed, a continuing series of revolts. The revolt is complex, more complex than I can here suggest. In terms of the discussion thus far, what happens in the modern period? To take only the worst and most famous case, let us reflect briefly on what happens to man at the hands of Karl Marx.

What is fundamental and to the point comes out early in Marx's career. In Thesis VI of the *Theses on Feuerbach* of 1845, *man* becomes a nodal point gathering in the sum total of social relationships. That means both man generically and each human being, since for Marx, individual essence has no reality apart from social life. Man is an "ensemble of social relations," no more and no less. What happened to the classic and Christian conceptions of man? Man—each man—is totally dissolved by Marx into the class structure of the society. He has *no* being apart from his social being. What lies behind that is suggested by a clue given in Thesis XI: "The philosophers have only *interpreted* the world in various ways; the point, however, is to *change* it." *Marx's* dissatisfaction lies with both science and reality. Scientists and philosophers, if the word *interpret* is given its due, have been trying (as Sir Francis Bacon said) to understand nature in order to command it.[17] To arrive at a truthful understanding or inter-

16. *Cf.* Exod. 18:13–26; Num. 11:16–17, 24–30; also Flavius Josephus *Antiquities of the Jews* III. 4. 1. The "Hebrew republic" was a commonplace of preachers during the American Revolution, as can be seen from Samuel Langdon's 1775 election sermon, later quoted in Chap. 5, p. 143.

17. Sir Francis Bacon, *New Organon*, Bk. I, Sec. 3.

pretation of reality is the very definition of science. This is not enough for Marx, who wishes to be a revolutionary. He wants a New Man and a New World, for the old man and the old world will not do. He therefore abandons both philosophy and science, and sets out as a revolutionary at the ripe old age of twenty-seven. He was a little depressed that Hegel had solved all philosophical problems, so all that an ambitious young man could aspire to do was *change* the world itself. All that is needed, he says, are *New Men*. A minor requirement! Karl Loewith marveled that Marx never seems to have blinked at the enormity of this program.

What is then afoot here is a question of how to get a New Man and a New World. Indeed, Marx requires a New Man who matches what Thomas Aquinas in the *Summa* gave as the famous definition of *God* as self-subsistent being. Marx applies this to *man*, who is alienated from his true being unless he is self-subsistent.[18] This is a particularly striking passage because it is just here that Marx specifically refuses to engage in philosophical discussion. Marx at least has the virtue of telling what he is about. Consider, after all, that he earned a doctorate in philosophy at age twenty-three and that he wrote his dissertation on Greek philosophy (it was accepted in 1841), quoting from Aeschylus for the epigraph. Marx there claims that the motto of modern philosophy can be taken from Prometheus' line, "In one word, I hate all the Gods." This hatred of divine being is the very motto of philosophy itself, as Marx will come to understand philosophy. But the next line from Aeschylus, which is not quoted by Marx, is spoken by Hermes: "Yes, but that is madness."[19] The irrationality or madness of man apart from divine being was clearly understood by Aeschylus. Hatred of divine being is the mark of the radical modern, and specifically of Marxian revolt.

As mentioned, this is driven home in a further line of the passage referred to in the 1844 manuscripts. There, Marx has an imaginary

---

18. Karl Marx, *Economic and Philosophic Manuscripts of 1844*, ed. Dirk J. Struik, trans. Martin Milligan (New York, 1964), 144–46; cf. Thomas Aquinas *Summa Theologica* I. q. 44. a. 1.

19. See Karl Marx, *Die Frühschriften*, ed. Siegfrid Landshut (Stuttgart, 1953), 246–48. Cf. Aeschylus *Prometheus Bound* lines 975–78. For a fuller discussion see Ellis Sandoz, *Political Apocalypse: A Study of Dostoevsky's Grand Inquisitor* (Baton Rouge, 1971), 114–18 and *passim*.

interlocutor ask pertinent questions, the fundamental one at issue being, where did reality come from? He said, who am I? The question, what is man? There is a little evasiveness on the part of Marx in this imaginary colloquy, and several uneasy rhetorical responses ensue, but the imaginary interlocutor properly insists. Finally, he will be put off no longer: I want to know where did I come from? "Who begot my father? Who is his grandfather? . . . Who begot the first man, and nature as a whole?" What is the origin and source of being? He asks, as we see, the question of questions, *the* fundamental question of all metaphysics. It is answered at the opening of Genesis: "In the beginning God created the heaven and the earth." It is answered by Aristotle in terms of the *arche,* or Prime Mover, the first cause that is itself uncaused, who is God and pure Mind.[20] The question is of the Ground of being, of the *beginning* in philosophical speculation, of the ultimate Reason of things (as Leibniz called it), of the divine beginning as we have it in the first verses of the Gospel of John—"In the beginning was the Word (*Logos*)"—and so on and so forth. The fundamental question of all thought is posed. What does Marx answer? At this point we touch the core of the modern radical revolt in its ontological and epistemological aspects. Marx prohibits the asking of the question: "Don't think, don't ask me (*Denke nicht, frage mich nicht*)." Stick to the reality under your eyes. A *socialist* man does not ask such irrational questions!

That response is the ominous signal not only of the abandoment of philosophy but also of any kind of rationality that can be called scientific, in so far as the first principles themselves have been abandoned and, along with them, any opportunity to arrive at an understanding of human reality. Dogma supplants reason and science, only so the murder of God can be sustained and the Socialist Superman—the paradigmatic New Man—can successfully usurp his place in a Second Reality of dreamworld imaginings. This verdict is elaborated by Albert Camus, who remarks, "Marxism is only scientific today in defiance of Heisenberg, Bohr, Einstein, and all the other greatest minds of our time."[21] Marx's "humanism" *obliterates* man by dissolving his

20. Aristotle *Metaphysics* XII. 6. 1–9. 6. 1071b4–75a11.

21. Albert Camus, *The Rebel: An Essay on Man in Revolt,* trans. Anthony Bower (New York, 1956), 222.

essence into sociology and abandoning noetic participation in favor of the dogmatic assertion of *libido dominandi* in radical rebellion and closure against divine being.

V

An alternative modern conception of man and democracy is associated with the English philosopher John Locke, the American founders, and what generally is called "liberal democracy." A complex set of new problems emerge at this juncture, as will be seen more fully in subsequent chapters. One acute problem is this: the turmoil of the breakdown of traditional societies through the rise of nation-states, the breakup of the universal church, eight wars of religious persecution in France alone in the sixteenth century, and a king beheaded in England in the next century. At the roots of much of this turmoil lie religious questions. A part of the extensive spiritual crisis revolved around the fact that, in the name of Christianity and the religion of love, everyone in Western civilization seemed to be doing his best to annihilate the human race. This grotesque situation pervades much of the debate in Europe in the sixteenth and seventeenth centuries, not least of all in England where the execution of Charles I (1649) greatly impressed Thomas Hobbes and influenced his attempt to find a basis for re-establishing order.

Enter John Locke, a physician. In general, medical doctors are, for all their expertise, pragmatic people. Locke, viewed as a famous political philosopher, was such a man. An epistemologist and natural philosopher, Locke was a friend of Newton, whose own keen mind embraced a high philosophical interest. Yet Locke, the *political* philosopher, was a man who wanted, somehow, to find a new basis for peace and liberty in society. However unsatisfactory any given peace may or may not be, it generally is better than the war it avoids.

Essentially, Locke was seeking a way out of a century of bitter animosities and the great difficulties that affected England and the West. To be sure, other factors were present, too. The fall from faith is part of the phenomenon of this contending sectarian strife that so divided English society as well as the Continental societies. Locke fomented resistance to the tyranny decried in the Stuart kingship, so he was no advocate of peace at any price, as was Hobbes. Rather, Locke's chief thrust, as I reflect on what Locke was about, was to find a new foundation for political association other than the one that had obtained through the long 2,000 years since Aristotle as modified by Christianity in the intervening centuries—namely, reliance upon the principle of a mutually agreed upon conception of justice and injustice of an intellectual and spiritually satisfactory kind. Locke sought a new basis because of the intractable turmoil of his times. He looked in the inventory of human characteristics, and he lowered his sights a bit by largely (but not entirely) abandoning the political goals of inculcating virtue and righteousness in citizens or subjects. He modified in the process the social contract theory whereby more modest goals become central. On this approach, it is agreed that human beings order society for the purpose of securing their lives, liberties, and estates, which Locke then calls *property* as a portmanteau term. *All that one is*—his life, liberty, and possessions—constitutes his property.[22] Men then enter into society and impose law and government upon themselves, Locke says, so as mutually to enjoy life and liberty in peace and also to enjoy their possessions, to pursue wealth, to accumulate without stint, and to satisfy *generally* the desire to have (*amor habendi*).

Now the pivotal significance of the desire to have physical possessions, that is, property, is justified all the way back to Aristotle. One cannot exercise the virtue of a friend unless one has property, he writes; moreover, property matters fuel revolution. He criticizes (and distorts) Plato's proposal in the *Republic* of a communism of women, children, and property on the ground of their widespread unacceptability to civilized people, either as dubious novelties or as ideas long known but seldom embraced.[23] Not only are philosophers rational, but other human beings are as well, and tradition and custom are not devoid of reason, Aristotle suggests. What Edmund Burke in the eighteenth century would call the accumulated wisdom of the ages raises fundamental doubts about Socrates' proposals in the *Republic*. The other point, however, is if we cannot invite a friend down to the beach; if we have no boat to go sailing in when we get there; if we

22. *Cf.* John Locke, *Second Treatise of Government* [1689], Sec. 123.
23. Aristotle *Politics* II. 2. 10. 1264a2; II. 5. 4. 1269a19–33.

have no house in which to entertain him; if, in short, we have no property with which to express our generosity and affection, then our existence is indeed thereby impoverished of virtue and happiness. So there is a metaphysical justification of private property already in antiquity.[24]

Locke is aware of this as a student of political writing. He also understands the natural desire to have what is *good* and to possess, which is fundamental in the whole analysis of love itself. *Philia* and *Eros,* as they appear in Plato and Aristotle, and even the Christian *caritas* of the mystic's rise to the Beatific Vision, in various senses involve the desire to attain the thing loved. Love and possession of one's own comprise the bonds of personal and social relationship. Departure from the state of nature and the creation of society through the contract, as recounted by Locke, build on these ideas to order society so men are secure in what they love most: life, liberty, and estates.

The *end* of social and political existence, Locke however stresses, is to *secure* property, and the enjoyment of property is the fundamental characteristic and justification of government itself. We can, with justification, read this as materialism and as proto-*laissez faire* capitalism, but it is clearly more than this because of Locke's broad meaning of *property*. Moreover, he says, not only are we our own property, but we are also God's property. What at first appears to be a rather crass conception is also found in the work of the angelic doctor Thomas Aquinas, in his *Treatise on the Law* and his understanding that the world is indeed God's property.[25]

It is a fundamental notion that the end of government is modest: the goal of government is to secure life, liberty, and property. Politics does not exhaust human reality. The role of government is not to go out and conquer the world. It is not, by Locke's account, to translate human existence into a paradise or perfection of man and the world. Quite to the contrary, it is to put a lid on human action so liberty does not degenerate into license as happiness is pursued by individuals and groups. It is to remember that justice is both the end of civil society and, inevitably, imperfect because it is human. Human exis-

24. *Ibid.,* II. 2. 6–7. 1263a43–b14; II. 3. 5. 1265a29–39.
25. Thomas Aquinas *Summa Theologica* I–II. q. 94. a. 5.

tence, grand as it is, has *limits*. We may recall the grandeur seen by the psalmist quoted at the outset. Locke knew his Psalms, and he knew his New Testament. Whatever may have been his relationship to Christianity, he constantly cited the Bible and knew it thoroughly. He understood clearly traditional natural law, which he refers to as the foundation of all other law, an utterance commonplace among English common law jurists.

The notion is thus: there are abiding principles of justice; the law of nature is superior in obligation to every other law; and municipal law—the law of nations and of lesser communities, the positive law that is legislated by assemblies or even by the referenda of people—is *subject* to the demands of natural and divine law as being permanent categories of *Justice*. While the assertion of the primacy of natural *rights* brings a different and novel perspective to the argument, it is in significant part the traditional view that Jefferson is thinking about almost a century after John Locke wrote when, in the Declaration, he talks about *the laws of nature and of nature's God*. Locke was not Hobbes, nor was Jefferson. Whatever majorities do, whatever particular rulers undertake, indeed they do have great liberty; *but* they are obliged as the condition of maintaining their true magistracy to rule *justly*. If they do not, then the people are not obliged to obey. Even a philosopher as cautious as Thomas says that.[26] The state is an association of *free* men. *Consent* is a fundamental element in the whole Western political tradition. Even a king, Aristotle already says, must rule by consent of the people (*politeuma*) who are the true constitution (*politeia*), but "a tyrant is still a tyrant, though his subjects do not want him."[27] The notion of consent is fundamental to *political* regimes and forms the very distinction between a political and a totalitarian regime, for instance. The Soviet Union has a totalitarian regime; Poland has a totalitarian regime. The citizen has no role to play in governing. He does not rule and exchange turns being ruled according to law; rather, he simply obeys. This is to be unfree and less than a man, since man is a *politikon zoon*. Such regimes are dis-

26. *Ibid.* I–II. q. 96. a. 4.
27. Aristotle *Politics* V. 8. 22–23. 1313a1–16; III. 6. 11–12. 1282a–24–42; 9. 4. 1285a1–10. Cicero *Republic* I. 25. 39; III. 31. 43; Plato *Laws* 832B–D.

tinctly unfit for human habitation because they are apolitical, thereby doing violence to human nature. Perhaps in 1989 this is about to change.

The various factors that I have recalled in an illustrative (*not* comprehensive) way are brought together in modern political thinking in the West and not least of all in the thought of the American founders. James Madison, John Adams, Thomas Jefferson, and the others are indebted not only to Locke, common law, and seventeenth- and eighteenth-century English experiences. Their debt is much wider. The common tradition lying behind their handiwork is shared by Continental as well as English writers, by Protestant as well as Catholic thinkers. We find it in John Calvin's *Institutes,* for example, on the order of 150 citations of the *Summa Theologica.* The common ground of the Latin Middle Ages—Judaic, Hellenic, and Roman antiquity—informs the development of Western constitutionalism as that finds unique expression in 1787.

There are good reasons why the United States Constitution has endured for 200 years, longer than any other written constitution that remains in effect. Part of it is luck, and another great part is historical circumstance. No small part is that the American founders were graced with strong common sense, a shrewd feel for the possible, a willingness to compromise, and a marvelous repertory of political experience and accumulated wisdom. Modern democratic theory must inevitably look to this greatest example of democratic practice to be properly informed by the relevant evidence. At the center of both theory and practice in this instance lies a unique dedication of political order to the fostering of Everyman's liberty, justice, and happiness. The vivifying conception of man is broad and eclectic, combining in resourceful ways the notions I have tried to delineate. One of the minor figures of the Convention, Pierce Butler of South Carolina, struck the tone that prevailed in subsequent weeks and months when he spoke on June 5, 1787: "We must follow the example of Solon who gave the Athenians not the best Government he could devise; but the best they would receive."[28] Utopian schemes were out of place in this gathering.

28. Max Farrand (ed.), *Records of the Federal Convention of 1787* (1911; rev. ed. in 4 vols., 1937; rpr. New Haven, 1966), I, 125.

The American founders did not dream (as they reflected on the hierarchial structure of reality) that the protection of property and the erection of an extended commercial republic contradicted their dedication *to* individual liberty or *to* the continuation of a Christian commonwealth moored in toleration of a denominational diversity and disestablishment. They were quite capable of reconciling Locke, the Italian republic tradition, Montesquieu's interpretation of constitutionalism, and the teachings of Aristotle, Polybius, and Cicero in devising their plan of government. *Any* doctrinaire interpretation of their thought and work that narrows it to one or another controlling factor is almost certainly misleading if not distorted, whether the factor is as fascinating and important as the place of Locke or of the Old Country Whig tradition or the influence of the Scottish Enlightenment. To be sure, there *is* an American consensus grounded in a universal and even passionate devotion to liberty and rule of law, the government of laws and not of men esteemed by Aristotle no less than James Harrington and assimilated on this side of the Atlantic from the English model. What all that comes to forms a larger matter for inquiry in the pages that lie ahead.

What I would finally say here by way of introduction to those pages is that a grand but limited conception of man and government emerges as the counsel of all sensible writers on democratic theory. The proponents of radical revolt and socialist man cannot be included in that number. Rather, they are enthusiasts to be guarded against if democracy, liberty, and justice are to have any chance of prospering together in viable political forms and affording effective governance of societies fit for human habitation. James Madison spoke for realists of all ages in a famous page of the *Federalist No. 51*, which is quoted more than once in this book. "Ambition must be made to counteract ambition. The interest of the man must be connected with the constitutional rights of the place. It may be a reflection on human nature, that such devices should be necessary to controul [sic] the abuses of government. But what is government itself but the greatest of all reflections on human nature? If men were angels, no government would be necessary. If angels were to govern men, neither external nor internal countrouls on government would be necessary." Madison nonetheless affirms that "justice is the end of government. It is the end of civil society. It ever has been, and ever will be pursued, until it be obtained, or until liberty be lost in the pursuit." He sees no contradiction.

Man—in the lofty sense that we have glimpsed him in reflecting upon our birthright from Western civilization—stands at the center of politics in our tradition just as surely as God stands at the center of religion. Yet in our tradition man is a being who partakes of things providentially ordained, things immortal. Neither the cynic nor the zealot deserves credence in assessing the human condition and prospect. Truth lies in-between, as Madison also said:

> As there is a degree of depravity in mankind which requires a certain degree of circumspection and distrust: So there are other qualities in human nature, which justify a certain portion of esteem and confidence. Republican government presupposes the existence of these qualities in a higher degree than any other form. Were the pictures which have been drawn by the political jealousy of some among us, faithful likenesses of the human character, the inference would be that there is not sufficient virtue among men for self-government; and that nothing less than the chains of despotism can restrain them from destroying and devouring one another.[29]

In the pages that follow, I shall explore the themes raised in this introduction in an attempt to flesh out the ways in which millennial concerns of contemplative human beings in the Western tradition came to bear on the American founding of the late eighteenth century. The thrust of the inquiry is theoretical rather than antiquarian or simply historical. The assumption is that the order devised in the founding persists into the present, whatever the modifications and adaptations worked by intervening centuries might be.

The inquiry continues with a consideration of the roots of political obligation in fundamental experiences of reality and the tensions that arise among rival experiences that accent this or that stratum of the hierarchy of being, from the material and brutish to the rational and spiritual. The urgent need for a satisfactory account of ultimate reality in a secularizing modern age next engages attention, with a focus on the general problem of civil theology and the particularly ingenious and influential myth of the origins and shape of human reality provided by modern thinkers and, especially, by John Locke. Chap-

29. Jacob E. Cooke (ed.), *Federalist* (Middletown, Conn., 1961), 378 (No. 55).

ters Three through Five deal with a series of neglected questions regarding the force of classical philosophy and biblical religion in the shaping of the American mind, public order, and the core consensus in the period of the founding. "Liberty as Law" is the theme of the penultimate chapter. It analyzes and brings together the array of constitutional, religious, and theoretical strands that were woven together to form the unique texture of the American Republic during the three decades from 1761 to 1791. The concern in the concluding chapter is to understand the ways in which the founding is a unique anti-modernist rearticulation of Western civilization, one rooted in a differentiated understanding of reality profoundly indebted to classical and Christian influences. It is seen to reaffirm in new institutional configurations the central principles of medieval constitutional theory by establishing limited government and rule of law in direct opposition to modern tendencies toward statism, absolutism, tyranny, ideological politics, and totalitarianism. All of these the American founders opposed and somehow avoided in their successful revolution. The enduring quality of their embodying liberty under law in a resilient public order mindful of the infinite worth of every human personality is seen as one of the supreme feats of political history.

But what of the noble visions of civic order in the face of the stubbornly brutish in man? We turn now to reflect on that question.

CHAPTER 1 Political Obligation and
the Brutish in Man

The discussion begins with a meditative analysis of the nature of political obligation in its theoretical aspect. It then moves to relate the theory of obligation in its theoretical aspect to the historical emergence and identification of the problem in seventeenth-century England. The probable role of rediscovered Roman law categories in this process is suggested, and the impoverished conception of the political community in Hobbes, Locke, and some of their English and American successors is contrasted with the reach of the parallel notion in medieval constitutionalism. It is argued that the American interpretation of existence, as heir to both the older transcendentalist experiences incorporated into and symbolized by the "Ancient Constitution" and the modern immanentist symbolisms of the "market society," has attempted a reconciliation of these two complexes of thought and has oscillated between them. The resultant ambiguities that have arisen through the interplay of two principal strands of American national consciousness are said to generate an acute crisis in political obligation when they are, in turn, placed under pressure of urgent pragmatic exigencies, such as tensions rooted in ethnic diversity, rapid urbanization, and chronic warfare. Finally, it is suggested that political obligation is an incomplete and too narrowly defined category which, in view of the full range of specifically human experience, requires supplementation through an analysis of political aspiration.

I

The sense of obligation is a fundamental experience of man, growing out of awareness of his participation in a reality so structured as to be an order rather than a chaos. As beneficiaries of this order, however it is apprehended (whether through myth, philosophy, revelation, or science), its modes comprise a stratified experience-symbolization of obligation.

Order in existence is experienced as a preserve secured from the forces of disorder and chaos, one that is essential to man's physical as well as to his psychic and spiritual well-being. This rational order in its whole range of levels, from the moral to the political and the metaphysical, is forever in jeopardy of lapsing into the irrational chaos and destruction whence it has been wrested. Hence, the fundamental obligation is experienced as conforming with the truth of being, and this is symbolized as a concrete order essential to man's existence as human. The sense of obligation is drawn from two different experiential directions: (1) existence in attunement to the order of being, which is requisite if man is to be truly himself and not perverse and less than human; and (2) disaffection from the truth of being, which can only mean a defection to the irrational chaos whence order has been wrested. In an alternative symbolism, defection from the *is* of being can only mean a fall into the nothingness of non-being—the ultimate act of rebellion, existential annihilation, and suicidal self-destruction.

The ontological obligation to seek to know the truth of being and to live in accordance with it, both personally and politically, is felt to be the price that must be paid to secure human existence itself. The symbolisms that represent this fundamental experience in its various modes are present in every society and are relied upon to form the essential fabric of political order.[1]

1. On the meaning of *participation* as the term is used in the preceding paragraphs see Plato *Sophist* 248; *Phaedo* 100; *Parmenides* 129; *Symposium* 208. See also Aristotle *Metaphysics* II. 1. 5. 993b20; XII. 3. 2. 1070a4; 7. 8. 1072b20; Aristotle *Nicomachean Ethics* X. 8. 4. 1178a26, and the indispensable theory of consciousness developed out of these texts by Eric Voegelin in "Was ist Politische Realitaet?," Pt. 3 of Voegelin, *Anamnesis: Zur Theorie der Geschichte und Politik* (Munich, 1966), English trans. Gerhart Niemeyer (Notre Dame, 1978). See also Sandoz, *Voegelinian Revolution*, Chap. 6.

II

Having stated these fundamental points by way of preliminary clarification, it will be noted that obligation is no more than a secondary
problem in political theory. Consideration of the problem of obligation, however that term is understood, is not, as far as I can see, the
main concern of any great work in the history of political theory,
with the possible exception of T. H. Green's essay on the *Principles of
Political Obligation,* a posthumous work published by Green's students from lectures delivered in 1879–1880.[2] The truth of this assertion could not, of course, be established without taking inventory of
the whole history of political theory; nor do I mean to say that the
question of obligation is of no account in political theory, since its
importance is affirmed by our preliminary consideration of it. Still,
the main thrust of political theory may be said to have been to gain
insight into the order of being and into human moral and political
existence as parts of this general order. Philosophers have not overly
argued the obvious point that men are obligated to conform to the
truth of being as articulated into the several realms of which they are
cognizant. That there is indeed such an objective and hence obligatory order of being, the truth of which is substantially ascertainable,
seems to comprise the central thread of political speculation in the
classical Hellenic no less than in the medieval Christian periods. This
same assumption underlies the thought of the Roman Stoic school
and infuses writings of the natural law thinkers. Despite substantial
recasting of the problem, Kantian transcendentalism is compatible
with this assumption, and so also is modern gnostic speculation, from
Joachim of Flora to Hegel, Marx, and Comte.

It may then be correct to say that the problem of obligation is a
phenomenon intimately related in its rise to prominence to the emer-

2. John R. Rodman remarks: "A little reflection on the text of the *Principles of Political
Obligation* will suggest that these lectures might just as appropriately have been titled 'The
Principles of Political Freedom.' Their central preoccupation is with rights. . . ." Quoted from
John R. Rodman (ed.), *Political Theory of T. H. Green* (New York, 1964), 38–39. More pre-
cisely to the point is Henri Bergson, *Two Sources of Morality and Religion,* English trans. R. A.
Audra and C. Brereton (New York, 1935), Chap. 1. There seems to be a consensus that political
obligation is "one of the oldest problems in political theory." H. B. Mayo, *An Introduction to
Democratic Theory* (New York, 1960), 170. See Cicero *De officiis;* Thomas Aquinas "Treatise
on Law" *Summa Theologica* I–II. qq. 90–108.

gence of political and moral relativism, and especially to the shatter-
ing of the "givenness" of existence as symbolized in the hierarchical
representation of being.[3] This event occurred with social effectiveness
in the periods of the Renaissance and Reformation. With the collapse
of the medieval *Christianitas* and the emergence of the plurality of
contending churches and nation-states, each in evident contradic-
toriness claiming universal truth for itself, the givenness of existence
was broken. With the modern crisis of truth and its givenness, as it
had been consolidated in medieval Europe through Church and Empire, there also inevitably occurred existential, intellectual, and pragmatic crises of conformity with radically uncertain truth. From this
matrix there appeared the speculative concern with spiritual, moral,
and political obligation. In short, the question of obligation became
acute in the context of revolution.

Into the disoriented existence of Western man there poured the Roman law as part of the learning of antiquity recovered in this period.
This became one important means of rationalizing the nascent spiritual and secular communities.[4] A central constituent of the Roman
law, of course, is the Law of Obligations. The tale of the impact of
Roman Civil Law on European constitutionalism need not be retold
here.[5] We may note, however, that the value of the Roman law as
an instrumentality of absolutism had already received monumental
recognition by Frederick II of Hohenstaufen in the thirteenth century.
Its modern "reception" is integrally related to the rise of the uni-
versities to which the *Stupor Mundi* lent impetus.[6] Sixteenth- and

3. With respect to the *givenness* of the order of being see Eric Voegelin, *Science, Politics, and Gnosticism*, trans. William J. Fitzpatrick (Chicago, 1968), 53–73.

4. *Cf.* Myron P. Gilmore, *Argument from Roman Law* (Cambridge, Mass., 1941), 26–30, 127, and *passim*; also J. G. A. Pocock, *Ancient Constitution and the Feudal Law: A Study of English Historical Thought in the Seventeenth Century* (1957; rpr. New York, 1967), esp. Chaps. 1 and 2. Reissued with a retrospective concluding essay (Cambridge, England, 1987). All citations in this chapter to Pocock's volume are to the 1967 edition unless otherwise indicated.

5. See, for example, the summary in William C. Morey, *Outlines of Roman Law, Compris-ing Its Historical Growth and General Principles* (2nd ed., rev.; New York, 1914), 167–218; also Max Radin, *Handbook of Roman Law* (St. Paul, 1927), Secs. 181 *et seq.*, and Max Radin, *Handbook of Anglo-American Legal History* (St. Paul, 1936), esp. Chap. 9. Not available when this chapter was written was the admirable study by Harold J. Berman, *Law and Revolu-tion: The Formation of the Western Legal Tradition* (Cambridge, Mass., 1983).

6. See Ernst Kantorowicz, *Frederick the Second, 1194–1250* (New York, 1957), 233–40. Also Julius Stone, *Social Dimensions of Law and Justice* (Stanford, 1966), 89–94.

seventeenth-century European absolutism eagerly availed itself of the Roman categories. It is germane to note that both John Calvin (author of the *Institutes of the Christian Religion* in 1535) and Jean Bodin (father of the modern conception of sovereignty in the *République* of 1576) were civil lawyers and that both wrote against the background of civil war. It is equally unnecessary at this juncture to explore the intricate relationship of English law to Roman law from Glanvil onward or to explain why Tudor and Stuart absolutism ultimately failed politically in what may or may not have been the conscious attempt to foster "reception" of the Justinian Code as the political and legal foundation of rulership in England.[7] We should observe, however, that English constitutionalism remained substantially anchored to its traditional moorings and by 1688 had effectively rejected the Roman legal system that otherwise had swept Western Europe. The reluctance of Anglo-American lawyers to utilize Roman law concepts is reflected in the fact that the Constitution of the United States was itself made to include the phrase "obligation of contracts" (Art. I, Sec. 10), we are told,[8] only on the insistence of James Wilson, a Scot trained in the Civil Law. John Marshall in applying the clause studiously avoided the term obligation in the Dartmouth College case (1819).

If there was great reluctance among common law barristers to use the Civil Law categories, the opposite was true of the English political theorists of the seventeenth century and later. The works of Hobbes, Locke, Bentham, and Austin all reflect a considerable debt to the conceptions and vocabulary of the Civil Law, now put to use in political and legal theory.[9] While Locke may be mindful that contracts can create obligation only *in personam* and not *in rem*, and so speaks in the main simply of "rights," Hobbes and then Bentham and Austin employ the term obligation to mean the general duty which the law

7. On Roman law influence on early English law see Radin, *Anglo-American Legal History*, Secs. 162 *et seq.*; on the Tudor period see Frederic W. Maitland, *English Law and the Renaissance* (Cambridge, England, 1901); Sir William Holdsworth, *A History of English Law* (London and Boston, 1903–38), IV, 253–70; *cf.* Radin, *Anglo-American Legal History*, 116; G. R. Elton (ed.), *Tudor Constitution: Documents and Commentary* (Cambridge, England, 1960), 152n; see also Pocock, *Ancient Constitution*, 32.

8. Edward S. Corwin (ed.), *Constitution of the United States of America: Analysis and Interpretation* (Washington, D.C., 1953), 332.

9. Gilmore, *Argument from Roman Law*, 13, has observed that "the revival of the Roman law made possible the construction upon certain misunderstood texts, like those which dealt with the *merum imperium*, of a political theory which was completely unrelated to the original

imposes on all to respect those rights sanctioned by the law.[10] Locke's discussion is especially in terms of property rights, which are taken to include personal freedom, security, and character—startlingly indeed, one's very self is property in Locke[11]—and which impose the corresponding duty on all to avoid molestation of the right. In this way an approximation is made to the Civil Law conception of Property as securing rights *in rem* and against the world.[12] The laws of Hobbes' sovereign and the conception of law as command advanced by Bentham and Austin[13] seem to have as their true common parent the *lex regia*, whereby the Roman citizens relinquished all their power and authority to the prince whose word was, therefore, law. But, of course, in Locke as well as in Hobbes, the entire fabric of obligation rests primarily if not wholly upon contract, although the former is careful to call it a compact and the latter a covenant. It can at least be doubted whether Hobbes' employment of the term meets any definition whatsoever of contract.[14] Finally, both Hobbes by his "contract" and Locke by his peculiar distension of "Property" effectively pervert not only the Roman but also the Christian conception of *Person*.

III

The critical point is not that Civil Law categories have been imported wholesale into political theory and then misused, although this cer-

---

meaning of the texts, but nevertheless was represented as being the inevitable deduction from them." The misuse of the Roman law concept of *obligation* by Jeremy Bentham and John Austin is noted by W. R. Anson, *Principles of the English Law of Contract*, ed. J. C. Knowlton (2nd American ed.; Chicago, 1887), 6–7. *Cf.* A. P. d'Entreves, *Notion of the State: An Introduction to Political Theory* (Oxford, 1967), 97–105; George H. Sabine, *A History of Political Theory*, (3rd ed.; New York, 1961), 277–280, 400, 404.

    10. Anson, *Principles of the English Law of Contract*, 6–7; see H. L. A. Hart, *Concept of Law* (Oxford, 1961), 230–54. *Cf.* G. W. Paton, *A Text-Book of Jurisprudence* (Oxford, England, 1946), 107–20.

    11. John Locke, *Second Treatise of Government*, Sec. 27. For the argument that this is "normal usage" for Richard Baxter and other of Locke's contemporaries see John Locke, *Two Treatises of Government: A Critical Edition with an Introduction and Apparatus Criticus*, ed. Peter Laslett (1960; rpr. "with amendments," Cambridge, England, 1963), 100–10, 305n.

    12. For these distinctions in the Roman law see Morey, *Outlines of Roman Law*, 341–51.

    13. See the critique of the "simple imperative theory" in Hart, *Concept of Law*, 16–17, 62–63, 234–37.

    14. *Cf.* the classic passages: Locke, *Second Treatise of Government*, Secs. 95–100; Thomas Hobbes, *Leviathan, or The Matter, Forme and Power of a Commonwealth, Ecclesiastical and Civil*, ed. Michael Oakeshott (Oxford, England, n.d.), Chap. 17.

tainly was done. (Did not Plato with considerable success analyze political order in the language of the Hellenic physicians?) Rather, it is that the controlling political symbolism of the period since Hobbes has been contrived by theorists from the conception of Roman secular law so that the whole fabric of societal relations has tended to be reduced to Property and Contract, thereby leaving out of account controlling sources of order in human affairs. Crisis in political obligation can at least partly be traced to this strand of development. The spiritual and ontological ground of philosophical anthropology and of political order is obliterated in the Hobbesian-Lockean schema of the "market society," as C. B. Macpherson terms it.[15] Man becomes the "possessive individual" engaged in the ceaseless competitive pursuit of felicity, according to a hedonistic and utilitarian calculus of acquisition of wealth, status, pleasure, and power. From this perspective, society is bound together by the community of lusts; it is engendered by the fear that violent death might ensue should public peace be broken. Government becomes a protective agency empowered to preserve and foster men's rights and opportunities to indulge greed according to established rules. Obligation is grounded in a recognition that forbearance of overt violence is essential to continued physical existence. This recognition finds particular expression in rules armed with sanctions that are promulgated by sovereign authority as obligatory law. Obligation resides in the law; the sense of obligation arises from what Locke calls the "Law of nature," that is, man's urge to self-preservation.[16] Political science, in this horizon, becomes the knowledge of power and decision making. It relays who gets what, when, and how.[17]

To be sure, Hobbes, Locke, and their successors did not *cause* the market society but proceeded on the basis of empirical observation to

15. C. B. Macpherson, *Political Theory of Possessive Individualism: Hobbes to Locke* (Oxford, England, 1962), 271–77.

16. Locke, *Second Treatise of Government*, Sec. 233, quoting William Barclay.

17. *Cf.* Harold Lasswell, *Politics: Who Gets What, When and How* (New York, [1936]); William T. Bluhm, *Theories of the Political System: Classics of Political Thought and Modern Political Analysis* (Englewood Cliffs, N.J., 1965), Chap. 9; Carl J. Friedrich, *An Introduction to Political Theory: Twelve Lectures at Harvard* (New York, 1967), Chap. 9; Bernard Crick, *American Science of Politics: Its Origins and Conditions* (Berkeley, 1967), Chap. 10; Herbert J. Storing (ed.), *Essays on the Scientific Study of Politics* (New York, 1962), Chap. 4; Dante Germino, *Beyond Ideology: The Revival of Political Theory* (New York, 1967), 198–214.

give it theoretical formulation, each illuminating different aspects of the same complex structure. Of course, Locke was more circumspect than Hobbes and retained enough of the traditional English viewpoint encompassed by a pale penumbra of natural law to qualify for the title "Father of Modern Constitutionalism." Of both of them we may say that their prescience is such as to make their works nearly prophetic, for the kind of social reality they reflect has developed apace since the seventeenth century to climax in the nineteenth century in England and America—unless that climax is yet to come. To deduce virtue from vice and harmonious order from the discordant jangle of the passions is no mean theoretical achievement and must command our respect. Yet it remains so that human existence outruns merely libidinous existence. If the upper ranges of man's existence finds no representation in the controlling political symbolisms whereby societies interpret their existence, then the long-range results can only be grave psychic and social disorders that can in their late stages be treated only with the complete Hobbesian therapy. In that extremity recovery is, at best, improbable. The eclipse of God and the components of natural law by the symbolism of the market society—no less than by ideologies of left and right—may be said, in principle, to achieve just this perilous effect through their deformations of reality.

English constitutionalism and the common law tradition—like the whole of European constitutionalism of the Middle Ages—developed out of feudalism[18] on the basis of faith (Latin *fides,* German *Treue*) as the central experience controlling man's existence and his understanding of it. Our constitutional tradition did not find its historical origin in any Lockean-like social contract.[19] Rather in feudal Europe, especially during the centuries from 1000 to 1300, the central experi-

18. "Feudal law is not a special law applicable only to one fairly definite set of relationships, or applicable only to one class of men; it is just the common law of England." Frederick Pollock and Frederic W. Maitland, *History of English Law Before the Time of Edward I* intro. by S. F. C. Milsom, (2nd ed. reissued; Cambridge, England, 1968), I, 235–36. The discovery of this relationship between common law and feudalism in seventeenth-century England is analyzed by Pocock, *Ancient Constitution.*

19. This is not simply to say that the Lockean account is unhistorical but to notice that it is ahistorical as well. See Pocock, *Ancient Constitution,* 236–40. On the compact in the founding fathers see, for example, the following: C. F. Adams (ed.), *Letters and Other Writings of James Madison* (Philadelphia, 1865), IV, 63, 294, 392–93, 422. Farrand (ed.), *Records of the Federal*

ence of *fides*—the source of what we are here discussing as obligation—truly constituted the existential community or body politic upon which government rested. In England it found a wide variety of temporal expressions, none more important in political terms than the ceremony of liege homage and the oath of fealty.

As recounted by Bracton in *De Legibus* (ca. 1250), homage was done by the tenant kneeling before the lord, placing his hands between those of the lord as the essential gesture of submission, and saying, "I become your man of the tenement that I hold of you, and faith to you will bear of life and member and earthly worship, and faith to you shall bear against all folk who can live and die, saving the faith that I owe to our lord the king." "The lord then kissed the man and received him into his protection. Homage being 'done' fealty (*fidelitas*) is then 'sworn.' The tenant stands up with his hand on the Gospels and says: 'Hear this my lord: I will bear faith to you of life and member, goods, chattels and earthly worship, so help me God and these holy Gospels of God.'"[20] These bonds were reciprocal, with the man exchanging his services for the lord's protection. Homage and fealty were given both to the immediate lord and to the king.

When William the Conqueror completed the conquest, he demanded fealty or fidelity of every male of the age of twelve years. Those who would not swear it had no right to remain in his kingdom. William's oath of allegiance (*ligeantia*) became the due of subsequent kings of England, the bond of the community, and the foundation of political obligation. It restrained the nobility from using its power against the king. Within the realm so constituted, the people then enjoyed the king's justice and peace, as well as the protection of their lesser lords. This pledge of faith was a more powerful cement than we in a secular age are apt to imagine. The pledge of faith (*fides*) is the pledge of the giver's Christianity itself; as Pollock and Maitland state it, "he pawns his hope of salvation."[21] Should the lord fail to

---

Convention of 1787, I, 54, 250, 314–15, 324; III, 140, 166. Alexander Hamilton, "H. G. Letter XII," March 8, 1789, in Harold C. Syrett and Jacob E. Cooke (eds.), *Papers of Alexander Hamilton* (New York, 1961–87), V, 294. Thomas Jefferson's letter to James Madison of September 6, 1789, in J. P. Boyd (ed.), *Papers of Thomas Jefferson* (Princeton, 1950–), XV, 392–95.

20. Quoted from Pollock and Maitland, *History of English Law*, I, 297–98.
21. *Ibid.*, II, 190.

perform his duties, the man is free of his bond.[22] The law which exists binds the king and the emperor no less than it does the lord and free-man, as the *Sachsenspiegel* (before 1233) explicitly states. On both sides of the Channel, the law in question is the customary law of the respective realms. Hence, Eike of Repchow calls his code the "Mir-ror of the Saxons," since it shows the Saxons as they are, just as a "woman's mirror reflects her countenance."[23] The notion of limited royal powers was not invented as an ad hoc principle by the lords spiritual and temporal at Runnymede. The only "sovereign" of the high Middle Ages was God Himself, and all men stood under Him and His law.

IV

The thesis that can be advanced in light of the foregoing illustra-tive analysis is that what Jefferson called "Americanism," from the time of its formal inception in 1776, has been woven not only from the materials distinctive to the political theorists from Hobbes and Locke down to the utilitarians, but that it also substantially incor-porates elements of the old political tradition of England and West-ern civilization. This second complex of institutions, symbols, and experiences appears likely to have been conserved especially in the common law tradition as transferred to the United States and in the general Christianity of the nation. To the degree to which these two strands of our national consciousness contradict each other, they produce ambiguity, clashes, and dissensus within the generally preva-lent "liberal tradition" in America.[24] It is, of course, manifestly im-possible to assert flatly the existence of a simplistic hard-and-fast di-chotomy of this kind in our politics. This is so because of interaction and transposition between the two complexes of ideas and also be-

22. This principle is clearly formulated in the *Schwabenspiegel* (late thirteenth century) as follows: "Wir sullen den herren darumbe dienen, daz si uns beschirmen. Beschirmen sie uns nit, so sind wir in nit dienstes schuldig nach rechte [We should serve the lord so that he protects us. If he does not protect us, then under law we are not obliged to serve him]." Quoted from Otto Brunner, *Land und Herrschaft: Grundfragen der territorialen Verfassungsgeschichte Oester-reichs im Mittelalter*, (4th ed.; Wien-Wiesbaden, 1959), 240.

23. K. A. Eckhardt (ed.), *Sachsenspiegel* (Hanover, 1933), lines 175–82, pp. 8–9.

24. The classic study is Louis Hartz, *Liberal Tradition in America: An Interpretation of American Political Thought Since the Revolution* (New York, 1955).

cause other factors deserve consideration. Moreover, even Hobbes and certainly Locke convey important elements of the older tradition with which they were themselves, to varying degrees, at odds. Yet if it cannot be supposed that the American political tradition is susceptible of analysis in terms of a formula, it still seems possible, on the basis of foregoing considerations, to identify and throw into relief certain key symbolisms formative of the American consciousness. These will perhaps prove to be of use in clarifying political obligation.

(1) A *"Nation under God."* In terms of the Judaeo-Christian tradition, the political order of the United States and the moral and ontological order of the individual persons who comprise its citizenry look to participation in and conformity with the revealed order of transcendent Being, as it is experienced and symbolized, as the ultimate ground of existence. By this familiar conception, a Creator-creature relationship is established on the basis of the primordial divine initiative, which is given authoritative representation in the creation myths of Genesis. The contingency and dependency of the intrinsically imperfect human order for its justness and reasonableness upon the divine and *given* order of the eternal presence are thereby postulated. Also asserted by direct implication is the conception of the limited obligation of man to human agencies, which is in contradistinction to the overriding and limitless obligation that men live in accord with the divine order. A corollary of this experience is that the public order of societies, no less than the private order of persons, must be consonant with the order of transcendent Being. What may be called the civil theology of the nation is understood to be a finite embodiment of this order, finding expression in such familiar notions as the American Zion, Manifest Destiny, and the providential role of America in the process of history.[25]

(2) *Foundation Myth.* The constitutional order of American society is built on the foundation of the consent of free and reasonable men as expressed in the myth of the social contract and in government as a trust established for limited purposes. Yet while key ingre-

25. Clear expression of this self-interpretation of Americanism is given in Ezra Stiles' great election sermon "The United States Elevated to Glory and Honor," preached on May 8, 1783. It appears in John Wingate Thornton (ed.), *Pulpit of the American Revolution; or, The Political Sermons of the Period of 1776* (1860; rpr. New York, 1970), 397–520. *Cf.* Sidney E. Mead, "The Nation with the Soul of a Church," *Church History,* XXXVI (1967), 262–83.

dients are Lockean, familiar conceptions of the *Second Treatise* as assimilated in America are embedded in the broader traditions of Western civilization and of English constitutional history. The chaos of the Hobbesian state of nature and the threatened collapse of the Lockean state of nature into the Hobbesian equivalent (Locke's state of war) reflect the Hellenic experience of cosmos as an island in the midst of ever-threatening existential chaos. The overt creation of society by means of the compact reflects an awareness of the necessity of a viable community if free government is to exist and if essentially human existence is to be secured against the onslaught of the passions whose rule is the very definition of disorder, tyranny, and rebellion against the rational order of being.

Whatever the distinctions that a full account would have to explore between the Aristotelian conception of community through friendship (*philia*)[26] and the Hobbesian and Lockean conceptions of community through shared *libido* (*pleonexia* and *amor habendi* in Locke),[27] the results for the theory of obligation are substantially the same. The man who enters into society as a member of the community or "people" is obliged to surrender his plenary autonomy of public action to the will of the new whole of which he is now only a part. Just as Socrates in the *Crito* acknowledges his obligation to abide by the laws of Athens even when they are perverted by rulers into injustice (if he cannot persuade society to act justly and if he does not exile himself from it), so the Lockean man submits himself to the will of the majority in certain public matters even if he dissents.[28] John Jay notes in the *Federalist No. 2* the necessity of individual relinquishment of certain natural rights to society if government is to have requisite power to act to secure the common good. Participation in a community then carries with it the obligation of abiding by the laws and decisions of the community in its properly public transactions, even when (like the commissary's landlady in Bentham) we disagree. Both the beast-man and the god-man who take the law into their own hands must be banished from society,

26. Aristotle *Nicomachean Ethics* IX. 3. 4–6. 4. 1166a1–1167b16; Aristotle *Politics* I. 1. 1–11. 1252a1–1253a18.

27. Voegelin, *Plato and Aristotle*, 33n; Leo Strauss, *Natural Right and History* (Chicago, 1953), 244.

28. Plato *Crito* 51B-D. Locke, *Second Treatise of Government*, Sec. 97. *Cf.* Jeremy Bentham, *Fragment on Government*, ed. F. C. Montague (London, 1891), 153–60.

according to Aristotle;[29] and Spinoza, Hobbes, Locke, and the Founding Fathers all agree. This is the essential condition of civil society, without which it cannot exist.

(3) *Constitutionalism.* Only a viable community can be governed freely. The self-imposition of a fabric of institutions, laws, and policies implies an effective consensus in a really experienced commonality, one sufficiently capable of reconciling disagreements so as to be able to move "in one direction." This community, however, is fashioned out of the whole cloth of human experience, not merely out of political (much less merely libidinal) aspects. It comprehends common language, heritage, race, religion, geography, customs, manners, principles of government, and a historical occasion, all of which weld refractory individual men together to form an identifiable "common sense," such as the one described in the *Federalist.* Only such a community can act to "appoint the form of the commonwealth" and to sustain free government.

Common sense is here used to designate the core consensus of the American community, or *Americanism,* as Jefferson coins it in a letter to Edward Rutledge of June 24, 1797, when he speaks of "the dictates of reason and pure Americanism."[30] The understanding of *Americanism* as the *common sense* of the nation further depends upon a conception of common sense that ranges from Vico ("Common sense is judgment without reflection shared by an entire class, an entire people, an entire nation, or the human race") to Thomas Reid ("There is a certain degree of it which is necessary to our being subjects of law and government, capable of managing our own affairs, and answerable for our conduct towards others: This is called common sense, because it is common to all men with whom we can transact business, or call to account for their conduct").[31]

29. Aristotle *Politics* I. 1. 9. 1253a7, citing Homer *Iliad* IX. 63.

30. A. A. Lipscomb and A. E. Bergh (eds.), *Writings of Thomas Jefferson* (Washington, D.C., 1905), IX, 409; *cf.* the use of the term by John Adams, letter to Benjamin Rush, July 7, 1805, in John A. Schutz and Douglass Adair (eds.), *Spur of Fame: Dialogues of John Adams and Benjamin Rush, 1805–1813* (1966; rpr. San Marino, Calif., 1980), 30.

31. See Giambattista Vico, *New Science,* ed. and trans. from 3rd ed. (1744) by T. G. Bergin and M. H. Fisch (abr. and rev. ed.; New York, 1961), para. XII, 142, p. 21; Thomas Reid, *Essays on the Intellectual Powers of Man* (1785; rpr. Cambridge, Mass., 1969), Essay VI, Chap. 2, 557. *Cf.* the reference to this fundamental consensus in Crick, *American Science of Politics,* 36, 43, 55, 234, and *passim.* See also Bergson, *Two Sources of Morality and Religion,* 96–100.

In terms of our constitutional tradition, powers are delegated to order the public sphere of action within substantive limits which are procedurally enforceable. They are exercised only in the specific ways agreed upon by the people as expressive of consent, given mediately or immediately. The laws and policies of constitutional government not only are limited in scope and grounded in consent, but they are bound to serve the well-being of the people of the society in general and of every single individual person in it, insofar as private good is compatible with public or common good.[32]

More than this, government and law must also be just and reasonable, not only in the view of the prevailing majority determination of these but also especially in view of conformity with higher law—the Declaration's "Laws of nature and of Nature's God." The "government of laws and not of men" of Harrington and Marshall is precisely an insistence that the tyranny of the passions (including those of the majority as well as those of the single tyrant) be averted by having "God and reason alone rule," as Aristotle first said.[33] The whole medieval tradition of constitutionalism as symbolized in the controlling relationship of *fides* as well as the common law tradition expressed from Glanvil to Coke and Blackstone testify to the centrality of this principle.[34]

This, then, is to note that "political obligation" pertains not only to the rights and obligations of subject and citizen but also with at least equal stringency to rulers and governors. By the Lockean account (as embedded in long tradition)[35] the rulers are obliged to exercise their powers only for the preservation of the liberties and properties of the people. The Declaration of Independence finds George III

32. Locke, *Second Treatise of Government*, Sec. 134.
33. Aristotle *Politics* III. 11. 3–4. 1287a19–32.
34. Sir William Blackstone's statement of the principle is clear enough. "This law of nature, being coeval with mankind, and dictated by God himself, is of course superior in obligation to any other. It is binding over all the globe, in all countries, and at all times: no human laws are of any validity, if contrary to this; and such of them as are valid derive all their force, and all their authority, mediately or immediately, from this original" (Blackstone, *Commentaries on the Laws of England*, I, 41). See Daniel J. Boorstin, *Mysterious Science of the Law* (1941; rpr. Boston, 1958), 49.
35. As Parker of Waddington, Lord Chief Justice of England, observed: "The great commentators, notably Bracton and Fortescue, paid great homage to the concept of the rule of law, Bracton laying it down that the King is under God and the law." Quoted from A. E. Dick Howard, *Road from Runnymede: Magna Carta and Constitutionalism in America* (Charlottesville, 1968), x.

to be a tyrant precisely because he has perverted his powers as monarch by overstepping limits imposed by both constitution and higher law to serve his own self-interest rather than to tend the common good of the Englishmen in America.

V

At this juncture the ground of civil disobedience in our tradition makes its appearance. It is well represented in the motto Jefferson inscribed on his personal seal: "Resistance to tyrants is Obedience to God." A regime that oversteps limited powers or imposes rule that fails to be just and reasonable by the standard of the higher law is in rebellion against the people and God. Since men are obliged to be obedient to God and to divine and natural law, they are (1) absolved from any further obligation to such a regime, and (2) both entitled and obliged to resist it, perhaps ultimately by force of arms.[36] Thus, not only is there a "right of revolution," but there is also a moral and metaphysical right and duty to refrain from participating as accomplices in the tyrant's rebellion by conforming as obedient subjects to

36. Locke, *Second Treatise of Government*, Secs. 23, 135, 149, 168, 233, 240. "The Obligations of the Law of Nature, cease not in Society, but only in many Cases are drawn closer, and have by Humane Laws known Penalties annexed to them, to inforce their observation. Thus the Law of Nature stands as an Eternal Rule to all Men, *Legislators* as well as others." This quotation from Section 135 contains one of Locke's rare uses of the term obligation; it is sandwiched between two quotations from Richard Hooker, the second of which is itself taken from Thomas Aquinas *Summa Theologica* I–II. q. 95. a. 3. As d'Entreves noted, "The greatest trick played by Locke on Hooker was that of presenting him as a forerunner of his own theory of the social contract" (d'Entreves, *Notion of the State*, 197n). See Locke, *Two Treatises of Government*, 376, 295–96.

The grounding of civil disobedience in resistance to tyranny is supported by David Hume in *A Treatise of Human Nature* (1740; rpr. London, 1911), II, 251–52. It is similarly justified by perhaps the most famous of American disobedients, Henry David Thoreau, who argues that "Government is at best but an expedient" and resolves all "civil obligation" into this expediency. He juxtaposes the "lawyer's truth" to "Truth," "prudence" to "wisdom": "Truth is always in harmony with herself, and is not concerned chiefly to reveal the justice that may consist with wrong-doing." His orientation is taken toward "the fountainhead" from which has trickled the relatively impure truth of "the Bible and the Constitution." See "Civil Disobedience" (1849) in Henry David Thoreau, *Walden and Other Writings*, ed. Brooks Atkinson (New York, 1937), 635, 639, 657–60. Cf. Bradford Torrey and Francis H. Allen (eds.), *Journal of Henry D. Thoreau* (1906; rpr. New York, 1962), II, 141, 179.

Finally, the most celebrated American disobedient of the mid-twentieth century takes the same ground and appeals to natural law and Augustine in "Letter from Birmingham Jail," in Martin Luther King, Jr., *Why We Can't Wait* (New York, 1964), 82.

his evil will. Indeed, this is the obligation of all men: to live justly as best as they can and to resist or perhaps even move to destroy unjust and perverse government. The truth of this is as applicable to the Stalins and Hitlers of the twentieth century as it ever was to the George IIIs of the eighteenth century. This principle is the foundation of the scenario enacted in our own American Revolution. The violation of both constitutional provision and higher law supplied the justification of the steps so reluctantly taken on that occasion, as the Declaration explicitly states.

The constitutional arrangements contrived by the Founding Fathers in 1787 were skillfully calculated to achieve the rule of law, of God and reason, rather than of men. The trouble with the rule of men, Aristotle had said and the founders knew, is that composite human nature carries in it base passions, the "wild beast" present in "even the best of men." [37] Hence, to achieve a government of laws and not of men, the beast in man must be chained, the demonic in politics exorcised. The founders' solution was, of course, the familiar separation of powers and system of checks and balances. But so far from being the mere institutional curiosity that Bagehot ridicules, [38] this arrangement was carefully designed to be the solution to the problem posed by the paradox that a rule of law rather than of men might be attempted when no angels were available to rule, only frail and imperfect men animated by the wild beast of desire. "Ambition must be made to counteract ambition," Madison states. [39] By the tripartite

37. Aristotle *Politics* III. 11. 4. 1287a30.

38. Walter Bagehot, *English Constitution and Other Political Essays* (rev. ed.; New York, 1877), 296.

39. *Federalist No. 51.* This key principle of the separation of powers and system of checks and balances had an immediate source in John Adams' *Defence of the Constitutions,* whose first volume appeared shortly before the Convention convened. For Madison's term *ambition* Adams employs *emulation;* see C. F. Adams (ed.), *Works of John Adams* (Boston, 1850–56), VI, 279. On the influence of Adams on the Convention see the letter of Benjamin Rush to Richard Price, June 2, 1787, quoted in Farrand (ed.), *Records of the Federal Convention of 1787,* III, 33. The theme of separation and equilibrium of powers is prominent in Adams' writings: *cf. Works,* IV, 391, 408 (citing Montesquieu), 410, 436; V, 10, 40, 273, 488; VI, 234, 246–48, 252, 271–72, 284, 297–98, 323, 397, 399; VIII, 560; IX, 183. See the important letter of Madison to Jefferson of June 6, 1787, in C. F. Adams (ed.), *Letters and Other Writings of James Madison,* I, 332. Also the statements attributed to Luther Martin in the convention in Farrand (ed.), *Records of the Federal Convention of 1787,* I, 437–41. Blackstone's analogy of the parts of government with "three distinct powers in mechanics," so operating as to "form a mutual check upon each other" (Blackstone, *Commentaries,* I, 154–55) is intimately con-

separation of powers and the intricacies of the system of checks and balances, ambition (the desire for dominion and power) could be sufficiently neutralized, so that the outcome of the proper functioning of the constitutional mechanism would be reasonable and just government—a "government of laws." As Madison summarizes: "Justice is the end of government. It is the end of civil society. It ever has been and will be pursued until it be obtained, or until liberty be lost in the pursuit." [40]

Yet, as the *Federalist* repeatedly notes, the reliance of free government upon the people is ineluctable. [41] There really is no system so perfect that men do not have to be good, to paraphrase T. S. Eliot. Therefore, a real community of shared virtue is, by the Founding Fathers' analysis, ultimately essential if free government is to be supportable.

The question that emerges is whether, in concrete circumstances, rejection of obligation arises from the awareness of a violation of the terms of our constitutional arrangement and/or a collision between the public policy of the nation and the provisions of natural and divine law, or whether dissent is rooted in some other source or sources. It is, admittedly, hard to put the question in this way, since few people today on any side of an issue wish to talk overtly of "the laws of nature and of Nature's God," despite the indebtedness of American public order to the higher law. [42]

To formulate the problem is strange if not archaic to contemporary ears, and this fact in itself may supply a clue to the nature of the crisis in obligation, insofar as one may be said to exist in the United States. H. L. A. Hart observed that obligation exists to abide by law even if

---

nected with the principles of Adams and the Constitution; cited in Correa M. Walsh, *Political Science of John Adams: A Study in the Theory of Mixed Government and the Bicameral System* (New York, 1915), 233. It appears likely that the whole symbolism can be traced to Sir Isaac Newton's "System of the World," which appeared as Book Three of the *Principia* in 1687, and that the fundamental principle of the Constitution is based on a marriage of political physics and philosophical anthropology. *Cf.* Alexander Hamilton in *Federalist No. 9.* Also Montesquieu, *Spirit of the Laws*, Bk. XI.

40. *Federalist No. 51.*

41. *Ibid.*, Nos. 17, 28, 33, 45, 46, 49, 50.

42. See Edward S. Corwin, *"Higher Law" Background of American Constitutional Law*, (1928; rpr. Ithaca, N.Y., 1957).

there is no sense of obligation.[43] This is indisputably true, as the fore-going analysis has tried to suggest. Yet the fabric of laws and policies that carries political obligation cannot order a society from which the sense of obligation is absent, or at the least must fail to do so to the degree that this sense of obligation is missing. As has been seen, what is called "respect for law" in American society follows from the real existence of a viable community, one of sufficient virtue to be freely governed by laws with which well-being is identified. If this existential community is significantly eroded, free government loses the fundamental consensus indispensable to it. Alternatives of action then become, in the extreme case, either the revolutionary reconstitution of society in order to re-establish the community and the authority of government, or rule by authoritarian means through deployment of all relevant resources of power available to the regime. By the former means, political obligation is secured through a reciprocal reauthentication of the justice and integrity of the public order, after the pattern of the American Revolution of 1776; by the latter means, it is secured through paramount reliance upon fear of sanctions, habituation to obedience, and fear of overwhelming might.

This oversimplified, disjunctive way of stating the matters should not obscure the facts that in every community a significant fraction of the citizenry identifies might and right; a sizable segment of the society inevitably identifies authority and injustice; and the charisma of the evocative personality possesses a persuasive potentiality to create a following among the masses along lines made familiar by the plebiscitary totalitarian democracies of the twentieth century. In short, no neat formula can suffice. The best we can do is bracket the complex of problems in order to give them definition and intelligibility. Moreover, if we acknowledge the impossibility in this century of a revolution like that of 1776, then the alternative that remains for a disintegrating political order is radical revolution and the reconstruction of society through terror and the imposition of a messianic ide-

---

43. Hart, *Concept of Law*, 86, 168. This is not, however, to minimize the importance, indeed, the ultimate decisiveness of the *sense* of obligation to moral and legal systems (*cf. ibid.*, 196–210). Hart's considerations parallel much that d'Entreves has to say in *Notion of the State*, Pt. 3.

ology of either the Left or Right—a forbidding prospect of the demise of free government.

In sum, it can be suggested that American political experience symbolized the relevant sectors of existence through the market society on the one hand and the myth of the ancient constitution and the higher law on the other hand. The two symbolisms tend to coalesce. Thus, the myth of the ancient constitution designates the common law view of the English law and constitution as existing from time immemorial, or time out of mind, and containing all justice and liberty. The phrase and analysis are identified in current discourse, especially with J. G. A. Pocock's scholarship. The "myth" received full expression in the work of Sir Edward Coke in the early seventeenth century. Into the myth was woven the content of feudal law as well as divine and natural law as sources of common law. The myth is no doubt a fundamental symbolism of the Anglo-American civil theology. It finds expression at least in Blackstone and confirmation in Burke. It is abandoned by Hobbes, Locke, Bolingbroke, and Paine.[44]

The picture that emerges from Pocock's analysis as related to the present discussion is that of a clear rebellion by rationalist and empiricist theorists against the historically grounded myth of the common lawyers' ancient constitution and its evocative symbolization of the English transcendentalist political tradition. In the field of general philosophy, the same tendency is manifested: "English philosophy is, to this day [i.e., 1925], almost as empirical and positivistic as in the times of Bacon and Locke. We may even claim, in general, that England, though rich in thinkers of the highest order, has never had but a single school of philosophy, or, rather, that is has never had any, for its philosophy is a perpetual protest against Scholasticism."[45] The atrophy of American community from the solidarity reflected in Jay's analysis of it two centuries ago in *Federalist No. 2* has tended to move it *de facto* closer to the market society paradigm at the expense of the ancient tradition, although both strands of consciousness remain powerfully intact to this day. It was against a drift of this kind

44. Pocock, *Ancient Constitution*, 35–36, 51, 162–68, 232, 237, 241–46, 249.
45. Alfred Weber and Ralph Barton Perry, *History of Philosophy*, trans. Frank Thilly (rev. ed.; New York, 1925), 316.

that T. H. Green and the Idealists raised their voices in the latter half of the nineteenth century.

VI

Political obligation is, paradoxically, both central and peripheral to a theory of human existence. It moves to the forefront of concern when the givenness of existence and the established order of politics are endangered or shattered by revolutionary forces. Obligation becomes topical when the sense of obligation among men is impaired to a socially significant extent. When this occurred in Western Europe in the sixteenth and seventeenth centuries, the terminology of the Roman law came to be employed by political thinkers to contrive the symbolisms of the sovereign nation-state[46] and society as a competitive market system of property relationships among men whose most prominent attribute is acquisitiveness. These symbolisms have tended to be the controlling ones on the Anglo-American horizon for three centuries and supply the core of the Liberal tradition.

To say that they have been the controlling ones is not, of course, to say that they are the only ones. An undercurrent of opposition can be seen at two levels, that of theory and that of the public order. From the side of theoretical critique, the reductionism of the controlling symbolisms has been combatted by a variety of opponents, from the Cambridge Platonists of the seventeenth century and the Scottish "common sense" school and Edmund Burke of the eighteenth century, to Marx and T. H. Green in the nineteenth century, and (under the influence of Bergson) William James and Santayana in this century. From the side of institutional order, general Christianity and the tradition of higher law have served to correct and ameliorate the materialism and hedonism of the controlling symbolisms. Renewed interest in political obligation in America during the 1960s and the Vietnam trauma as well as subsequently is symptomatic of crisis in a precariously balanced public order that has endured since Locke.

Political obligation, then, comes to the forefront of concern as a

46. *Cf.* T. H. Green's comment, *Lectures on the Principles of Political Obligation*, ed. Lindsay, Secs. 136, 141. He speaks of the "Roman state."

straw in the wind in time of crisis; otherwise it is simply imbedded in the routine operation of the ongoing order. Obligation in the narrow legal meaning of the term is not dependent for its force upon the sense of obligation. The reverse of this is true when political obligation is broadly understood. A crisis of political obligation is a crisis of authority in society, a companion of the *anomie* that besets a society when the old gods are dead and the new ones have yet to be born. It is an expression of malaise and disorientation in the consciousness which is the substance of "society," symptomatic of a loss of the common sense essential to every community. It marks a crisis of political consciousness when the center does not hold, and the fragility of public order intimates the mortality of human life itself lest that, too, be forgotten.

Public authority is then something more than the equivalent of might or power.[47] It can better be understood to mean these together with reason, justice, and liberty. Such a conception of constituted authority was well expressed when Cicero said, "We all are the laws' slaves that we may be free."[48] It found optimal expression in the democratic horizon in Lincoln's famous formula of government of, by, and for the people. If the crises in obligation and authority are of a piece, it is worth remembering that this is a matter of specifics and particularities rather than something more, a matter of *what*, not *whether*. A Pyrrhonic skepticism, or a suicidalist despair, while not totally absent, is not widely characteristic of the contemporary crisis. Protest in all directions is rooted in a keen sense of obligation to various truths—often contradictory ones and often only dimly seen— that are sufficiently compelling to spark and sustain physical and metaphysical rebellion. Our own age of political iconoclasm vindicates Luther's dictum that "man always has either God or idols," a piece of wisdom whose enormous range of consequences was never better expressed than in Dostoevsky's "Grand Inquisitor."[49]

The contemporary crisis in political obligation, however, derives unique urgency from universal awareness of existence in the shadow of the impending catastrophe threatened from multiple sources, from

47. d'Entreves, *Notion of the State, passim;* Hart, *Concept of Law,* 196–200.
48. Cicero *Pro. A. Cluentio Oratio* 53, 146.
49. See Sandoz, *Political Apocalypse,* 241–54.

nuclear war to the greenhouse effect. This experience is of such melancholy profundity and pervasiveness as to create anxiety of existence of a magnitude perhaps unparalleled in human history. Yet the deepening uncertainty of existence is an experience that could occasion powerful spiritual and philosophical responses. H. L. A. Hart has well said, "Our concern is with social arrangements for continued existence, not with those of a suicide club."[50] Yet the issue of "survival" means more to man than mere biological subsistence. Moreover, the array of conventional justifications for obligation has been steadily undermined also on the liberal marketplace side by the dismaying experience of science and technology, and the modern economic order rooted in them. Governments themselves are key sources, not of happiness and well-being in existence but of death-dealing pollution, destruction of the natural order, exploitation of the impoverished, domestic violence, total war, state terror, and genocide horrors rampant from the Katyn Forest to Auschwitz and various Cambodian resorts of Pol Pot.

It is at precisely this juncture that a discussion of obligation takes the turn toward the discussion of freedom and aspiration to good, issues that emerge with unique force under the contemporary existential anxiety of a fall from being. This turn was earlier noted in the ambiguity of T. H. Green's discussion of political obligation. Such an ambiguity is not evidence of muddleheadedness but rather of solid insight. Herein lies the theoretical aspect of the paradox of the simultaneous centrality and peripherality of obligation as a political problem. Political obligation embraces the minimal set of duties, mostly negative, essential to man's survival and existence in society. It is built upon habituation as formed and enforced by education, law, and convention backed by sanctions at the disposal of established authority. This minimal order of the politics of obligation is complemented by the essentially unlimited order of the politics of aspiration and freedom.

50. Hart, *Concept of Law*, 188. For the psychological dimensions see Robert Jay Lifton, *History and Human Survival: Essays on the Young and the Old, Survivors and the Dead, Peace and War, and on Contemporary Psychohistory* (1961; rpr. New York, 1971), Chap. 15, "Protean Man." For theoretical analysis see Thomas A. Spragens, Jr., *Irony of Liberal Reason* (Chicago, 1981), Chap. 8, "The Quiet Demise of Liberal Reason."

The "ideals" of both Green and Hart rest upon the Aristotelian conception of man as a political, living being whose peculiar quality is that "he alone possesses a perception of good and evil, of the just and unjust" and that it is a "common perception of these things which makes a family and a polis."[51] The teleological conception of human nature as tending toward the good and the just as ontologically (not merely "normatively") requisite of man *qua* human—and the definition of this *telos* as more than merely mortal and as divine[52]—is foundational to the politics of freedom, to political science, and to the Western conception of political order alike. It is, finally, in the late work of Henri Bergson that the politics of aspiration is rediscovered in modern philosophy to find full expression as embracing the entire range of Judaeo-Christian mystical experience.[53] Bergson's analysis gives rise to the imagery of the closed society of obligation and the open society of aspiration and freedom.[54] The politics of obligation can only deal with a truncated man and existence. It is no more than a survival kit, essential but ultimately insufficient. The politics of aspiration alone can direct man toward his unknown destiny.

Political *obligation* and *aspiration*, therefore, are highly stratified experiences that complement each other. When taken together they may be said to define the field of the uniquely human in man's existence. Out of the reflective consciousness of men aware of their essential humanity as reasonable beings arises the aspiration to order the sphere of reality in which their participation is creative so as to achieve the goods of justice and happiness demanded of them by this same essential humanity. The aspiration to the good generates with it the existential obligation to live in accord with the truth apprehended by consciousness through reason and spirit in its noblest flights. The realization of the good in individual men and in societies is only possible if knowledge is translated into action; that is, only if taken to heart as obligatory.

51. Cf. Green, *Principles of Political Obligation*, ed. Lindsay, secs. 25, 251, and *passim*. Hart, *Concept of Law*, 177–80, 184–87. Aristotle *Politics* I. 1. 9–11. 1253a2–18 (trans. Ernest Barker).

52. Aristotle *Nicomachean Ethics* X. 7. 6–9. 1177b4–1178a9.

53. Bergson, *Two Sources of Morality and Religion*, 232–35, 280–84. See Ellis Sandoz, "Myth and Society in the Philosophy of Bergson," *Social Research*, XXX (1963), 171–202.

54. Cf. Bergson, *Two Sources of Morality and Religion*, 255–57.

Theoretical and praxiological derailments disruptive of public and private order occur if the attempt is made to divorce obligation and aspiration from each other or to treat them as contradictory terms. A preoccupation with obligation is oppressive and deadening: at best conducive to habituation productive of a minimal existential order and public peace through consensus; at worst stultifying of freedom and intellect, and liable to perversion into the reign of terror of a totalitarian power elite in a schismatic master-slave society, which has become commonplace in our century. A preoccupation with aspiration, on the other hand, while liberating and productive of the highest human achievement becomes, if left to itself, annihilatingly destructive of every psychic, social, and spiritual order. It is productive of anarchism or apocalyptic utopianism, of nihilism or the dream-world of the second realities of spiritual enthusiasm so familiar in modern ideologies. Yet as these formulations suggest, the structure of the differentiated human consciousness is such that it is in fact impossible to sever aspiration from obligation.

A balance between obligation and aspiration is requisite if a satisfactory human political order is to be maintained. The traditional obligations of a society inevitably comprehend within themselves and imply the aspirations of the generations of men who have lived before as the legacy and substance of a common sense that both secures and orients existence. For this reason Cicero viewed the law as not simply obligatory but liberating as well. Christians accept the proposition that only if revealed truth is known can one, through faith, be made free. The noetic structure of reality empirically explored by a philosophically grounded political science includes not only the insights and aspirations of the moment but also the cumulus of obligatory truths discovered by mankind throughout history. Only through remembering by attentive sifting of the whole known content of man's historical participation in being can the liberating truth of existence be recaptured, preserved, augmented, and institutionalized in social vessels accessible to everyman and constantly adapted by successive generations.

The modern liberal mode of politics is heavily indebted to events and personalities of the seventeenth century, especially John Locke. Despite all that the revisionists have said about him, Locke shaped an evocative view of human reality, which substantially underlies the orthodoxies of modern free government. The American Founders may not have been Lockean in any strict or dogmatic sense (however defined by various interpretations of the philosopher's thought), but his words echo in the Declaration of Independence and his political thought requires careful attention. We next turn to that aspect of the analysis.

CHAPTER 2 The Civil Theology of Liberal Democracy: Locke and His Predecessors

The concept *civil theology* is best known from its use, following the Stoics, by Marcus Terentius Varro (d. 27 B.C.) and its subsequent appearance in Augustine's *City of God* and from the work of Hobbes, Spinoza, and Rousseau in the seventeenth and eighteenth centuries. Giambattista Vico's *New Science,* moreover, is explicitly a "rational civil theology" in one of its principal aspects. Finally, Michael Oakeshott and Eric Voegelin have revived the notion as a technical term in contemporary political science.[1]

The political necessity for a generally accepted account of the ultimate reality does not diminish with the crisis or collapse of this or that particular account but instead tends to become more acute. Philosophers from time to time have sought to supply such rational grounds of spiritual and emotional concord (*homonoia*) through articulation of civil or political theologies. It is the purpose of this chapter to clarify the meaning and use of the notion of civil theology from the time of Plato onward and, more particularly, to relate it to the

---

1. Augustine *De civitate Dei* VI. 6.; Thomas Hobbes, *De cive* (1642), cap. 15, art. 15; Hobbes, *Leviathan* (1651), Chaps. 31, 32, and 42 to end. Vico, *New Science,* paras. 334, 342, 360, 364, 366, 385, 390, 990; Jean-Jacques Rousseau, *Du Contrat Social* (1762), Bk. IV, Chap. 8; Benedict de Spinoza (d. 1677), *Tractatus theologico-politicus,* Chaps. 3, 6.40, 8.46. Michael Oakeshott (ed.), "Introduction," in Hobbes, *Leviathan* (Oxford, n.d.), lxi–lxiv. Eric Voegelin, "Industrial Society in Search of Reason," in *World Technology and Human Destiny,* ed. Raymond Aron (Ann Arbor, Mich., 1963), 35–37; Voegelin, *New Science of Politics,* Chap. 3.

thought of John Locke. It will be argued that Locke's *Second Treatise of Government* is less a work of political philosophy than one in the genre of civil theology. This fact goes far to explain much of the vagueness and ambiguity in the *Second Treatise* itself and its relation to the *Essay Concerning Human Understanding*. In examining Locke's motivations, it will be urged that his chief purposes were (like those of both Hobbes and Spinoza) to foster civic peace in the face of political and religious enthusiasm and violence so as to secure for the people a modicum of public order and for himself and other thinkers the freedom and safety conducive to the life of reason. Hence, his primary political concern was with the peace that the show of truth can secure and not with the truth itself so loved by philosophers. At the same time, Locke's intentions were revolutionary, both as a partisan of Shaftesbury's Whig cause and as a political and philosophical thinker. The contours of this revolutionism will be sketched and some of the implications drawn.

The presentation is divided into six parts. The first two trace the notion of civil theology in Plato, Spinoza, and Hobbes, and provide an overview of the subject into the present. The last four examine Locke against this background, briefly relating his work to philosophy, myth, and constitutional history, and indicating the principal components of his own naturalistic political theology. His work effects a profound break with both the classical and Christian teachings, and it will be suggested that despite its enduring effectiveness in the self-interpretations of Anglo-American societies, it also laid the groundwork for the reductionist doctrines that emerged in the nineteenth century and became politically prevalent in the twentieth.

I

The question of a civil or political theology has its roots not among the Stoics but in Hellenic philosophy. It makes an appearance in Hesiod and in Xenophanes and becomes explicit with the coining by Plato of the neologism *theology*. This occurs in his analysis of the order of being, in relation to the true ethical and political order as given in the *Republic*, where he speaks of the "types of theology" (*typoi peri theologias*) (379A-B). The discussion in the *Republic* at this point is precisely of a true civil theology, one that the founders of a society must insist upon to replace the traditional mythological or fabulous theologies of the poets. Plato's civil theology occupies an intermediate position between deceptive mythological theology, on the one side, and the mystic-philosopher's profound insight into the divine Ground of being on the other—the later "natural theology" of the Stoics. Three types of theology are thereby distinguished. Mythological theology is rejected because it is false and misleading to an unacceptable degree, producing ignorance in the soul about the highest things. The mystical or noetic theology of the philosopher is so esoteric that it lies beyond the intellectual and experiential reach of ordinary men. Civil theology, therefore, occupies a middle ground in that it consists of key principles or doctrines discerned by philosophers to be true and essential to right order in man and society. These doctrines are to be persuasively embodied by poets into likely tales and images representing "gods and demigods and heroes" and the after-life of the soul (392A).

Civil theology in its first formal appearance consists then of propositionally stated true scientific knowledge of the divine order. It is the theology discerned and validated through reason by the philosopher, on the one hand, and through common sense and the *logique du coeur* evoked in everyman by the persuasive beauty of mythic narrative and imitative representations, on the other hand. The principal doctrines are outlined by Socrates-Plato, the philosopher-legislator, and then incorporated into mythic accounts in the dialogues by Socrates-Plato, the poet. Only after the true theology has been expounded can the truth of man become thematic to the *Republic* (392A-B), an insight into the demands of rationality preserved in Marx's dictum that "the critique of religion is the presupposition of all critique."[2]

The outline of the civil theology as a self-conscious enterprise on this first occasion involved assertion of a minimum dogma of creedal truths. In the *Republic* these are as follows: (1) God is truly good and the author of only good things and of nothing that is evil; (2) He does

2. "Für Deutschland ist die *Kritik der Religion* im wesentlichen beendigt, und die Kritik der Religion ist die Voraussetzung aller Kritik." Quoted from "Zur Kritik der Hegelschen Rechtsphilosophe," in Marx, *Die Frühschriften*, 207. Emphasis here and throughout the present chapter is as it appears in the original.

not lie to or deceive man through magic or in any other way; and (3) death and immortality need hold no terror for the good and virtuous man (379C-392A). These doctrines encourage citizens "to honour the gods and their parents, and to value friendship with one another" (386A) as the essential conditions to achieve a just political order. In the last dialogue, the *Laws,* which is overtly a theology, sacrilege is defined in terms of violation of the minimum dogma. "No one who in obedience to the laws believed that there were Gods, ever intentionally did any unholy act, or uttered any unlawful word; but he who did must have supposed one of three things,—either that they did not exist,—which is the first possibility, or secondly, that, if they did, they took no care of man, or thirdly, that they were easily appeased and turned aside from their purpose by sacrifices and prayers."[3] To the minimum dogma of the *Republic* are added two further principles: (4) divine providential concern for man is a reality; and (5) impenitent and perfunctory prayer and ritual are insufficient to appease divine wrath. Institutionalization of the minimum dogma of the *Laws* takes the form of a brief law, which includes punishment by death for incorrigible impiety. The expository and persuasive prelude (*prooemium*) to this law fills Book X.[4]

II

The effective collapse of the medieval *Christianitas* by the fifteenth century, the rise of Renaissance learning and of the new nation-states, and the turmoil of the Reformation and Counter-Reformation brought surging to the historical surface the undercurrent of apocalyptic enthusiasm till then restrained by Augustinian doctrine and checked by institutional concert. The great age of Western Revolution which thereby began provoked a reassertion of civil theology by such representative thinkers as Hobbes, Spinoza, Vico, and Rousseau—and in a unique fashion, also by Locke.

The differentiation through the civil theology of the public *cultus* from the life of reason was present in Plato's formulation of a minimum dogma. A glance will show that this distinction has been pre-

---

3. Plato *Laws* 885B (trans. Jowett). Noticed by Vico, *New Science*, para. 130.
4. See Voegelin, *Plato and Aristotle*, 263.

sented in a similar fashion by others throughout the long stretch of history since then. It was articulated after Augustine in 496 through the Gelasian system that sought to rationalize the spiritual and temporal dimensions of human existence by elaborating the doctrine of Church-Empire and Pope-Emperor as representative symbolisms. This solution sufficed until the thirteenth century, when Dante, under pressure from the new philosophical ferment prompted by the Averroists' rediscovery of classical thought, extensively modified the symbolisms of Emperor and Philosopher. As a result of changing historical and intellectual circumstances, comparable doctrines were advanced in the sixteenth century by Jean Bodin, who proposed the National Sovereign and Mystic Philosopher, and in the ideological climate of the nineteenth century by Auguste Comte, who contributed the symbolisms of Industrial Manager and Positivist Intellectual. Finally, in the twentieth century the life of reason has been substantially obliterated in favor of the "mental slavery" of the total man, who is the party stalwart of National Socialism or Communism. Civil theology has been engulfed by this or that party line and imposed through physical and psychological mass management and terror. For this predicament two appropriate epitaphs readily come to mind: Whitehead's "Modern philosophy has been ruined," and Solzhenitsyn's "Only the prisoners are free."[5]

The need for fundamental consensus through a minimum dogma beyond public debate was also a central element of Plato's civil theology. As we have noted, however, Plato regarded his dogmas to be superior to the old myths of the poets precisely because of their true representation of divine reality. The minimum dogma comprised a valuable prophylaxis against the "true lie" (*alethes pseudos*) and against the psychic "disease" (*nosos*) of ignorance in the soul about true being.[6] Among the seventeenth-century thinkers the purpose of the minimum dogma was less ambitious. It was intended merely to subdue the religious passions that were disruptive of the public peace and dangerous to personal security. At just this point, it may be said,

5. Voegelin, "Industrial Society," 36. Étienne Gilson, *Unity of Philosophical Experience* (New York, 1937), 294; Alfred North Whitehead, *Science and the Modern World, Lowell Lectures [of] 1925* (New York, 1967), 55. Aleksandr I. Solzhenitsyn, *First Circle*, trans. Thomas P. Whitney (New York, 1969), 370, 533, where the "epitaph" is implicit but not express.
6. Plato *Republic* 382A–B; *Laws* 888B.

that religion became in the view of intellectuals "the opium of the people," as Marx later spoke of it. From Bacon to Rousseau—and beyond him into the subsequent radical ideological phase down to the present—the dogmatism and superstition of Christianity in all its shades and manifestations is contrasted in increasingly absolute terms with the life of reason.

This disjunction is clearly expressed in Spinoza's *Tractatus theologico-politicus* (1670), whose fourteenth chapter is entitled "Definitions of Faith, the True Faith, and the Foundations of Faith, which is once for all separated from Philosophy." He there affirms that "faith does not demand that dogmas should be true as that they should be pious—that is, such as will stir up the heart to obey." He summarizes the distinctions and their merits as follows:

Between faith or theology, and philosophy, there is no connection, nor affinity. I think no one will dispute the fact who has knowledge of the aim and foundations of the two subjects, for they are as wide apart as the poles.

Philosophy has no end in view save truth: faith . . . looks for nothing but obedience and piety. Again, philosophy is based on axioms which must be sought from nature alone.[7]

If the interest of Spinoza in setting down these distinctions is on the side of insuring freedom of thought and personal security for the speculative philosopher, that of Hobbes in 1642 and 1651, while less clear, seems to lie on the side of establishing public peace as an end in itself. In neither thinker is there a shred of concern for the central issues of classical political theory, *i.e.*, the just life and the best regime for man *qua* human. These questions can be addressed only by individual men in the strictly private sphere of their existences, if at all. Of course, for Hobbes there is no supreme good but only the *summum malum,* the fear of violent death. Hobbes' justification of the civil theology finds typical expression as follows:

As for the sacred laws, we must consider . . . that every subject hath transferred as much right as he could on him or them who had the supreme authority. But he could have transferred his right of judging the manner how

7. Benedict de Spinoza, *Writings on Political Philosophy*, ed. A. G. A. Balz, trans. R. H. M. Elwes (New York, 1937), 13, 16. Fundamental to the understanding of Spinoza is Leo Strauss, *Persecution and the Art of Writing* (Glencoe, 1952), Chap. 5, esp. 180–86.

God is to be honoured, and therefore also he hath done it. . . . Wherefore subjects can transfer their right of judging the manner of God's worship on him or them who have the sovereign power. Nay, they must do it; for else all manner of absurd opinions concerning the nature of God, and all ridiculous ceremonies which have been used by any nations, will be seen at once in the same city. . . . It may therefore be concluded, that the interpretation of all laws, as well sacred as secular, (God ruling by the way of nature only), depends on the authority of the city, that is to say, that man or counsel, to whom the sovereign power is committed; and that whatsoever God commands, he commands by his [*i.e.*, the sovereign's] voice. And on the other side, that whatsoever is commanded by them [*i.e.*, sovereign power], both concerning the manner of honouring God, and concerning secular affairs, is commanded by God himself.[8]

Hobbes bases his doctrine on "reason" and the "principles of nature only." He designates the public system of divine worship as the *cultus Dei* and finds it distinguished from private worship by its division into the three parts of praise, magnifying, and blessing. In contrast, the "passions" of *love, hope,* and *fear* arise from private worship. He enumerates the actions and attributes of the public cultus, just as Spinoza would enumerate the essential dogmas, and specifies that they must be uniform throughout the commonwealth.[9] He defines the church to be "*a company of men professing Christian religion, united in the person of one sovereign, at whose command they ought to assemble, and without whose authority they ought not to assemble.*"[10] He affirms the sovereign's will to be binding in things both secular and spiritual through the "consolidations of the right politic and ecclesiastic in Christian sovereigns" by which they *are* therefore "the commonwealth and . . . the Church; for both State and Church are the same men."[11] As in Spinoza, the emphasis is placed on the regula-

---

8. Hobbes, *De cive*, 3.17; *cf.* Hobbes, *Leviathan*, Chap. 42.
9. Hobbes, *Leviathan*, Chaps. 32, 31; *cf.* Chap. 43. Spinoza's dogmas as formulated in Chap. 14 of the *Tractatus theologico-politicus* are the following: "I have now no further fear in enumerating the dogmas of universal faith or the fundamental dogmas of the whole of Scripture, inasmuch as they all tend (as may be seen from what has been said) to this one doctrine, namely, that there exists a God, that is, a Supreme Being, Who loves justice and charity, and Who must be obeyed by whatsoever would be saved; that the worship of this Being consists in the practice of justice and love towards one's neighbour, and that they contain nothing beyond the following doctrines. . . ." (Cited from Spinoza, *Writings*, 14–15).
10. Hobbes, *Leviathan*, Chap. 39.
11. *Ibid.*, Chap. 42.

tion of overt action, since the inward life of man is (in the seventeenth century still) beyond regulation by Leviathan; hence, it alone is the sphere of liberty.

The essential elements of the modern civil theologies may, then, be summarized generally as follows: (1) preservation of the distinction between the public *cultus* from the life of reason and contemplation; (2) recognition that a basic consensus or obligatory minimum dogma with respect to ultimate reality is essential if public peace is to be maintained; (3) identification of dogmatic Christianity itself as the mythological-civil theology with which the life of reason is to be contrasted; *or* alternatively, (4) after Hegel, elaboration and terroristic imposition of sectarian ideological creeds for the masses in society by party or intellectual elites who alone possess knowledge (*gnosis*) through the exercise of speculative reason; and (5) enforcement of the principles of the civil theology by government, either directly through positive law or indirectly through mythic evocation of natural rights and the institutionalization of religious toleration.

III

John Locke's *Second Treatise of Government* provides a historio-genetic explanation of society and government, the account apparently being assimilated to English constitutional history and to the classical and biblical traditions. Cogent analyses, however, have advanced the view that the presumed historical argument is, in fact, ignored. The *Treatise*'s apparent rapport with the classical and biblical tradition is deceptive and, therefore, an untenable assumption for a critical assessment of Locke's thought.[12] When we recognize the extent to which those of the seventeenth and eighteenth centuries acknowledged the necessity of a civil theology, as evidenced in the work of several political thinkers of the period as well as in Locke's philo-

12. See Pocock, *Ancient Constitution*, 237–38; Locke, *Two Treatises of Government*, 75–78; Richard Cox, *Locke on War and Peace* (Oxford, 1960), Chap. 1; Strauss, *Natural Right and History*, 202–51; cf. Macpherson, *Political Theory of Possessive Individualism*, 300. Laslett's "Introduction" in the 2nd edition (1967) of Locke's *Two Treatises* modified the passage cited above (to pp. 75–78) and partly replaced it by saying that the English "Constitution was undoubtedly in Locke's mind in 1689," p. 77. We must deal, of course, with what is said in Locke's book.

sophical affinities with both Hobbes and Spinoza (whatever his differences), it is not implausible to suppose that his covert intention in the *Second Treatise* may have been to advance a civil theology in the form of an evocative naturalistic myth of civil government. Civil theology typically incorporates doctrinal formulations of the insights of reason into order by using mythic imagery, and the mythic cast of Locke's work supports the surmise that at least a part of his real intention in writing may have been to communicate a civil theology. This line of interpretation finds a number of points of support.

The meaning of the ambivalence of Locke's work may first be considered. Santayana remarked, "Had Locke's mind been more profound, it might have been less influential." There is merit in this observation, for Locke's theoretical deficiency lies in a kind of shallowness that is often called common sense. His true profundity, however, is perhaps obscured by an ambivalence that was probably calculated and which followed from his systematic intention to break with the classical and Christian tradition in philosophy and religion while appearing to be the true advocate of that tradition. His "caution" may be understood, but not in terms of a reluctance to identify his intentions clearly. His "extraordinary furtiveness" (as Peter Laslett calls it) took such forms, among others, as never acknowledging during his lifetime authorship of the two *Treatises* (Spinoza, also writing in fear of persecution, was published only posthumously), of seeming to uphold the viewpoint of Richard Hooker and the most conventional English reading of the biblical tradition, and of apparently aiming his acknowledged philosophical work at the Cartesian doctrine of innate ideas.[13]

The ambiguities of Locke's writing make notoriously difficult the critical determination of the precise meaning of a particular work or

---

13. George Santayana, *Some Turns of Thought in Modern Philosophy: Five Essays* (Freeport, N.Y., 1933), 3. *An Essay Concerning Human Understanding*, published in 1689, bore Locke's name and appeared in December. The two *Treatises* and the *Letter Concerning Toleration*, published in translation earlier the same year, were anonymous and remained so until Locke's death in 1704. No fewer than sixteen passages from Richard Hooker, added as an afterthought in 1681, according to Laslett, are quoted in the *Second Treatise* (Secs. 15, 60, 61; and in the author's notes to Secs. 74, 90, 91, 94, 111, 134, 135, 136). There is little evidence that Locke ever read beyond Bk. I of Hooker's *Ecclesiastical Polity*. See Locke, *Two Treatises of Government*, 4–6, 37, 39, 57n (on Hooker); see also pp. 65–66, 69, 72, 81, 205n; Strauss, *Natural Right and History*, 207–11; Cox, *Locke on War and Peace*, 14–21, 48–63, 209;

the relation among his several books. If we assume the ambiguities are a part of the writer's calculated deceptiveness, it follows that we must read with a suspicious eye, as it were, on the assumption that Locke means more or less or something other than simply what he says. There seems but little doubt that the primary explanations of this deceptiveness are an inordinate intellectual sensitivity to criticism and a well-based fear of physical harm prompted by the disorder of the times in which he lived and wrote, and by his own disagreement with prevailing doctrine and politics. Algernon Sidney, after all, had been beheaded in 1683 for treason and regicide, and for holding doctrines common to those Locke already had expressed in an unpublished preliminary draft of the two *Treatises*. As late as 1703 Locke denied ever having read Sidney's *Discourses*, even though the book was in his library and he recommended it (side by side with Hooker and his own *Treatises*) in *Concerning Reading and Study*.

From 1666 on, Locke was intimately associated with the first Earl of Shaftesbury, who was eventually charged with treason, imprisoned in the Tower, and died in 1683 in Holland whence he had fled after release from imprisonment and vainly attempting to foment rebellion against the crown. He was also in personal contact with Essex, who was either murdered or committed suicide in the Tower, as well as with other "disaffected Englishmen," both in England and on the Continent. In the period from the Assassination or Rye House Plot until after the Revolution, *i.e.*, from 1683 till 1689, Locke was himself suspect and under surveillance. By the king's command he was deprived of his studentship and home at Christ Church, Oxford. A warrant was issued for his arrest, and he fled to Holland, where he continued conspiratorial activities in connection with the 1685 invasion of Scotland by Argyle; extradition was sought, and he used the alias "Dr. van der Linden" for a time. Locke's biographer writes that "Locke is an elusive subject for a biographer because he was an extremely secretive man. He modified a system of shorthand for the purpose of concealment; he employed all sorts of curious little cyphers; he cut

---

Locke, *An Essay Concerning Human Understanding*, abr. and ed. A. S. Pringle-Pattison (Oxford, 1924), xxxi–xxxiv; Locke, *An Essay Concerning Human Understanding; Collated and Annotated, with Prolegomena, Biographical, Critical, and Historical*, ed. A. C. Fraser (1894; rpr. New York, 1959), II, 268n, 291n. Further references to *Essay* are to this edition.

signatures and other identifiable names from letters he preserved; at one time he used invisible ink."[14]

Despite Locke's own denials, therefore, convincing evidence suggests that he can only be regarded as a genuine revolutionary in the full meaning of that term, living in a conspirator's fear of life and liberty for his political activities and views throughout most of the period during which he composed and published the *Letter Concerning Toleration,* the two *Treatises,* and the *Essay.* If this is accepted as true, it will be instructive to notice some of the ways in which he departed from the intellectual conventions of his turbulent age so as to be better able to gauge his polemical and theoretical purposes. As a Whig revolutionary strenuously in conflict with the Stuart Restoration government of both Charles II and James II, this opposition took literary form during the Exclusionist Controversy in his refutation in the *First Treatise* of Filmer's *Patriarcha.* The principles of the argument were then set forth in the *Second Treatise.* As Laslett has shown, the *Second Treatise* was in fact written first (probably during the winter of 1679–80) but was published only in 1689.

Locke was, however, far from being merely a traditional Whig. This may best be seen from the fact that neither of the two *Treatises* contains an appeal to the history of the Ancient Constitution, which was the polemical mainstay of every other Whig writer of the seventeenth century.[15] Again, the appeal of the argument is not to English

14. James L. Axtell, *Educational Writings of John Locke: A Critical Edition with Introduction and Notes* (Cambridge, England, 1968), 400n. A. C. Fraser (ed.), "Prolegomena," in Locke, *Essay,* I, xxxv. See the account of this period of Locke's life in Maurice Cranston, *John Locke: A Biography* (New York, 1957), xi, and Chaps. 15–19. Locke continued to be watched even in Holland, and he was expelled from Utrecht in 1686. He wrote to his friend Philip Limborch on December 12 of that year: "The expulsion of which you have heard I do not understand, nor do I wish it talked about." Quoted from *ibid.,* 262. Locke's secretiveness already was evident at age twenty. See John Locke, *Essays on the Law of Nature,* ed. Wolfgang von Leyden (Oxford, 1954), 15. Locke's early "conservatism" is argued by Philip Abrams in John Locke, *Two Tracts of Government,* ed. with intro., notes, and trans. by Philip Abrams (Cambridge, England, 1967); *cf.* Melvin J. Lasky, "The Birth of a Metaphor: On the Origins of Utopia and Revolution (II)," *Encounter,* XXXIV (1970), 35–37.

15. Pocock, *Ancient Constitution,* 235–38. Locke, *Two Treatises of Government,* 75–78, 118–19. On the revolutionary quality of Locke's political teaching and philosophical posture see Strauss, *Natural Right and History,* 248–51; *cf.* Laslett's exasperation with Strauss' analysis in his edition of Locke's *Two Treatises,* 105. See n. 12 given earlier. *Cf.* Richard Ashcraft, "Locke's State of Nature: Historical Fact or Moral Fiction," *American Political Science Review,* LXVII (1968), 898–915; and Richard Ashcraft, *Revolutionary Politics and Locke's Two Treatises of Government* (Princeton, 1986).

history, and it is also not directed to philosophical understanding or "reason," as Locke himself defines it in the *Essay*. Rather, it appeals to common sense and revelation as contained in Scripture.[16] The content of the *Treatises*, then, has a truth value, in Locke's own view, of only probability or persuasive belief and not of scientific knowledge.[17] In the first book of the *Essay*, Locke explicitly rejects the doctrine of innate principles and ideas *in the specific sense* of the Stoic *koinai ennoiai* (not the *koine aisthesis*), although he is in effect ironically appealing to this doctrine in the *Treatises*.[18] This rejection is critically understood, however, to run not only against the Cartesians but more specifically against the dogmatism of the Schoolmen and their "depraved Aristotelianism," and against certain of the Cambridge Platonists. While conducting the polemic against innate ideas, Locke introduces intuitive knowledge and self-evident principles in their stead.[19]

Without exploring in detail the complicated epistemological issues, it can be noted that an effect of these steps is to excise political theory from philosophy and reduce it to the level of uncritical or ignorant opinion (*doxa*), thereby undercutting the very possibility of a science

16. John Locke, *First Treatise*, Secs. 4, 60; Locke, *Essay*, Bk. II, 9–15. See the appeal to common sense itself in the midst of the attack on innate ideas and Hamilton's comment on Bk. I, 2. 4 in Locke, *Essay*, I, 68n.

17. Locke, *Essay*, Bk. IV, 14. 2. This distinction is upheld vigorously until Locke's last days and is basic to his view of political and theological understanding. See Locke, *Works of John Locke* (new ed. corrected; 1823; rpr. Aalen, Germany, 1963), *Third Letter for Toleration* (1692), VI, 143–46, 210, 402; *Fourth Letter for Toleration* (1704), *ibid.*, 566–67. Locke was engaged in the writing of the *Fourth Letter* at the time of his death. See Locke, *Essay*, I, lxxx, xciii, cvii, cviii; II, 429n.

18. Locke, *Essay*, Bk. I, 2. 1, 3. 4; *cf.* Bk. IV, 7. 11. On the Stoic theory of knowledge see Edward Zeller, *Stoics, Epicureans and Sceptics*, trans. O. J. Reichel (new and rev. ed.; New York, 1962), 75–91. For the belief in God as a *koine ennoia* see Cicero *De natura deorum* I. 16–17.

19. Locke, *Essay*, ed. Pringle-Pattison, xxxiii, 21n; Locke, *Essay*, Bk. I, 1–3; II, 1–2; IV, 2. 1, 7. 19, 17. 14. Since it is at least doubtful whether anyone (including the Stoics) ever held the doctrine of innate ideas in the sense attacked by Locke, Pringle-Pattison rightly notes that it was a "dead issue" and wonders "was it ever a live one?" Locke, *Essay*, ed. Pringle-Pattison, xxxiv. *Cf.* Locke, *Essay*, Bk. I, lxxi; also Zeller, *Stoics, Epicureans and Sceptics*, 80–82. This raises the question, what is the real purpose of Locke's critique? Probably he intended not only to continue the philosophically therapeutic rebellion begun by Bacon against late Scholastic dogmatism but also more generally to discredit the entire philosophical enterprise as it had been conducted from Plato to Thomas Aquinas. *Cf.* Bacon, *New Organon*, Bk. I, Secs. 61–68, 124–29. On *intuition* see Locke, *Essay*, Bk. II, 176, 190, 407, 417, 420, 422n, 427n, 428n, 429n, 433n, 434n, 453. *Cf.* the discussion in Richard I. Aaron, *John Locke* (2nd ed.; Oxford, 1965), 10–11, 220–27.

of politics. A further effect is to eliminate the historically developed common sense or *koinai ennoiai* by rejecting the classical and Christian notions of man's knowledge of divine Being through participation in it as, alternatively, the bearer of divine Reason (*Nous*), in Aristotle's sense, or as the creature who bears the divine image of his Creator so that "the spirit of man is the candle of the Lord."[20] The new "candle of the Lord" of Locke's *Essay* is "reason" in the narrow sense of discursive intelligence or the inferential faculty. It thereby becomes synonymous with *reasoning*, exclusive of common sense, on the one hand, and of the intuitive or noetic intelligence, on the other hand, on which all rationality ultimately depends. Such "reason" becomes the new test of all knowledge on the basis of the sensationalist (empirical) epistemology of the *Essay*. Together with what Locke then calls "intuition," "reason" determines the understanding in both practical and speculative aspects.[21] In sum, under the guise of defining the true limits of understanding, Locke manages to reject the core of classical and Christian anthropology and along with it, the tradition that was embodied in Western and English history. By a stunning disingenuous display of semantic legerdemain, he substitutes naturalistic reasoning for the Aristotelian *nous* and the Christian *ratio*, employing for this purpose a trifling argument in *ignoratio elenchi* against pretended Cartesian *koinai ennoiai*.

Finally, the argument of the *Second Treatise*, now understood to be essentially doxic and uncritical, appeals to traditional common sense, newly decked out in the garb of a natural law which is both fundamental and inexplicit in the work published by Locke but which, nonetheless, absorbs both reason and revelation. By a means effectively complementary to the entirely different attack of the *Essay*, the same naturalistic reduction is thereby achieved. On this reading, the "state of nature" of the *Second Treatise* is systematically identical to

20. Prov. 20:27, a favorite verse of Locke's in the *Essay e.g.*, Bk. I, 1. 5, Bk. IV, 3. 20. See Aristotle *Nicomachean Ethics* Bk. X. 7. 1. 1177a11. Locke expressly excludes from practical common-sense *knowledge* the proposition "that one should do as he would be done unto," which he simultaneously acknowledges to be "the most unshaken rule of morality, and foundation of all social virtue," thereby both rejecting the statement as knowledge and embracing it as *true opinion* (*Essay*, Bk. I, 3. 4). *Cf.* the discussion in John W. Yolton, *Locke and the Compass of Human Understanding: A Selective Commentary on the "Essay"* (Cambridge, England, 1970), 169–71.

21. Locke, *Essay*, Bk. I, 1. 1; Bk. IV, 17; *cf.* Locke, *Essay*, Bk. II, pp. 385n, 427n, 430n.

the *tabula rasa* of the *Essay* inasmuch as both negate the content of human experience in the respective modes of history and philosophy. By Locke's account, no less than by Hobbes', prudential science was an impossibility in an age of contending gnostic enthusiasms, precisely because science depends upon the elaboration of noetic insight into the order of being, including transcendent Being. From just the madness of divinely inspired sectarian paracletes, both these thinkers sought in their different ways to rescue political existence.[22]

IV

A completely cogent presentation of the analysis just summarized would very nearly entail a sentence-by-sentence commentary on at least both the *Treatises* and the *Essay*. This type of analysis has already been completed by Alexander Campbell Fraser in 1894 for the latter work. In large part the former has recently been done by Peter Laslett. Moreover, Leo Strauss and Richard Cox (among others) have distinguished the levels of argument in Locke and the differences in

22. Locke himself does not use the expression *tabula rasa* here, but "white paper"; see *Essay*, Bk. II, 1. 2. On *enthusiasm* in Locke see *Essay*, Bk. IV, 19; on "fiery zealots" in religion as those "striving for power over one other" see *A Letter Concerning Toleration*, in Locke, *Works*, VI, 5–6 and *passim*; on classical and Lockean prudence see Cox, *Locke on War and Peace*, 192–95; on prudence in Hobbes see *Leviathan*, Chap. 47; *cf.* Aristotle *Nicomachean Ethics* VI. 3. 1–13. 8. 1139b14–1145a12. The impossibility of political and prudential *science* is directly affirmed by Locke in an entry in his *Journal* dated June 26, 1681, at about the same time he was revising the two *Treatises* by inserting the quotations from Hooker. He wrote: "The well management of public or private affairs depending upon the various and unknown humours, interests and capacities of men we have to do with in the world, and not upon any settled ideas of things physical, polity and prudence are not capable of demonstration. But a man is principally helped in them by the history of matter of fact, and a sagacity of finding out an analogy in their operations and effects.

"[The truths of mathematics are certain.] But whether this course in public or private affairs will succeed well, whether rhubarb will purge or quinquina cure an ague, is only known by experience, but no certain knowledge or demonstration." Quoted from Locke, *Two Treatises, of Government*, 84–85, who cites from Richard I. Aaron and J. Gibb (eds.), *An Early Draft of Locke's Essay, Together with Excerpts from His Journals* (Oxford, England, 1936), 116ff., a volume not available to me. Again, the crux of the issue lies in distinguishing noetic and phenomenal science. *Cf.* Aristotle *Nicomachean Ethics* I. 2–3. 1094a19–95a13. An important recent study is Patrick Romanell, *John Locke and Medicine: A New Key to Locke* (New York, 1984), esp. 127–54; see also W. M. Spellman, *John Locke and the Problem of Depravity* (Oxford, England, 1988), 106–98, 205–14.

modes of discourse between his two principal works. The reader can thus be referred to these sources for details.[23]

Certain points, however, must be further supported and emphasized here as interpretative conclusions, each resting upon conflicting passages in Locke's writing. T. H. Green was justified in saying that the *Essay* is an incoherent "chaos of antinomies" from which a consistent meaning cannot be directly extracted, and Locke himself admitted to being an "inaccurate writer."[24] That was, indeed, a part of his technique, one essential to his purposes. Insofar as Locke in the *Essay* is true to his own philosophical principles, the drift of the argument is an anti-metaphysical flight from the oneness of being into the manifold particularities declared by the senses, a closure against the divine Ground which implies an anti-philosophical hatred of Being as the transcendental *ens realissimum*. Such a flight from the One is declared no less by Locke's reduction of experience to sensory perception and of reason to discursive reasoning than by his constriction of intuition to what may perhaps be termed "inward" perceptions and his separation of it from "reason" by his excessively narrow definition of knowledge, by his blurring of the distinction between logical and ontological "first principles," by his rejection of historical ("traditional") knowledge as mere hearsay, by his obfuscation of the concept of history so that it means only the chronological content of an individual person's experience, and most especially by his slighting of the category of being (*ousia*) in order to seek the *limits* of the understanding rather than the Ground of being.

The contrast with Aristotle is especially instructive. In the first book of the *Metaphysics*, Aristotle, after observing the universal desire of men to know, next observes that "all men suppose what is called Wisdom to deal with the first causes and the principles of things." Moreover, the nature of Wisdom can be suggested by considering the character of a "wise man." Such a man, he says, will not be concerned with sensory perception because "sense perception is com-

---

23. Works by Fraser, Laslett, Strauss, and Cox have already been cited (see nn. 12 and 13 above). A good summary of the Straussian viewpoint can be found in Bluhm, *Theories of the Political System*, Chap. 9. See also T. H. Green's "Introduction," in David Hume, *Philosophical Works*, ed. T. H. Green and T. H. Grose (1886; rpr. Aalen, Germany, 1964), I, 1–299.

24. Green, *Philosophical Works*, I, 112. Locke, *Works*, IV, 448.

mon to all, and therefore easy and no mark of Wisdom"; rather, "the wise man knows all things, as far as possible." The first principles then are identified with the first causes, and these are specified to be the good and God.[25] Thus, when Aristotle considered the question of limits of human knowledge, his response was the opposite of Locke's. Philosophy begins in wonder and is sustained by it. The philosophical man—no less than he who framed the old myths—seeks to know the genesis of particular realities, and hence of the cosmos itself.

And a man who is puzzled and wonders thinks himself ignorant (whence even the lover of myth is in a sense a lover of Wisdom, for the myth is composed of wonders); therefore since they philosophized in order to escape from ignorance, evidently they were pursuing science in order to know, and not for any utilitarian end. . . . The possession of it might be justly regarded as beyond human power; for in many ways human nature is in bondage, so that according to Simonides "God alone can have this privilege", and it is unfitting that man should not be content to seek the knowledge that is suited to him [i.e., practical rather than theoretical knowledge].

Yet Aristotle rejects the latter view. He holds that

the most divine science is also most honourable; and this science alone must be, in two ways, most divine. For the science which it is most meet for God to have is a divine science, and so is any science that deals with divine objects; and this science alone has both these qualities; for (1) God is thought to be among the causes of all things and to be a first principle, and (2) such a science either God alone can have, or God above all others.

In the *Nicomachean Ethics* he adds, "We must not follow those who advise us, being men, to think of human things, and, being mortal, of mortal things, but must, so far as we can, make ourselves immortal, and strain every nerve to live in accordance with the best thing in us."[26] And that is noetic reason, the divine something in man whereby first principles are grasped and through which he participates in divine *nous* itself.

While Locke is prepared to acknowledge the intuitive self-evidence of such principles of knowledge as contradiction and identity, he passes

25. Aristotle *Metaphysics* (trans. W. D. Ross), I. 1. 17–2. 14. 981b28–30, 982a6, 12, 982b10, 983a8.
26. *Ibid.*, I. 2. 8–14. 982b12–983a10. Aristotle *Nicomachean Ethics* X. 7. 8–8. 1. 1177b31–1178a1, 1178a9–10, VI. 6. 1–7. 5. 1140b31–1141a8.

over the intuitive apprehension of being itself and insists that God is known only through demonstration (even though with absolute certainty) and not innately or through direct intuitive self-evidence.[27] Étienne Gilson discriminates Locke's misapprehension in the general remark, "The most tempting of all the false first principles is: that *thought*, not *being*, is involved in my representations."[28] Locke's proof of God's existence is a modification of the cosmological proof or the proof from design. It begins from the intuitive certainty that "I exist," as this is apprehended in turn through self-consciousness. "It is for want of reflection that we are apt to think that our senses show us nothing but material things. Every act of sensation, when duly considered, gives us an equal view of both parts of nature—the corporeal and spiritual. For, whilst I know, by seeing or hearing, that there is some corporeal being without me—the object of that sensation, I do more certainly know that there is some spiritual being within me that sees and hears."[29]

Despite this sensitivity (rare in the *Essay*) to the implications of the experience of participation in being, Locke denies that noetic experience in the divine Ground is in any way evidenced. At the end of his life, he wrote: "I am content with my own mediocrity. And though I call the thinking faculty in me, *mind*, I cannot, because of that name, equal it in anything to that eternal and incomprehensible Being, which, for want of right and distinct conceptions, is called *Mind* also, or the eternal Mind."[30] Locke's idea of God is, in anticipation of Feuerbach, the infinite projection of the highest faculties of man, the magnification of sensory perceptions and simple ideas, and a "putting them together" to "make the complex idea of God," rather than the idea of Active Reason immanent to nature and spirit.[31] Insofar as

27. Locke, *Essay*, Bk. IV, 10 *passim; cf.* Bk. I, 3. 8–16.
28. Gilson, *Unity of Philosophical Experience*, 316.
29. Locke, *Essay*, Bk. II, 23. 15.
30. Letter to Anthony Collins, June 29, 1704, quoted in *Essay*, I, 419n. Eric Voegelin has remarked that Locke suffered from a "severe spiritual disturbance." "I say advisedly from a *spiritual* disturbance, not from a mental; Locke was not a clinical case and his disease does not come under the categories of psychopathology. He is a case of spiritual disease in the sense of the Platonic *nosos;* it belongs to the pneumatopathology of the seventeenth century of which Hobbes was the masterly diagnostician." Quoted by Peter J. Opitz, "John Locke," in *Zwischen Revolution und Restauration: Politisches Denken in England im 17. Jahrhundert*, ed. Eric Voegelin, List Hochschulreihe Geschichte des politischen Denkens (Munich, 1968), 144, 159.
31. Locke, *Essay*, Bk. II, 23. 33–36; Bk. I, 3. 7–18.

Locke's God participates in reality, He is the deistical mechanic of Newton's mechanistic universe.

The assault on metaphysics as such was perhaps clearest in Locke's slighting of the category of being (*ousia*) or substance which, from Aristotle onward, is the foundation of ontological speculation. Locke's treatment of both "substance in general" and God, viewed as one and the same, is proto-positivistic. He asserts that there is no knowable distinction between nominal and real essence (in more recent language, between phenomenon and essence) since our ideas are narrowly dependent upon sensory experiences, and these are always particular and never general or universal. Along with his conviction, however, that "we can attain to nothing but those simple ideas, which we originally received from sensation or reflection," Locke feels compelled to hang back one step from the philosophical nihilism of pure positivism by clinging to "a supposition of *something* to which they [particular ideas of substances] belong, and in which they subsist."[32] So Edward Stillingfleet's acute observation that Locke had "almost discarded substance out of the reasonable part of the world" was accurate.[33] For despite the clarifications and concessions wrung from Locke by the Bishop of Worcester in their extensive controversy as to the mysterious but not necessarily irrational origins of the admittedly "vague" ideas at the root of knowledge, Locke's philosophical heir David Hume flatly discarded substance from philosophy because (like Locke) he too was unable to find "any impression corresponding to the general idea of substance."[34]

32. *Ibid.*, Bk. V, 23, 37.
33. Quoted *ibid.*, I, 423n.
34. Hume quoted Locke, *ibid.*, I, 423n. To Hume, therefore, substance is an "unintelligible chimera," for "neither by considering the first origin of ideas, nor by means of a definition are we able to arrive at any satisfactory notion of substance; which seems to me a sufficient reason for abandoning utterly that dispute concerning the materiality and immateriality of the soul, and makes me absolutely condemn even the question itself." David Hume, *A Treatise of Human Nature*, Pt. 4, Secs. 3 and 5, in Green and Grose (eds.), *Philosophical Works*, I, 508, 518; cf. *ibid.*, I, 324, 327. Note the prohibition of questioning vigorously laid down by Hume in the quoted passage. This significantly anticipates Marx's stance in the *Economic and Philosophic Manuscripts of 1844*, quoted in the Introduction on pp. 34–35 above. Broadly characteristic of ideological thought, the prohibition against metaphysical questions is analyzed in Marx and Comte by Voegelin, *Science, Politics, and Gnosticism*, 15–49; and more exhaustively in Eric Voegelin, *From Enlightenment to Revolution*, ed. John H. Hallowell (Durham, NC, 1975), 136–94, 240–304.

At all of the places in which he considers it in the *Essay,* Locke denigrates and ridicules the idea of "substance in general," only accepting its attenuated conception as a last resort.[35] Whether it is against "the Stagyrite [*sic*] himself" or only the "poor secondary tralatitious system of modern and barbarous schoolmen" that Locke contends, as James Stanhope assumes,[36] Locke signals his meaning by repeatedly slighting the category of being, by barely considering the category of causation that informs the speculation of Aristotle and the Scholastics,[37] and by denying both the innateness and the self-evidence or direct intuitive knowledge of God. He also signals it by providing a circular argument in proof of God's existence, which— so far from being "equal to mathematical" certainty[38]—is obviously flawed and also carries the clear implication that divine Being is *not* a "first principle" since first principles must be intuited or grasped noetically and cannot themselves be demonstrated. Moreover, Locke's proof does not undertake to demonstrate that the Eternal Being must be intelligent (the essence of God in Aristotle) even though in the polemical literature of the day this was understood to be, as Samuel Clarke said in 1704, "the main question between us and the Atheists." Leibniz chided Locke for the insufficiency of his "proof." "I assure you, sir, with perfect sincerity, that I am extremely sorry to be obliged to say anything against this demonstration: But I do it in order to give you an opportunity to fill up the gap in it. . . . I find ambiguity in it."[39] Fraser comments on Locke's demonstration: "The infinite cannot be logically concluded from the finite. We are practically obliged to *presuppose* immanent active Reason, in order to conceive the finite and changing, but we cannot, *by logical argument,* sustain the presupposition. Our 'perception' of God is not the conclusion of a syllogism: it is the necessary assumption in all reasoning, whether about our sensuous or our spiritual experience, and the

35. *Cf.* Locke, *Essay,* Bks. I, 3. 16; I, 6; II, 13. 17–20; III, 6; IV, 3. 4–11; see Fraser's note on the Aristotelian *hyle prote* in connection with Locke's disquisition on the "Abuse of Words," *ibid.,* II, 135n.

36. See Axtell, *Educational Writings,* 31.

37. Locke, *Essay,* Bk. II, 26. 1–2.

38. *Ibid.,* Bk. IV, 10. 1.

39. G. W. F. von Leibniz, *New Essays on the Human Understanding* (1704), quoted from Philip P. Wiener (ed.), *Leibniz: Selections* (New York, 1951), 471.

foundation of all certainty. Assume it—rest life upon it—and the universe and life become harmonious."[40]

Perhaps most indicative of all of Locke's intention to reject *noesis* is his reiterated ridicule of the search for the divine Ground through use of the simile of the "poor Indian philosopher," who "imagined that the earth also wanted something to bear it up." It is too bad, Locke says, that, unlike Western philosophers, the Indian did not know of the "word *substance*." Had he known it, then "he needed not to have been at the trouble to find an elephant to support it [the earth] and a tortoise to support his elephant: the word substance would have done it effectually."[41] The Indian philosopher's "*something, he knew not what*" is the unmovable eternal substance, Aristotle's God, First Principle, and divine Ground of being, encountered above. Indeed, Locke protects himself by virtually assuming the concept of substance in the *Essay*. He repeatedly refers to the "support" of our complex ideas of particular substances; he even provides a classification of substances that approximates Aristotle's.[42] Yet he could have done no less than this without, in a religious age, being labelled an atheist, and Locke was a cautious revolutionary, as we have seen. Stillingfleet clearly perceives the fact and philosophical consequences of Locke's "ridicule [of] the notion of substance, and [of] the European philosophers for asserting it" and argues that, upon Locke's "principles we cannot come to any certainty of reason."[43] All of this, of course, Locke denies. By the drift and emphasis of the *Essay*, however, the issue is beyond doubt. Locke consistently flees from Being into the particularities, descending rather than ascending toward the One, avoiding at every step speculative questions and impugning the worth of the noetic enterprise wherever he touches on it.

It is quite true that we cannot come to any "certainty of reason" if the noetic experiences of the Ground of being and their philosophic

40. Locke, *Essay*, II, 309n.
41. *Ibid.*, Bk. II, 13. 19; *cf.* Bk. II, 23. 3.
42. "We have the ideas but of three sorts of substances: 1. *God*. 2. *Finite intelligences*. 3. *Bodies*. First, *God* is without beginning, eternal, unalterable, and everywhere, and therefore concerning his identity there can be no doubt." *Ibid.*, bk. II, 27. 2; *cf.* Bk. IV, 9–11; *cf.* Aristotle *Metaphysics* XII. 1–6. 1069a18–72a17.
43. Edward Stillingfleet quoted by Locke in his "Mr. Locke's Reply to the Right Reverend the Lord Bishop of Worcester's Answer to his Second Letter," in Locke, *Works*, IV, 448–49.

symbolizations are cast aside by an epistemology that rests exclusively upon sensory perception and ideas formed through reflection upon it, by a logic that is unaware of the conditions of rational discourse, and by a disposition to ridicule away the great insights into the mystery of being upon which the whole of philosophical activity depends. The search for the divine Ground is represented in the mythic imagery of the "Indian philosopher" no less than in the inquiry of Aristotle in the *Metaphysics*. From the beginning of philosophical thought, *something* upon which all reality, order, and rationality depend has been apperceived as the foundation of man's humanity and the sovereign reprieve from Chaos, first of the gods.[44] Whether in myth, mysticism, or philosophy, beyond the rational Ground of being lies the mysterious Unground. This symbolism of the ultimate mystery enveloping reality is, as Leibniz so well says in propounding his two great questions, both the beginning and the limit of noetic speculation, behind which the mind cannot penetrate. He lays down as the "*Great principle*" the axiom that "*nothing happens without a sufficient reason.*" "The first question which should rightly be asked, will be, *Why is there something rather than nothing?* For nothing is simpler and easier than something. Further, suppose that things must exist, we must be able to give a reason *why they must exist so* and not otherwise." Leibniz does not leave the answer in suspense. Beyond the particularities of contingent things in series must lie a necessary being, he writes, "carrying the reason for its existence within itself. . . . And this final reason of things is called *God*."[45]

V

The rejection of the *koinai ennoiai* with all of the consequences this entailed was the preamble to an assault calculated to be a body blow against dogmatism in philosophy and enthusiasm in politics as well as a vindication of naturalistic and pragmatic reason as the monitor and foundation of knowledge and order. Aaron remarks with regard

44. See Hesiod *Theogony* line 116; *cf.* G. S. Kirk and J. E. Raven, *Presocratic Philosophers: A Critical History With Selection of Texts* (Cambridge, England, 1960), Chap. 1.
45. Leibniz, *Principles of Nature and Grace, Based on Reason* (1714), quoted from Wiener (ed.), *Leibniz*, 527–28.

to the argument against innate ideas, "The practical bearing of the polemic too should not be forgotten; it aimed a shrewd blow at the obscurantism of the day in religion and worship and made fresh thinking in these fields essential."[46] By the middle of the eighteenth century Locke's efforts—especially his exploration of epistemological issues in the *Essay*—had led to Humean scepticism and a malaise in philosophy from which it has not yet fully recovered and which has substantially deprived modern mankind of an essential instrument of rational existence. As T. H. Green observed in the 1880s, the *Essay* exercised such influence as to become "a sort of philosopher's Bible in the last century."[47]

Hume's scepticism of the possibility of knowledge is memorably expressed in many places. In the *Enquiry* he writes:

It seems to me that [the] theory of the universal energy and operation of the Supreme Being is too bold ever to carry conviction with it to a man, sufficiently apprized of the weakness of human reason, and the narrow limits to which it is confined in all its operations. . . . We are got into a fairy land, long ere we have reached the last steps of our theory; and *there* we have no reason to trust our common methods of argument, or to think that our usual analogies and probabilities have any authority. Our line is too short to fathom such immense abysses."[48]

His abandonment of philosophy itself and withdrawal into the ataraxy of complete scepticism already had been expressed in the *Treatise.*

Sceptical doubt, both with respect to reason and to the senses, is a malady, which can never be radically cur'd, but must return upon us every moment, however we may chace [*sic*] it away, and sometimes may seem entirely free from it. 'Tis impossible upon any system to defend either our understanding or senses; and we but expose them farther when we endeavor to justify them in that manner. As the sceptical doubt arises naturally from a profound and intense reflection on those subjects, it always increases, the farther we carry our reflections, whether in opposition or conformity to it. Carelessness and in-attention alone can afford us any remedy. For this reason I rely entirely

---

46. Aaron, *Locke*, 98.
47. Green and Grose (eds.), *Philosophical Works*, II, 1.
48. David Hume, *An Enquiry Concerning Human Understanding*, Sec. 1, Pt. 1. para. 57, in David Hume, *Enquiries Concerning the Human Understanding and Concerning the Principles of Morals*, ed. L. A. Selby-Bigge (2nd ed.; Oxford, 1902), 72.

upon them; and take for granted, whatever may be the reader's opinion at this present moment, that an hour hence he will be persuaded there is both an external and internal world."[49]

Politically the immediate results were happier than they were philosophically, for Locke and his successors contributed the naturalistic political theology that, despite profound shortcomings, remains evocative in England and in America to this day. Yet even politically, the losses have been great, for the ultimate effect of the Lockean assault on the *cognitio fidei* and on noetic reason has been paradoxically to foster the triumph throughout most of the West—and by way of Westernization throughout the world—of precisely the politics of despotic enthusiasm that he set out to defeat in England.[50]

Locke's rejection of enthusiasm as a valid ground of assent was clearly understood by Leibniz, who wrote in the *New Essays:* "Enthusiasm was originally a good term. Just as 'sophism' properly indicates an exercise of wisdom, so enthusiasm signifies that there is a divinity in us (*Est deus in nobis*). But men having consecrated their passions, fancies, dreams, and even their anger, as something divine, enthusiasm began to signify a mental disturbance attributed to the influence of some divinity. . . . Since then, we attribute it to those who believe without foundation that their impulses come from God."[51] The legitimate grounds of assent, according to Locke, are reason and revelation in a man who searches for truth out of love for it: "For he that loves it not, will not take much pains to get it; nor be much concerned when he misses it." The terms are defined as follows:

Reason is natural *revelation,* whereby the eternal Father of light, and the Fountain of all knowledge, communicates to mankind that portion of truth

---

49. Hume, *Treatise of Human Nature,* Sec. 2, Pt. 4, in Green and Grose (eds.), *Philosophical Works,* I, 505.

50. On the emergence of liberal and totalitarian democracy out of Enlightenment thought see Jacob L. Talmon, *Origins of Totalitarian Democracy* (New York, 1951); Jacob L. Talmon, *Political Messianism: The Romantic Phase* (New York, 1960); on "Westernization" see Arnold J. Toynbee, *A Study of History* (Oxford, 1934–64), VIII, 501–21; IX, 405–644.

51. Quoted from Leibniz's *Nouveaux Essais,* in Locke, *Essay,* ed. Pringle-Pattison, 360n. See Locke, *Essay,* Bk. IV, 19. On enthusiasm as the divine gift (*theia moira*) whereby the poet transmits his inspiration to the audience (Leibniz's "good term") see Plato *Ion* 533C, and the discussion in Bruno Snell, *Discovery of the Mind: The Greek Origins of European Thought,* trans. T. G. Rosenmeyer (1953; rpr. New York, 1960), 299–301.

which he has laid within the reach of their natural faculties. *Revelation* is natural *reason* enlarged by a new set of discoveries communicated by God immediately, which reason vouches the truth of, by the testimony and proofs it gives that they come from God. So that he that takes away reason to make way for revelation, puts out the light of both; and does much-what the same as if he would persuade a man to put out his eyes, the better to receive the remote light of an invisible star by a telescope.[52]

Revelation is the handmaid of the inferential intellect which performs as a censor either to affirm or to deny and suppress the truth of both Scripture and immediate experiences of a pneumatic or noetic kind. Thereby is the life of the spirit as an independent ordering source in existence brutally suppressed and wholly absorbed by an immanentist naturalism. Not only is the conventional division between the vulgar life of the masses who rely on dogma and that of the philosopher who lives by the truth of philosophical reason delineated, but also philosophy itself is impoverished by the excision of noetic reason from even private meditation. Noetic reason is systematically excluded as irrational, as are existential faith and perverse enthusiasm, which are indistinguishably the same.[53]

The view that emerges from a consideration of the tangled relation between Locke's politics and his philosophy enforces the argument that one bridge between the aspects of his thought is the desire to compose an effective civil theology that would secure peace and, therewith, the liberty of the speculative thinker, not least of all that of Locke himself. To this issue we must now turn more directly.

Whatever the other consequences of that effort for political science or philosophy, Locke the physician and practical man of affairs employed his theoretical talents in the *Treatises* in such a way as to do what neither Hobbes nor Spinoza had accomplished. He composed a civil or popular philosophy and, as a part of that, a political theology, which so appealed to and marshalled the prejudices and common sense of his countrymen that it was accepted as the basis for the "liberal" self-interpretation of Anglo-American society. If Spinoza was

52. Locke, *Essay*, Bk. IV, 19. 1 and 4. *Cf.* Richard Hooker, *Of the Laws of Ecclesiastical Polity*, ed. Christopher Morris (New York, 1907), "Preface" [3.10], I, 101–102.
53. See Locke, *First Treatise*, Secs. 62–67, 100; also n. 60 in this chapter.

bolder in doctrine than Hobbes, Locke was yet bolder than either, equally dogmatic, and infinitely more imaginative and politic.[54] The *Second Treatise* avoids not only the whole historical argument and deeply stratified tradition of English constitutionalism but also supplies virtually no definitions of terms. It contains no discussion of either conscience or obligation, no mention of religious toleration, no occurrence of the words moral, morals, or morality, and no appeal to the philosophical reason and little to authority. These facts drive the editor of the *Treatises* to see in their author a combination of common sense existentialism and dogmatic rationalism, whose very imprecision he counts a strength.[55]

Whatever it may "mean," there can be little doubt that Locke contrived a controlling symbolism of the Anglo-American public order. Out of the experiential rubble of fragmented history, disintegrated philosophy, and faction-ridden Christianity, Locke creates a scientistic myth of man, society, and civil government that evokes a sense of history and satisfies the demands of common reason in men seeking earthly peace and eternal salvation. It generates sufficient consensus, in support of a civil authority dedicated to the preserving of human liberty, to conform will to the new natural order glimpsed by

54. Locke in 1698 states, "I am not so well read in Hobbes or Spinosa [*sic*];" Locke, *Two Treatises of Government*, 73. There is reason to believe Locke was less than well educated philosophically. As a student at Oxford, his companionship rather than his scholarship was most prized, and he seems not to have been fond of reading extensively. He finally turned to natural science and medicine and eventually became a practicing physician, although not a medical doctor. Fraser suggests that Locke was theoretically illiterate. "He was too little read in the literature of philosophy to do full justice to those who, from Plato onwards, have recognised implicates in our physical and moral experience that deeply concern the ultimate destiny of man, and the reality of the universe." Locke, *Essay*, I, lxxii; *cf. ibid.*, I, cxxxiii, 80, 526n. To similar effect, Leibniz remarks of Locke's discussion of the self-evidence of maxims (Locke, *Essay*, Bk. IV, 7. 1.): "This investigation is very useful and even important. But you must not imagine, sir, that it has been entirely neglected. You will find in a hundred places that the scholastic philosophers have said that these propositions are evident *ex terminis*, as soon as their terms are understood." Leibniz, *New Essays*, in Wiener (ed.), *Leibniz*, 468. On Locke's Oxford life see Cranston, *Locke*, Chaps. 3–6; Locke, *Essays*, ed. von Leyden 19n, 16–39; Axtell, *Educational Writings*, 31, 43, 50, 85–86. *Cf.*, however, Romanell, *John Locke and Medicine*, esp. Chaps. 2 and 7.

Locke had, however, read Hobbes' *Leviathan*, and he purchased Spinoza's *Tractatus theologico-politicus* in 1674 (Locke, *Two Treatises*, 144). He could hardly have been oblivious to the bold attempts made by both writers to contrive solutions for the same vexed problems which so disastrously affected him throughout his own lifetime.

55. *Cf.* Locke, *Two Treatises of Government*, 92, 96, 115; also 76, 84–85, 87, 89, 91, 118.

Bacon and raised to clear awareness by Locke's friend Newton. The strength of the construction is not so much its intellectual imprecision as its effective representation in concrete images of the commonplace and vulgar experience of an existence purged of all authority except that of the marketplace and of nature itself. The *Second Treatise* is told in mythic imagery, designed to persuade Everyman of its truth through common sense, the reason whereby men attune themselves to the love of life in the shadow of ineluctable death. God's and nature's law encompass the earthly drama, surrounding the suspense of time in the infinitude of benevolent eternity. Reason is the voice of God in man, which narrates how it is that power in society comes to be fixed in the hands of those who rule. The tale begins: Once upon a time in the primordial state of nature when every man was equally his own master, free, and rational.

The force of the account is at least mainly attributable to its clarity of expression and to its psychological immediacy. Locke's man is, like most men, animated by an erotic lust to possess, to enjoy, to accumulate without limit as the prime measure of his being and happiness. This concupiscence, while morally deplorable, is intrinsic to fallen man and limited only by desire itself and, of course, by wastage and violence since these contravene the natural order whose necessity is the very definition of rationality.[56] The divine economy and the philosophical anthropology find expression in terms of property and property rights. This primitive presentation has the merit of accentuating naturalistic immediacy. It appeals to the most vulgar experience of self and of existence, and it appeals in powerful if staid language that effectively defines the substantive relations among ordinary men passionately engaged in the combat of existence. It easily makes sense to see in the collision of acquisitive and lustful men the occasion that stimulates formation of society on the basis of mutual advantage and self-love, and so also of government. But the story need not be retold again.

Neither Locke's other published works nor the journals and the other manuscript materials first opened to scholarly scrutiny in 1948 betray any interest on the part of the author in *property* prior to the

56. Locke, *Second Treatise*, Sec. 111.

writing of the *Second Treatise.*This suggests that property is not only the primary means for expressing the principles of constitutionalism, but that it is a literary device whereby the analogy of the marketplace (which next to passionate nature itself comprises the most pungent experiential sector of man's existence) is put to use in composing the myth of civil society. Philosophers do not need civil theologies, and the *Second Treatise* was not written for them. Yet even in this regard, no philosopher before Locke ever sought to present the whole range of divine and human affairs through the symbolisms of property and contract.[57] Here, too, Locke broke with the philosophical tradition in voicing a materialistic anthropology and theology of existential verve that, even if dogmatic and shockingly reductionist, was nonetheless comprehensible and fresh, and cut through the inane dogmatism of the schools he so despised.

Finally, it is a fundamental tenet of political theory from Plato onward that the collapse of the justice discerned and fostered by the noetic and spiritual experience of individual men through ethical and political order means the upsurge to hegemony of unbridled passion. From the perspective of political theory, this was the condition of the society that supplied the empirical setting for the work of both Hobbes (who experienced no *summum bonum,* only a *summum malum* controlling human affairs) and Locke. A serious attempt to reestablish through skillful persuasion a minimal order in the midst of catastrophic existential disorder could scarcely be undertaken by Locke at all except through the medium he employed, namely, the rationalization of the passionate element in man's social existence on grounds of the rudimentary reason of natural necessity and the logic of marketplace biology. Perhaps there was no other common ground of "reality" left but this, so profound was the debauchery of an England standing on the threshold of the unmitigated rottenness of the Gin Age.[58]

57. See, however, Thomas Aquinas *Summa Theologica* I–II. q. 94. a. 5. The conception of Christian stewardship as a dimension of man's dominion over God's nature is central to traditional teaching, a teaching blunted in Locke but not wholly absent.

58. On the debauchery of the period 1675–1750 see W. E. H. Lecky, *A History of England in the Eighteenth Century* (Cabinet ed.; London, 1892), II, Chap. 5. See also the novels of Henry Fielding, esp. *Amelia* (1749) and *Tom Jones* (1751). M. Dorothy George states in her *London Life in the Eighteenth Century* (1925; rpr. New York, 1964), "The orgy of spirit-

VI

The *Second Treatise* offers no discussion of toleration, an essential aspect of democratic civil theology. Locke's intention is, in part, to restrain the disruptive activities of apocalyptic and millenarian enthusiasts, a problem common to all of the authors of civil theology considered here. He achieves by means of toleration what Hobbes and Spinoza had hoped to achieve through their enforced dogmas, namely, public peace. Hobbes' *Leviathan* was the king of the proud, whose rule would break the pride of men for whom community on terms other than fear of violent death was ineffective, and he took from Job 41 both the title and the motto of his work. Locke's men seem scarcely less afflicted by pride than were those of Hobbes, although Laslett professes to see a "doctrine of natural political virtue" implicit in the Lockean reliance on compact and trust as foundations of the community and of representative government.[59] While this poses an important issue in political theory, it is here contended that Locke was inexact and vague in theoretical points just because he was composing a broadly evocative myth and a civil theology. Hence, the strictly theoretical debate should be abandoned unless we wish to press upon the author a purpose that was not his. At a minimum it seems essential not to interpret the *Second Treatise* as preeminently political philosophy, a fact that Locke himself acknowledged.

Community arises out of mutual recognition of the need to preserve life, liberty, and property from criminal rapacity. The concerted exercise of power in a society of human beings by a government operating within limits for the stated purpose of mutual well-being is the only definition of community explicitly given by Locke. If a Rousseauist natural political virtue is part of the Lockean man's humanity, he has neither said so directly nor implied it clearly. This is to say that men possess virtue not because they are Lockean but because

---

drinking . . . was at its worst between 1720 and 1751, due to the very cheap and very intoxicating liquors, which were retailed indiscriminately and in the most brutalising and demoralizing conditions." "Gin was threatening to destroy the [English] race." "But the dangerous tendencies of spirit-drinking [already] had been seen twenty years earlier" (*ibid.*, 27, 30, 35). Admittedly, it is hard to imagine the horrors of the Gin Age as we try to live through the far greater horrors of the Heroin and Cocaine Age.

59. Locke, *Two Treatises of Government*, 108–20.

they are men. The tone instead suggests the poem *Fable of the Bees* by Locke's young contemporary Bernard Mandeville.

> So vice is beneficial found,
> When it's by justice lopp'd and bound;
> Nay, where the people would be great,
> As necessary to the state,
> As hunger is to make 'em eat.
> Bare virtue can't make nations live
> In splendor; they, that would revive
> A golden age, must be as free,
> For acorns as for honesty.[60]

Locke's espousal of the principle of the heteronomy of ends may not be "crypto-capitalist," but it is consistently laissez-faire; nor, as the quotation from Mandeville proves, is it anachronistic to suppose this to be an element in Locke's myth.

The theoretical validity of Laslett's perception lies in the facts, first that contract and trust cannot *create* virtue or the sense of obligation that is essential to their performance, for this must antedate either action in order to make a binding commitment possible. From this it next follows that the foundation of social and political order does *not* lie in either the contract or the trust itself but in the antecedent sense of honor arising from the broadly historical common sense and morality of the society—traditional elements utterly indispensable to the existentially obligatory, freely consensual compact described in the *Second Treatise* and expunged from the account. In sum, the real foundations of the social and political order described by Locke are neither physical laws nor a Roman law conception of obligation, but rather the socially pervasive common sense of the historically developed English constitutional and Christian tradition now evoked in a novel universalist symbolism. It is thus to be understood that the "contract theory" is no theory at all but merely a vulgar opinion or dogma (*doxa*) valuable in a myth but useless to political theory, as Plato knew and as Locke himself may well have realized.[61]

60. From "The Grumbling Hive" (1705), in Bernard Mandeville (1670–1733), *Fable of the Bees, or Private Vices, Publick Benefits*, ed. Irwin Primer (New York, 1962), 38.

61. *Cf.* Plato *Republic* 359A. That Locke himself realized the systematic unimportance of the social compact is suggested by his neglect of it after Sec. 81. He mentions it only three times in the last half of the *Second Treatise* (*i.e.*, Secs. 122, 171, 172).

Locke's doctrine of toleration completes the civil theology and asserts the liberty of worship and conscience of churches and sects except for those that insist on making a political issue of religion. The latter groups, which must not be tolerated and are denied civil status, include by implication Catholics, Mohammedans, Antinominans, and Levellers. "The civil government operates on the premise that the way of life of a liberal-protestant community must and will become the way of life of the nation."[62]

The discussion, divided into a consideration of "outward worship" and "articles of faith," presumes that "all men know and acknowledge that God ought to be publicly worshiped" and that the "only business of the Church is the salvation of Souls." Everything in outward worship ought to be tolerated that is by the laws permissible "in any private house." Locke denies that the "law of Moses" is "obligatory to us Christians," for it is not part of the positive law of the Commonwealth.[63] The articles of faith are considered under their "speculative" and "practical" aspects. The civil laws and magistrates have nothing to do with the former, since they are "opinions . . . which are required only to be believed" and are purely "inward." The latter, however, being fruitful of "moral actions," are both inward and outward, and hence fall also within the jurisdiction of the civil government. They are "both of the magistrate and conscience." Anyone may employ persuasion to encourage a fellow man to true religion, "but all force and compulsion are to be forborne." If legislation infringes conscience, a man may disobey and accept punishment, "which it is not unlawful for him to bear" since "obedience is done, in the first place, to God, and afterward to the laws."

The limit of toleration is at last reached. Locke specifies as just grounds for intolerance the following: (1) opinions, which he terms "madness," contrary to the interest of society or to the moral rules necessary to its preservation; (2) secret teaching in violation of oaths and treason to the king, *e.g.*, "that faith is not to be kept with here-

---

62. Voegelin, "Industrial Society," 37.
63. But, of course, "nobody intends that everything, generally, enjoined by the law of Moses, ought to be practised by Christians." John Locke, *A Letter Concerning Toleration* (1689; the *Epistola de Tolerantia* of 1685 as translated by William Popple) in Locke, *Works*, VI, 37.

tics" and "that kings excommunicated forfeit their crowns and king-doms"; and (3) the doctrine that "dominion is founded in grace," which really lays "claim to the possession of all things" as the only truly pious and faithful. This *last* point also implies a "peculiar privilege or power above other mortals, in civil concernments," an "authority over such as are not associated with them in their ecclesiastical communion," and a refusal to "own and teach the duty of tolerating all men in matters of mere religion." All of these and "like doctrines signify . . . that they may, and are ready . . . to seize the government . . . the estates and fortunes of their fellow subjects." A further ground for intolerance is (4) the "*ipso facto*" service through a religious communion of "another prince," thereby establishing a "foreign jurisdiction" within the commonwealth, and finally, (5) the atheism of all "who deny the being of God."

Anyone or any church or society that teaches any of these things has "no right to be tolerated by the magistrate," Locke states, and he expresses his basic axiom in these words: "The law of toleration [must be] once so settled that all churches [are] obliged to lay down toleration as the foundation of their own liberty, and [to] teach that liberty of conscience is every man's natural right, equally belonging to dissenters and to themselves; and that nobody ought to be compelled in matters of religion either by law or force. . . . 'The sum of all we drive at is that every man may enjoy the same rights that are granted to others.'" [64]

The solution, then, is to erect the principles of toleration and articles of intolerance (or persecution) just summarized into a compulsory minimum dogma enforced by positive law and justified by appeal to natural law. A result is the radical privatization of the life of spirit and the interpretation of civil government as the expression of universal providence immanent to history in the natural order of human reason.

In Locke's civil theology, therefore, we confront not only a brilliantly effective solution to the vexed problems of political existence of his day and a legacy efficacious into the present but also the incipient formulation of a radically immanentist conception of human

---

64. *Ibid.*, VI, 51. Locke's anonym as author of the toleration letters was Philanthropos.

existence. As mediated through the *philosophes* and the French Revolution, this doctrine stimulated the rise of totalitarian democracy as the malformed brother of liberal democracy. This Cain-Abel relationship found expression in nineteenth-century French and German ideologies that assumed the privatization of reason and spirit to be tantamount to a denial of the substantive reality of either and hence proclaimed as rationality the political apocalypse of the Great Being Man and of the Realm of Freedom ironically glimpsed in the pages of "Philanthropos." Its twentieth-century expression is the chronic terror of existence in the shadow of universal barbarism and annihilation.

The complexities of the American public order arise from the fact that it is an intricate texture of processes and structuring elements. It is Lockean but not radically so. It is any number of other things that historians and political philosophers readily inventory. A kind of pragmatic balance washes back and forth in this complex texture to affirm the core principles of a social order that insists upon liberty and law and is leery of excesses. At the center of this self-equilibrating order are the understandings of human existence and ultimate reality shaped in classical antiquity and in the sacred history recounted in the Bible. These are mediated into American society through the British medieval Christian culture and especially through the dissenting strand of the Reformation, whose nurture of individual accountability and self-reliance became signatures of American social order itself.

It is to a closer inspection of these central formative elements of American experience that we turn attention in the next chapters.

CHAPTER 3 Classical and Christian

Dimensions of American Political Thought

I shall here take the advice of William James and try to apply it to the American political experience. He wrote:

Place yourself . . . at the center of a man's philosophic vision and you understand at once all the different things it makes him write or say. But keep outside, use your post-mortem method, try to build the philosophy up out of the single phrases, taking first one and then another and seeking to make them fit, and of course you fail. You crawl over the thing like a myopic ant over a building, tumbling into every microscopic crack or fissure, finding nothing but inconsistencies, and never suspecting that a center exists.[1]

What is this vision, where this center, if one seeks them in Jamesian fashion? It is the synthesis authoritatively expressed by the generation of founding fathers, preeminently but not exclusively in the familiar words of the Declaration and Constitution. The key elements accord with the crucial insights of classical and Christian thought and give them renewed force in the emergent nation. Jefferson and John Adams called the amalgam "the dictates of reason and pure Americanism."[2] The self-interpretive symbols of American nationhood denoted in the quoted phrase look in two directions: toward the truth of man's existence personally, socially, and historically, on

---

1. William James, *A Pluralistic Universe*, in *Essays in Radical Empiricism; A Pluralistic Universe*, ed. Ralph Barton Perry (1942; rpr. Gloucester, Mass., 1967), II, 263.

2. Thomas Jefferson to Edward Rutledge, June 24, 1797, in Lipscomb and Bergh (eds.), *Writings of Thomas Jefferson*, IX, 409. For "Americanism" in John Adams see his letter to Benjamin Rush, July 7, 1805, in Schutz and Adair (eds.), *Spur of Fame*, 30.

the one hand; and toward the persuasive and evocative articulation of that truth in the foundation myth of the new community, on the other hand. In short, the articulation by reason of the truth of Americanism is a rearticulation of the existential and transcendental truth of the Western civilization, of which America is representative. The vision at the center of American politics, then, is structured by insights into human reality taken to be universally valid for all mankind, even as they are adapted to the concrete conditions of time and place at the moment of the articulation of the new nation as an entity politically organized for action in history.[3]

Neither the pragmatic nor the purely parochial aspects of the founding should be permitted to obscure the universalist elements. In human experience, the universal is encountered only in concrete and particular events, which existentially form the participatory reality of men's lives in the In-Between of time and eternity, birth and death. This tensional reality of existence in the In-Between (including the apperceptive insights that the Whole is structured by the indices of immanence and transcendence, and that the development of human existence in time is a directional process unfolding historically and ontologically from a divine Beginning toward an equally divine goal of fulfillment) composed the consciousness of the human beings who essayed the founding as heirs of classical philosophers and of Christian civilization. To be sure, the founders were heirs to other influences of cardinal importance as well, such as the Old Whig or Country "ideology" of English politics so meticulously explored by Bernard Bailyn and other scholars. Yet the larger framework of the American vision reached beyond Plymouth and Jamestown, beyond the institutional and theoretical structures of Anglo-American civilization, and even of Western civilization itself as conventionally understood. The contemporary recognition of this universal reach of their vision explains the founders' sense of exclusiveness and election rather than ethnocentricity, tribalism, or simple nationalism. John Pocock has from time to time argued that, so far from being the first act of modernity, "the American Revolution and Constitution . . . form the

3. For the theories of articulation and representation implicit here see Voegelin, *New Science of Politics*, Chaps. 1–3.

last act of the civic Renaissance."[4] He might better have said that they form the rebirth of classical and medieval constitutionalism. For, although influenced and conditioned by all that had gone before it, the thought of the founders sought its headwaters in the oldest traditions of the civilization and partook in no essential way of the currents of radical secularist modernity already swirling around them.

The warp and woof of American political thought in the period from 1761–1791 was the movement toward truth and virtue, and the quest for a just and stable order in the wake of the Revolution.[5] The standards of these several goals, and others they subsume such as liberty, equality, and happiness, were supplied by the great tradition of Western thought now revalidated. The sense in which this assessment is true can be established through an illustrative analysis of our subject matter.

I

For the purposes of this discussion, the American Revolution may be considered to be a meaningful complex of experiences and symbolisms articulated with especial force and clarity during the thirty-year period just indicated. The spectrum of understanding here summarized ranges from self-interpretation by the authors and their contemporaries to the level of theoretical formulation. Since, however, the American Revolution was enacted and reflected upon by persons often deeply rooted in the controlling theoretical symbolisms of philosophy and revelation, the self-interpretive end of the spectrum necessarily partakes of theoretical formulation, and the lines of distinction blur.

From the founding of the nation through the Declaration of Independence (explicit in the opening line: "When . . . one people [N.B.!] . . . dissolve[s] the political bands which have connected them with another"), to the framing of the Constitution and its exegesis by

4. J. G. A. Pocock, *Machiavellian Moment: Florentine Political Thought and the Atlantic Republican Tradition* (Princeton, 1975), 462.

5. The period indicated is from James Otis' speech against the writs of assistance of February 1761 to the ratification of the Bill of Rights in December 1791, the beginning and end of the Revolution.

Publius in the *Federalist,* to the declaration of "the great rights of mankind secured under this Constitution" in the Bill of Rights, the Revolution is dominated by actions intended to restore a true and just social and political order.[6] The *restorative* dimension of the Revolutionary experience is, therefore, dominant and determinative. It is adumbrated in the deeds and language of lawyers, politicians, and preachers, *i.e.,* by the intellectual leadership of the country. The rights, privileges and immunities of the free men of the English colonies were being systematically violated and had to be restored. The English constitution was perverted by multiple means, to the end that balance among the Estates had been destroyed and liberty itself thereby imperiled. Political influence and corruption were but palpable manifestations of the deeper spiritual malaise of *sin* and iniquity whose rot portended divine retribution unless the people (individually and collectively) repented, prayed for forgiveness, and returned to Christ in humility and faith. "The Biblical conception of a people standing in direct daily relation to God, upon covenanted terms and therefore responsible for their moral conduct," Perry Miller writes, "was a common possession of the Protestant peoples," who overwhelmingly comprised the country's population.[7] The general sentiment of the times was that America was a land blessed of Divine Providence, inhabited by a Chosen People, and led through Divine Grace by Christian men of heroic stature. And, while repentance for iniquity, constant struggle with temptation and evil of every form, and fasting and prayerful supplication for forgiveness and fortitude must accompany her every step, America's righteousness and adherence to the true faith must inevitably bring the reward of victory over Great Britain and a high place in history such as can only be achieved by the godly among nations.

The union of the temporal and spiritual communities on these general terms might be illustrated in countless ways. The intimate con-

6. The phrase "great rights of mankind" is attributed to Madison, who borrowed it from Blackstone. It is taken from his speech on June 8, 1789, in the House of Representatives, in which he introduced the Bill of Rights for adoption as amendments to the Constitution. Quotes from Bernard Schwartz (ed.), *Bill of Rights: A Documentary History* (New York, 1971), II, 1024.

7. Perry Miller, "From Covenant to Revival," in *Religion in American Life,* ed. J. W. Smith and A. L. Jamison (Princeton, 1961), I, 325.

nection is perhaps best suggested by the Continental Congress' practice of repeatedly calling upon the fledgling nation to observe days of "publick humiliation, fasting and prayer" as well as days of "thanksgiving." One such occasion was decided upon on June 12, 1775, even prior to declaring independence. A communication, sent from Philadelphia to the thirteen colonies and published in newspapers and handbills, called for observance of a day of public humiliation on July 20 "that we may with united hearts and voices unfeignedly confess and deplore our many sins, and offer up our joint supplications to the all-wise, omnipotent, and merciful Disposer of all events; humbly beseeching him to forgive our iniquities, to remove our present calamities, to avert those desolating judgments with which we are threatened."[8] The ritualistic form of this resolution, adopted unanimously by Congress, involves a national confession of sin, followed by repentance, supplication for forgiveness, and prayer that punishment be stayed. Clearly expressed is the pathos of the emergent people who experienced themselves as—beyond the personal hope of salvation of individuals who have entered into covenant with their maker—"explicitly merged with the society's covenant" with the " 'great Governor' " of Creation in a "living sense of a specific bond between the nation and God."[9]

Thus, the dynamic of fall from faith and restoration to grace visibly traced in revolutionary events defined the substance of man's existence in the world for Americans of this age. The immediate experiential power arose from its universality among people of a Christian nation who eagerly and fervently hoped for redemption and peace despite lapses and frailty. Corruption of religion and its restoration through the Reformation is a major motif of modern European history. The restoration sought was conceived to be recovery of the original purity instilled by foundation of the church by Jesus and the Apostles. Similarly, the Renaissance was a restoration or rebirth of learning to the level attained in distant antiquity. The cycle of fall and restoration was repeatedly enacted in English politics in the seventeenth and eighteenth centuries, from Coke onwards, with appeals even beyond Magna Carta (itself a restoration) to the Ancient Con-

8. *Ibid.*, 322.
9. *Ibid.*, 326, 361.

stitution, whose misty immemorial beginnings lay in the Saxon for-
ests of the fifth century (Jefferson) or, perchance, in the remnant of
settlers led by the mythical Brutus of Troy to ancient Albion's shore
(Coke). The eternal and natural law, safeguarded in timeless custom,
assured justice and the liberty due freemen. Politics as such was an
embedded dimension of the natural and divine order of reality, whose
hierarchical texture was epitomized in man's existential participation
in history and being, as Aristotle's analysis of composite human nature in *Ethics I* and *Politics I* taught. Thus, King Charles I in 1642
could think of no better way to counter the Long Parliament's demands for enlarged powers than to conclude his *Answer to the XIX
Propositions* by repeating the celebrated words of the assembled barons of the Merton parliament of 1236: *Nolumus Leges Angliae mutari* (We do not want the Laws of England to be changed).[10] And
James Otis, in 1764, appealed beyond the incipient convention of absolute parliamentary sovereignty to the unchanging natural and divine order in this striking language.

To say Parliament is absolute and arbitrary is a contradiction. The Parliament cannot make 2 and 2, 5: omnipotency cannot do it. The supreme
power in a state is *jus dicere* [to speak law] only: *jus dare* [to give or make
law], strictly speaking, belongs alone to God. Parliaments are in all cases to
declare what is for the good of the whole; but it is not the *declaration* of
Parliament that makes it so. There must be in every instance a higher authority, viz., GOD. Should an act of Parliament be against any of *his* natural
laws, which are *immutably* true, *their* declaration would be contrary to eternal truth, equity, and justice, and consequently void. . . . All power is of
GOD. Next and only subordinate to Him in the present state of the well
formed, beautifully constructed British monarchy, . . . [whose] pillars are
fixed in judgment, righteousness, and truth, is the King and Parliament.[11]

It is difficult to imagine a more perfectly medieval view of human law
in its relationship to natural and eternal law than Otis' statement.[12]
The point to stress for the moment, however, is that this sentiment
infused the restorative thrust of the Revolution, for the reasonable

---

10. *Cf.* Corrine Comstock Weston, "Beginnings of the Classical Theory of the English Constitution," *Proceedings of the American Philosophical Society*, C (1956), 144.
11. James Otis, *Rights of the British Colonies Asserted and Proved*, in *Pamphlets of the
American Revolution, 1750–1776*, ed. Bernard Bailyn (Cambridge, MA, 1965), 454, 456.
Emphasis as in original.
12. *Cf.* Thomas Aquinas *Summa Theologica* I–II. qq. 90–97.

and just ordering of human affairs was to be restored so human and divine governance would again harmonize in natural concord. Nor was this solely or even primarily a matter of secular or civil concern. To the contrary, ecclesiastical polity and religious liberty were equally at issue. The strength of Americans' reaction against obnoxious trade regulations and taxes, tending (they were convinced) toward the enslavement of freemen, was powerfully augmented by a growing conviction that the very terms upon which salvation itself depended were, for each of them, profoundly jeopardized by a comprehensive conspiracy against liberty.

Too much emphasis cannot be laid on the fact that sooner or later there was something in British policy that directly affected, or seemed to threaten, the religious or political liberties of every individual in the English colonies. Each successive step toward further commercial and political control by authority external to the colonial assemblies was apparently accompanied by parallel proposals to extend ecclesiastical control. This almost rhythmic or periodic sequence of external regulations and piling up of events during the sixties induced a situation that was highly charged with emotion. . . .

The sustained secular drift of our own times must not be permitted through sheer ignorance or cynicism to black out of history the potent fact that religion was the central concern for most Americans, not only throughout the entire century and a half of settlement on this continent but of the era of the Revolution as well. Who can deny that for them the very core of existence was their relation to God? . . . No less eminent personage than the [great evangelist] George Whitefield gravely warned two prominent ministers at Portsmouth, New Hampshire, in April 1764: "There is a deep laid plot against both your civil and religious liberties, and they will be lost. Your golden days are at an end."

When the Grenville reform program took effect in 1764 and 1765, many colonials had come to the conclusion that the Sugar, Currency, and Stamp acts and the plan for [an Anglican] bishop were all part of one concerted plan. . . . John Adams . . . urged all printers to spread news of this imminent catastrophe throughout the land. Obviously he accepted the idea of a conspiracy to subvert American liberties and sought to link civil and religious tyranny in the minds of his readers.[13]

The repeal of the Stamp Act in March 1766 was immediately followed by enactment of the Declaratory Act in which Parliament asserted its right to bind the colonies "in all cases whatsoever." The cry

13. Carl Bridenbaugh, *Spirit of '76: The Growth of American Patriotism Before Independence, 1607–1776* (New York, 1975), 117–19.

of "Tyranny!" that then went up, beginning with James Otis' "black regiment, the dissenting clergy," and his committees of correspondence, thundered through America in a steady crescendo to climax in Independence and Tom Paine's *Crisis Papers* a decade later.[14] Published in the deep gloom of retreat the day before Washington's famous crossing of the Delaware on Christmas Eve, 1776, *Crisis I* captured the somber resolve and pathos of the Revolution in these bitter words.

Britain, with an army to enforce her tyranny, has declared that she has a right (not only to TAX) but "to bind *us in* ALL CASES WHATSOEVER," and if being *bound in that manner,* is not slavery, then is there not such a thing as slavery upon earth. Even the expression is impious; for so unlimited a power can belong only to God. . . . Not all the treasures of the world . . . could have induced me to support an offensive war, for I think it murder; but if a thief breaks into my house, burns and destroys my property, and kills or threatens to kill me, or those that are in it, and to "*bind me in all cases whatsoever*" to his absolute will, am I to suffer it? What signifies it to me, whether he who does it is a king or a common man; my countryman or not my countryman; whether it be done by an individual villain, or an army of them? . . . Let them call me rebel and welcome, I feel no concern from it; but I should suffer the misery of devils, were I to make a whore of my soul by swearing allegiance to one whose character is that of a sottish, stupid, stubborn, worthless, brutish man.[15]

The paradigm of Revolution itself, then, was conceived similarly to *stasis* in Aristotle, but with biblical overtones added. Outrage over property matters and unconscionable injustice lay at the root of American discontent. The perversion (*parekbasis*) at the hands of George III, the ministry, and their parliamentary accomplices of the monarchy that Otis so admired into the tyranny Paine so loathed aroused a sense of injustice in the citizenry to the point that stability finally gave way. The people withdrew allegiance from a ruler who wantonly had violated his trust. The Lockean "appeal to Heaven" might be cited, and indeed it was, but a potent strand of medieval Christian constitutional and political theory as well lay squarely behind the American determination. The pungency of Paine's words in *Crisis I* arises partly

14. *Ibid.*, 120–21.
15. Philip S. Foner (ed.), *Complete Writings of Thomas Paine* (New York, 1945), I, 50, 55. Emphasis as in original.

from the skill with which he brings to bear the older elements of the political heritage in concert with the newer elements supplied by the contract theorists. From William the Conqueror onward, the English community was founded on *fides,* first symbolized in ceremonies of liege homage and the oath of fealty in a reciprocal act of faith between man and lord in which service and allegiance were promised in return for protection, peace, and justice. The mutual bonds of obligation so covenanted were cemented by the pledge of the man's Christianity itself, or as Pollock and Maitland state it, "he pawn[ed] his hope of salvation."[16] If either party failed to meet his obligations, then the other was freed from his. The essentials of this relationship were retained into modern times and symbolized in the English coronation ritual.

The teaching of Thomas Aquinas also is apposite, not as the voice of the "popish" church roundly despised by most of our revolutionaries as the reign of the Antichrist overthrown at the Reformation, but as a great spokesman of the medieval Christian synthesis.[17] Thomas asserts, "Just as the government of a king is the best, so the government of a tyrant is the worst."[18] The end of rule befitting freemen is the common good of the multitude. Such rule is right and just when it conduces to the happiness of men, their natural and eternal end. Such is kingly rule, or true rule, whether by one, a few, or the many. Perverse rule, of which the worst is tyranny in its absolute form, does not aim at the common good but at the private good of the ruler(s) and is, therefore, unjust.[19] The tyrant, more specifically, is one who "oppresses by might instead of ruling by justice."[20] How can a people rid themselves of a tyrant? Among other alternatives, Thomas offers these:

16. Pollock and Maitland, *History of English Law,* II, 190. *Cf.* Chap. 1 herein.

17. *Cf.* Ernest L. Tuveson, *Redeemer Nation: The Idea of America's Millennial Role* (Chicago, 1968), 17–19 and *passim.* This view of Reformation and papacy is not uniquely American. For example, for the *Pope as Antichrist* by Melchior Lorch see the plate, as well as the general analysis, in Norman Cohn, *Pursuit of the Millennium: Revolutionary Messianism in Medieval and Reformation Europe and Its Bearing on Modern Totalitarian Movements* (2nd ed.; New York, 1970), 48 and *passim.*

18. Thomas Aquinas *On Kingship* I. 3. 21.

19. *Ibid.,* I. 1. 10.

20. *Ibid.,* I. 1. 11.

If to provide itself with a king belongs to the right of a given multitude, it is not unjust that the king be deposed or have his power restricted by that same multitude if, becoming a tryant, he abuses the royal power. It must not be thought that such a multitude is acting unfaithfully in deposing the tyrant, even though it had previously subjected itself to him in perpetuity, because he himself has deserved that the covenant with his subjects should not be kept, since, in ruling the multitude, he did not act faithfully as the office of king demands. . . . Should no human aid whatsoever against a tyrant be forthcoming, recourse must be had to God, the King of all, who is a helper in due time in tribulation. . . . But to deserve to secure this benefit from God, the people must desist from sin, for it is by divine permission that wicked men receive power to rule as a punishment for sin. . . . Sin must therefore be done away with in order that the scourge of tyrants may cease.[21]

And, finally, Thomas counsels in this vein: "Man is bound to obey secular princes in so far as this is required by the order of justice. Wherefore if the prince's authority is not just but usurped, or if he commands what is unjust, his subjects are not bound to obey him."[22] The drift of Thomas' words closely accords with the logic of the American revolutionaries (however vehemently they might have scorned the association), as the pathos of national days of "publick humiliation" and all that went with it eloquently suggests. Moreover, the Declaration's persuasive dynamic echoes the common heritage of classical and Christian civilization shared by the thirteenth-century philosopher and our eighteenth-century founders. Its initial and final appeals to God and the natural order of reason and justice for ultimate justification bracket a bill of particulars wherein "absolute Tyranny" is proved against George III. Far from securing peace, protection, and justice essential to the common good of his people, "He has abdicated Government here, by declaring us out of his Protection and waging War against us." In doing so, monarchy has been perverted into tyranny, with the justifiable and necessary consequences that faith is broken and obligations covenanted between king and people dissolved: "The good People of these Colonies . . . are Absolved from all Allegiance to the British Crown, and . . . all political connection between them and the State of Great Britain . . . is and ought to be

21. *Ibid.*, I. 4. 49, 51, 52; quoted from Dino Bigongiari (ed.), *Political Ideas of St. Thomas Aquinas: Representative Selections* (New York, 1969), 190–92.
22. Thomas Aquinas *Summa Theologica* I–II. q. 104. a. 6. reply obj. 3.

totally dissolved." [23] In brief, the action is to depose the monarch because he has become a tyrant and to declare independence for the reconstituted community and its new polities, the States. The guiding sentiment of the action is perhaps best captured by the motto Jefferson chose in 1776 for his personal seal: "Rebellion to tyrants is obedience to God." [24]

Jefferson claimed he looked at no books in drafting the Declaration. "All of its authority rests then on the harmonizing sentiments of the day, whether expressed in conversation, in letters, printed essays, or in the elementary books of public right, as Aristotle, Cicero, Locke, Sidney, etc., & c." [25] The classical, as well as feudal, cast of Jefferson's thinking is underscored by his language of the time as used elsewhere, and it sustains the account of the meaning of the Declaration in certain of its key aspects just summarized. Thus, the "Composition Draft" of the Declaration containing the charges against the king was substantially identical with Jefferson's drafts for the pertinent part of the Virginia Constitution of 1776. It opened with these words: "Whereas George Guelph King of Great Britain & Ireland and Elector of Hanover, heretofore entrusted with the exercise of the Kingly office in this government, hath endeavored to pervert the same into a detestable & insupportable tyranny[:] 1. by putting his negative on laws the most wholesome & necessary for the public good. . . . 16. and finally by abandoning the helm of goverment & declaring us out of his allegiance & protection." [26]

23. Quotations from the Declaration are from Charles C. Tansill (ed.), *Documents Illustrative of the Formation of the Union of American States,* 69th Cong., 1st Sess., House Doc. No. 398 (Washington, D.C., 1927), 24–25.

24. Boyd (ed.), *Papers of Thomas Jefferson,* I, 677–79. Boyd concludes that Benjamin Franklin probably originated the motto.

25. Worthington C. Ford (ed.), *Writings of Thomas Jefferson* (New York, 1892–99), X, 343. The statement is hooted at by Garry Wills, *Inventing America: Jefferson's Declaration of Independence* (New York, 1979), 174. Recommending John Locke's *Second Treatise* to another, despite Jefferson's own supposed ignorance of the text himself, says Wills, was no more "dishonest" than "his crediting Aristotle (of all people) with formation of the background for his Declaration." Wills' argument aims to disabuse us of the traditional and "useful vagueness of Jefferson" by proving him to have been specifically or "quintessentially a man of the Enlightenment; he lived in the world of Catherine and Diderot" (*ibid.,* 368). Jefferson, however, lived in some other worlds as well. Wills' argument is tendentious.

26. Boyd (ed.), *Papers of Thomas Jefferson,* I, 427, 419. Cf. the wording of the Virginia Constitution (adopted June 29, 1776), *ibid.,* 377–78. For true and perverse rule and their relation to the common good see Aristotle *Politics* III. 4. 7–5. 10. 1279a18–80a38.

In his "First Draft" of the Virginia Constitution, Jefferson wrote that "public liberty may be more certainly secured by abolishing an office which all experience hath shewn to be inveterately inimical thereto, and it will thereupon become further necessary to reestablish such ancient principles as are friendly to the rights of the people." A later passage continues: "It is declared that the said colonies are in a state of open Rebellion & hostility against the king & his parliament of Great Britain, that they are out of their allegiance to him & are thereby also put out of his protection," whereupon Jefferson quotes from "the original charter of compact granted [by Queen Elizabeth] to Sr. Walter Raleigh on behalf of himself & the settlers of this colony & bearing date the 25th of March 1584," whose terms supply justification for "lawfully, rightfully, & by consent of both parties divest-[ing George Guelph] of the kingly powers." [27] In the "Second Draft," "he is hereby deposed from the kingly office within ys. government & absolutely divested of all it's [sic] rights & powers." [28] In the "Third Draft," because of his "misrule George Guelph has forfeited the kingly office and has rendered it necessary for the preservation of the people that he should be immediately deposed from the same." [29]

A king who perverts his rule is a tyrant. He corrupts it by abandoning public good in favor of using his power against the people for private good, that is, for the good of only a part of the community. For this, the people can justly depose him *if* it is within their purview to provide themselves a king. We have seen that these were thoroughly medieval Christian notions, with roots in the teachings of Aristotle and Thomas, but they were equally American conceptions by 1776. What of the missing links? Did the king's authority rest on the people's consent? As early as 1765, John Adams delivered this warning to the English in reacting to the abusive policies of Grenville and his henchmen: "Do you not represent [the King and Parliament] as forgetting that the prince of Orange was created King William [III in 1689], *by the people*, on purpose that their rights might be eternal and invio-

27. Boyd (ed.), *Papers of Thomas Jefferson*, I, 339–40. Boyd dates this and the other two drafts "Before 13 June 1776."
28. *Ibid.*, 347.
29. *Ibid.*, 357.

lable?"[30] Aristotle's teaching plainly undergirds Adams' caustic reminder of the English constitution's principles. "Kingship implies government with consent as well as sovereignty over the greater part of affairs . . . for when subjects cease to consent, a king is no more a king; but a tyrant is still a tyrant, though his subjects do not want him."[31]

To depose the king clearly lay within the right of the people, but on what specific terms? In the unfolding debate over American rights and the place of the colonies in the British empire, arguments were conducted on a variety of levels, political theory and natural rights perhaps being the ones most fashionable with scholars. Obviously, however, the constitutional debate was central historically, and within that, the questions of authority and allegiance were pivotal. This brings to view the feudal relationship between America and the English monarchy within the empire, for from 1773 onward, in rejecting the authority of parliament to legislate for them (to bind them "in all cases whatsoever," as the unrepealed Declaratory Act of 1766 obnoxiously and alarmingly asserted), the Americans turned to the king. Led by the Boston Adamses, Sam and John, they argued that personal allegiance to the king in the reciprocal bonds of protection, homage, and fealty constituted the *sole* bond of community with England. John Adams' scathing denunciation of the feudal system and its covert popery of 1765 did not prevent his shifting the debate to the new ground by 1774. Earlier, Adams had derided bitterly the notion of the personal relationship between mother and child which the court claimed underlay the detestable policies of Great Britain toward the colonies. It reminded him (with "horror") of Shakespeare's depiction of another mother, Lady Macbeth, who

> Had given suck, and knew
> How tender't was to love the babe that
> milked her,
> but yet, who could
> Even while't was smiling in her face

30. C. F. Adams (ed.), "Dissertation on the Canon and Feudal Law," in *Works of John Adams*, III, 447–64, at 461. Emphasis added.

31. Aristotle *Politics* V. 10 [V. 8. 23. in Loeb ed.] 1313a14–16 (trans. T. A. Sinclair [Baltimore, 1962]), 224.

> Have plucked her nipple from the boneless gums,
> And dashed the brains out.[32]

In the *Resolutions* adopted by the First Continental Congress on October 14, 1774, Adams prevailed over the stubborn opposition of Joseph Galloway to win approval of this familiar language:

That the foundation of English liberty, and of all free government, is a right in the people to participate in their legislative council; and as the English colonists are not represented, and from their local and other circumstances, cannot properly be represented in the British parliament, they are entitled to a free and exclusive power of legislation in their several provincial legislatures, where their right of representation can alone be preserved, in all cases of taxation and internal polity, subject only to the negative of their sovereign, in such manner as has been heretofore used and accustomed.

In their petition to the king adopted on October 26, Congress called England "that nation" with which the Americans are in contention and stated, "We wish not a diminution of the prerogative."[33]

The basis of this final and rather astonishing constitutional position of the Americans lay in reasoning elaborated at length in Adams' *Novanglus* and succinctly displayed in a Massachusetts document of 1773. The position taken there rested, in turn, primarily on the precedent of *Calvin's Case*, decided in 1608. By the feudal basis of the relation of realm to dominions, lordship and dominion are vested solely in the king; all power is his. Feudal principles "afford us no idea of parliament." Considered as merely feudatory, "we are subject to the king's absolute will, and there is no authority of parliament, as the sovereign authority of the British empire." Moreover, no allegiance is due by Americans to "the crown of England." The tie is a strictly *personal* one: "Every man swears allegiance for himself, to his own king, in his natural person." Coke's opinion in *Calvin's Case* is quoted: "'Every subject is presumed by law to be sworn to the king, which is to his natural person. The allegiance is due to his natural body.' . . .

---

32. C. F. Adams (ed.), "Dissertation on the Canon and Feudal Law," in *Works of John Adams*, III, 461. Adams paraphrases Lady Macbeth from William Shakespeare, *Macbeth*, Act I, Scene 7. For the shift in Adams' emphasis see his *Novanglus*, in *Works*, IV, 1–177, which fully explores the feudal-medieval theory of the English constitution as sketched herein.

33. Quoted from Charles H. McIlwain, *American Revolution: A Constitutional Interpretation* (New York, 1923), 114–16.

If, then, the homage and allegiance is not to the body politic of the king, then it is not to him as the head, or any part of that legislative authority" vested in Parliament. Rather, "our ancestors received the lands [in America], by grant, from the king; and, at the same time, compacted with him, and promised him homage and allegiance, not in his public or politic, but natural capacity only." It then follows that "the right of being governed by laws, which were made by persons in whose election they had a voice, [our ancestors] looked upon as the foundation of English liberties. By the compact with the king, in charter, they were to be free in America as they would have been if they had remained within the realm; and, therefore, they freely asserted that they 'were to be governed by laws made by themselves, and by officers chosen by themselves.'" To hold otherwise and subject Massachusetts' people to the arbitrary will of a Parliament in which they had no voice, one claiming authority to make laws binding upon them in all cases whatsoever "without our consent," could only be "destructive of the first law of society, the good of the whole." [34]

This feudal conception of the English constitution is distinctly contrary to the Whig principle—whether New Whig or Old Whig—of vesting sovereignty in parliament. In plain fact, this is the medieval conception of the English constitution. It supplemented the appeal to natural law and rights in the late phases of the debate leading to independence, and it alone makes intelligible both Jefferson's designation of the king as "George Guelph" and the stress placed in both the Virginia Constitution and the Declaration of Independence as adopted on proving the political sins of the monarch, with only minimal attention being paid Parliament. The personal relationship was central, as were the bonds of faith between persons in America and the person of the king. The king had broken his faith by perverting just rule into misrule, thereby freeing the Americans from their obligations of allegiance and service. Parliament's role in this scenario (whatever its actions) was constitutionally negligible, since by this American theory it had no valid claim whatever to authority over them.

It is worthwhile to give the last word to John Adams in this rather

34. Quoted and summarized *ibid.*, 130–36; *cf.* pp. 92–95 for the details of *Calvin's Case*.

technical argument, although the testimony of Benjamin Franklin, James Wilson, John Dickinson, and Thomas Jefferson might also be adduced. In *Novanglus* he summed up the cardinal point this way:

Lands are holden according to the original notices of feuds, of the natural person of the lord. Holding lands in feudal language, means no more than the relation between lord and tenant. The reciprocal duties of these are all personal. Homage, fealty & c. and all other services, are personal to the lord; protection, & c. is personal to the tenant. And therefore no homage, fealty, or other services, can ever be rendered to the body politic, the political capacity, which is not corporated, but only a frame in the mind, an idea. No lands here, or in England, are held of the crown, meaning by it the political capacity; they are all held of the royal person, the natural person of the king. . . . As soon as [the colonists] arrived here, they got out of the English realm, dominions, state, empire, call it by what name you will, and out of the legal jurisdiction of parliament.[35]

II

It is, of course, no novelty to point out that Christianity is basic to American politics. This has been done before by many writers in many ways, few more incisively than Tocqueville, who published this view in 1840:

It was religion that gave birth to the English colonies in America. One must never forget that. In the United States religion is mingled with all the national customs and all those feelings which the word fatherland evokes. For that reason it has peculiar power. . . . Christianity has kept a strong hold over the minds of Americans, and . . . its power is not just that of a philosophy which has been examined and accepted, but that of a religion believed in without discussion. . . . Christianity itself is an established and irresistible fact which no one seeks to attack or to defend.[36]

Ralph Barton Perry, over a century later, reports that America is a "Christian country" whose "general Hebraic-Christian-Biblical tradition embraces ideas so familiar that, like the air, they are inhaled

35. C. F. Adams (ed.), *Works of John Adams*, IV, 176–77. *Cf.* McIlwain, *American Revolution*, 138–47. The views stated by Adams were voiced already by Franklin as early 1766; see McIlwain, *American Revolution*, 147.
36. Alexis de Tocqueville, *Democracy in America*, ed. J. P. Mayer, trans. George Lawrence (Garden City, N.Y., 1969), 432. The first volume of *Democracy in America* appeared in 1835, the second volume (from which the quotation is taken) in 1840.

without effort or attention." [37] He identifies the "fallacy of difference" in the delineation of Puritanism by writers who unwarrantedly ignore the fundamentally common ground shared by Puritans with all other Christian communions—a point of consideration for an argument that cites Thomas Aquinas in viewing the American Revolution as a study in restoration. "Puritanism was an offshoot from the main stem of Christian belief, and Puritans, equally with Catholics, claimed descent from St. Paul and Augustine." He also defines Puritanism as "theocratic, congregational–presbyterian, Calvinistic, protestant, medieval Christianity." [38] Persuasive scholarship has traced the rise of *Americanism* itself to the Great Awakening of the 1730s onward as the beginning of a series of waves of revivalism rising and falling down to the end of the eighteenth century and even beyond. This surge of renewed faith can be seen as the decisive factor in the emergence of an American national consciousness by the 1760s. The Great Awakening, Herbert Osgood flatly states, "was an event of general human significance" marking an "epoch" in our history. [39]

The citations might go endlessly on. The curiosity is that relatively little detailed connection with political theory has been traced after the decline of Puritanism toward the end of the seventeenth century. The influence of the classical philosophers is minimized even more, despite the fact that scarcely a paragraph of the political literature of the revolutionary period can be read without stumbling on direct classical allusions and steady use of the Greek and Roman categories of thought. In his exciting analysis, Bernard Bailyn identifies at the outset five major sources of revolutionary thought, including classical antiquity and New England Puritanism. The former he decides is universal but merely illustrative rather than determinative of thought, while the latter is important for the covenant theology, the contribution of the notion of the cosmic, providential sweep of America's destiny, ubiquitous, but ultimately incoherent and filled with conflicts. Enlightenment thought is directly influential but superficial apart

37. Ralph Barton Perry, *Characteristically American* (New York, 1949), 93.
38. Ralph Barton Perry, *Puritanism and Democracy* (New York, 1944), 82–83.
39. Herbert L. Osgood, *American Colonies in the Eighteenth Century* (1924; rpr. Gloucester, Mass., 1958), III, 409. Carl Bridenbaugh confirms the judgment in numerous places, *e.g.*, *Cities in Revolt: Urban Life in America, 1743–1776* (New York, 1955), 64, 150–56, 424.

from Locke, who is centrally important; and the common law is historically important but not determinative. Dominant and determinative for our revolutionaries, Bailyn finds, is the "radical social and political thought of the English Civil War and Commonwealth period." Milton, Harrington, and especially Sidney composed the "textbook of the Revolution." This strand of thinking, Bailyn contends, drew together and harmonized all other elements into the distinctive synthesis seen in the formative period.[40]

I can only say that in so concluding, I think Bailyn is wrong, even if elegantly so. Christianity and classical theory together constitute the matrix of both the sense of community and the "ancient principles" of man and government, whose synthesis distinguishes the founders' thought. This synthesis they and I call by the familiar name Americanism. McIlwain is close to the fact when he asserts that "1768 was the high-water mark of Whiggism in America. There it stopped."[41] Alan Heimert, a Harvard colleague, once remarked of Bailyn that he wrote almost as though the preachers did not exist. While too much need not be made of a casual observation, there is indeed in Bailyn's account a suspicion of what Perry Miller called "obtuse secularism." As to the mobilizing sentiment of the American Revolution, Miller adds, "A pure rationalism such as [Jefferson's] might have declared the independence of these folk, but could never have inspired them to fight for it."[42] Neither Louis Hartz's "irrational Lockianism" nor Wills' or others' Enlightenment thought nor Bailyn's Country ideology deserves first regard in our understanding of the mind of the American founders—significant as all three may be in the sophisticated and highly stratified consciousness of that uncommonly well-educated generation.[43]

The meaning of equality and happiness as held by such *aristoi* as Jefferson and Adams, and the esteem in which the *people* are held in

40. Bernard Bailyn, *Ideological Origins of the American Revolution* (Cambridge, Mass., 1967), 23–35, 53.
41. McIlwain, *American Revolution*, 157.
42. Miller, *Religion in American Life*, I, 336n, 343. For Heimert's settled views see Alan Heimert, *Religion and the American Mind: From the Great Awakening to the Revolution* (Cambridge, Mass., 1966).
43. See Hartz, *Liberal Tradition in America*, 62 and *passim*.

the repeated references to them in the Constitutional Convention are quite mystifying unless the classical and Christian notions of a common human nature present to all men *qua* men and the dignity of man as created in the divine image and loved of God are borne in mind.[44] As John Adams asserted in 1765:

A native of America who cannot read and write is as rare an appearance as a Jacobite or a Roman Catholic, that is, as rare as a comet or an earthquake. It has been observed that we are all of us lawyers, divines, politicians, and philosophers. . . . [A]ll candid foreigners who have passed through this country, and conversed freely with all sorts of people here, will allow, that they have never seen so much knowledge and civility among the common people in any part of the world. . . . Be it remembered . . . that liberty must at all hazards be supported. We have a right to it, derived from our Maker. But if we had not, our fathers have earned and bought it for us, at the expense of their ease, their estates, their pleasure, and their blood. And liberty cannot be preserved without a general knowledge among the people, who have a right, from the frame of their nature, to knowledge, as their great Creator, who does nothing in vain, has given the understanding, and a desire to know.[45]

III

A passing glance at the constitutional and historical perspectives commonplace to the founders permit me to stress a few of the central points. Richard Gummere is indubitably right in his judgment that "the delegates to the Constitutional Convention assembled at a time when the influence of the classics was at its height. They were not interested in mere window dressing or in popular slogans filched from history books. They dealt with fundamental ideas and considered them in light of their applicability."[46] Aristotle, Cicero, and Polybius were central. The majority of delegates to the Convention

44. For the discussion of *aristoi* (best men by nature) see Lester J. Cappon (ed.), *Adams-Jefferson Letters: The Complete Correspondence Between Thomas Jefferson and Abigail and John Adams* (1959; rpr. New York, 1971), 387–92, Jefferson's letter dated October 28, 1813; also the other letters in this period, *ibid.*, 365–99.

45. C. F. Adams (ed.), *Works of John Adams*, III, 456. Cf. Aristotle *Metaphysics* I. 1. 1. 980a22, first line: "All men by nature desire to know."

46. Richard M. Gummere, *American Colonial Mind and the Classical Tradition: Essays in Comparative Culture* (Cambridge, Mass., 1963), 174; for the college curriculum and its thorough education of Americans in the classics see pp. 55–59.

knew the classics, as Gummere shows and as can easily be concluded by reading through the character sketches of fifty-three of the participants done by William Pierce of Georgia at the Convention.[47]

The central principle of the Constitution, as establishing a rule of law and not of men, took its rise from Aristotle's *Politics*, Book III, Chapter 16, as did the fundamental insight into human nature of the passage that Madison and his colleagues institutionalized in the separation of powers and system of checks and balances—expounded in *Federalist Nos.* 47–51—and as Edward S. Corwin taught six decades ago and we have forgotten.

"To invest the law then with authority is, it seems, to invest God and reason; to invest a man is to introduce a beast, as desire is something bestial, and even the best of men in authority are liable to be corrupted by passion. We may conclude then that the law is reason without passion and it is therefore preferable to any individual. . . ." The opposition which [Aristotle's formulation] discovers between the desire of the human governor and the reason of the law lies, indeed, at the foundation of the American interpretation of the doctrine of the separation of powers and so of the entire system of constitutional law.[48]

The mediation of common notions of rule from antiquity by such important writers as Harrington, Bolingbroke, Montesquieu, and many others ought not confuse the fact that the original sources were Greeks and Romans. The framers knew not only the mediators but also the originators themselves, thoroughly and often in the original languages. Madison's repeated clarification of the "ends" of man and government as happiness and justice, and the echoing agreement with him on all sides trace to the headwaters of Plato and Aristotle as confirmed in Cicero and Polybius. Toward the close of *Federalist No. 51*, Madison's summary is clear and may again be quoted: "Justice is the end of government. It is the end of civil society. It ever has been and ever will be pursued until it be obtained, or until liberty be lost in the pursuit." After opening the *Ethics* with the clarification that the highest good attainable by action is Happiness, Aristotle went on to

---

47. *Ibid.*, 178. *Cf.* "Notes of William Pierce [Ga.] in the Federal Convention of 1787," in Tansill (ed.), *Documents Illustrative of the Formation of the Union*, 96–108.

48. Corwin (ed.), *"Higher Law" Background of American Constitutional Law*, 8–9.

his analytical inquiry, arriving at the pertinent juncture that "the laws make pronouncements on every sphere of life, and their aim is to secure . . . the common good of all. . . . Accordingly, in one sense we call those things 'just' which produce and preserve happiness for the social and political community."[49]

To be sure, the founders kept the context of their efforts constantly in mind in fashioning the Constitution, an attitude strongly present also in Plato's *Laws* and Aristotle's *Politics,* for all of the amplitude of their vision of transcendental truth. As Gouveneur Morris said in the Convention's proceedings, in America "the people are the king."[50] Yet the *Justice* to which the Constitution was dedicated was that of the higher Law of God and Reason—the "Law coeval with mankind" in Cicero's phrase, as Blackstone had reaffirmed for the hundredth time in 1765, when the first volume of the *Commentaries* appeared.[51] In short, it is divine and natural Justice as embedded in common law that supplies the standard of what is lawful and within the reach of the consent of the people under their Constitution.

The historical vista is accordingly wide. The sobriety of Americans in politics also characterizes their view of history and the nation's destiny. Apocalypticism is a potent factor from the early years of settlement onward, but I think it was never a dominant one. Still, there is the understanding of special favor and an intimacy with God that supplies peculiar meaning to America's pilgrimage through time. Americans, for all their enthusiasm in religion from time to time, could never forget the fundamental of the faith: "My kingdom is not of this world." At the founding, the New Order of the Ages was, in fact, proclaimed; Manifest Destiny was prefigured before the eighteenth century was out. And if the end of history and the translation of time into eternity at the millennium are eagerly anticipated, along with America's special role in this final fruition of faith, then the representative attitude is suspenseful and hopeful rather than dogmatic and certain. The flavor is caught by the illustrious Ezra Stiles in his election sermon of 1783.

49. Aristotle *Nicomachean Ethics* V. 1. 13. 1129b16–18 (trans. Martin Ostwald).
50. Farrand (ed.), *Records of the Federal Convention of 1787,* II, 69.
51. Cicero *Republic* III. 33; Cicero *Laws* I. 18. Blackstone, *Commentaries,* I, 41.

I have thus far shown wherein consists the true political welfare of a civil community or sovereignty. The foundation is laid in a judicious distribution of property, and in a good system of polity and jurisprudence, on which will arise, under a truly patriotic, upright, and firm administration the beautiful superstructure of a well-governed and prosperous empire. . . . Already does the new constellation of the United States begin to realize . . . glory. . . . And we have reason to hope, and I believe, to expect that God has still greater blessings in store for this vine which his own right hand hath planted, to make us high among the nations in praise, and in name, and in honor. The reasons are very numerous, weighty, and conclusive.[52]

The intertwining of politics and religion in American experience posed the knotty problem of how the two could be both combined and kept distinct. The fervor for liberty during the Revolution took on all the existential urgency of a quest for salvific religious truth. Common ground was found in Americanism, and a solution that endured worked through the half-century following the Declaration of Independence. Central to this process in all of its stages were John Adams and Thomas Jefferson, and it is especially their understanding of power and spirit in the founding that we next consider.

52. Stiles, "United States Elevated to Glory and Honor," in Thornton (ed.), *Pulpit of the American Revolution,* 438–39. An abbreviated version of this sermon is reprinted in Conrad Cherry (ed.), *God's New Israel: Religious Interpretations of American Destiny* (Englewood Cliffs, N.J., 1971), 82–92, which also contains useful bibliographies. For a large collection of related material see Ellis Sandoz (ed.), *Political Sermons of the American Founding Era, 1730–1805* (Indianapolis, 1991).

CHAPTER 4 Power and Spirit in the
Founding: Thoughts on the Genesis of Americanism

Despite the misgivings of the American founders themselves, the patriotic consciousness of the country from the very first insisted that the founding was an activity of men more than merely mortal done in close cooperation with the Deity himself. It is my purpose here to sketch the founders' "divine science of politics" as the noetic ground of popular consciousness and of the symbolisms articulating the order of our constitutional democracy in Americanism. I propose to do this by considering the authority of the founders, the character of the consensus that emerged in the formative period, and the science of politics with its penumbra of foundation myth and civil theology. The "divine science of politics" is John Adams' symbol. The equation of "the dictates of reason and pure Americanism" originates with Thomas Jefferson.[1]

I

It is evident that the authority of the founders, or Founding Fathers (habitually capitalized, as befits heroic and celestial beings), has been

1. John Adams to James Warren, June 17, 1782, in C. F. Adams (ed.), *Works of John Adams*, IX, 512; *cf.* John to Abigail Adams ("Portia"), "early 1780," in C. F. Adams (ed.), *Letters of John Adams* (Boston, 1841), II, 68; Thomas Jefferson to Edward Rutledge, June 24, 1797, in Lipscomb and Bergh (eds.), *Writings of Thomas Jefferson*, IX, 409; *cf.* John Adams to Benjamin Rush, July 7, 1805, in Schutz and Adair (eds.), *Spur of Fame*, 30.

and remains great in the American consciousness. A French visitor to the country understated the case when he reported in 1939 that "America is the only country in the world which pretends to listen to the teaching of its founders as if they were still alive." [2] We listen to them much better than if they were still alive. The founders themselves would have been amused by the twentieth-century report but scarcely surprised by it. The "canonization" of the founders began with the Revolution and Constitution, and culminated in the "emotional outburst" that swept the country on the fiftieth anniversary of the Declaration of Independence when the news broke that both John Adams and Thomas Jefferson had died on that day, "the point at which the American people came to remember the Revolutionary fathers for what they had agreed upon rather than for their disputes with one another." [3] But the founding generation was fully aware at the time that epochal events were unfolding, that history had taken a new turn, and that *novus ordo seclorum* was being imprinted upon America and the world itself by the heroic mind of remarkable men in its midst. Contemporaries were also aware that this is the stuff myths are made of, and they entered into the fabulous articulation of the tenor and significance of events never regarded as merely secular and pragmatic by leading participants. Jefferson called the Federal Convention "an assembly of demigods." Not to be outdone, Adams soon afterward and with customary irony magnified the framers as "heroes, sages, and demigods" for whom he hoped to become one of the "underworkmen." Yet at the very end of their lives Jefferson gently uttered the final encomium when he wistfully wrote of "the Heroic age" of the founding and of himself and his dear old friend Adams as among its "Argonauts." [4]

Perhaps the leading participant who was, at once, most alive to the

2. Raoul de Roussy de Sales, "What Makes an American?" *Atlantic Monthly* (March 1939), as quoted in Dixon Wector, *Hero in America: A Chronicle of Hero Worship* (1942; rpr. Ann Arbor, Mich., 1963), 81.

3. Wesley Frank Craven, *Legend of the Founding Fathers* (1956; rpr. Ithaca, N.Y., 1965), 87–88.

4. Thomas Jefferson to John Adams, Aug. 30, 1787, in Cappon (ed.), *Adams-Jefferson Letters*, I, 196; John Adams to John Jay, Sept. 22, 1787, in C. F. Adams (ed.), *Works of John Adams*, VIII, 452. *Cf.* Max Farrand, *Framing of the Constitution of the United States* (New Haven, 1913), 39–41; Thomas Jefferson to John Adams, Mar. 25, 1826, Cappon (ed.), *Adams-Jefferson Letters*, in II, 614.

momentous, portentous, and comic dimensions of the founding was John Adams. "It has been the will of Heaven," he wrote in January 1776, "that we should be thrown into existence at a period when the greatest philosophers and lawgivers of antiquity would have wished to live. A period when [we have] an opportunity of beginning government anew from the foundation. . . . How few of the human race have ever had any opportunity of choosing a system of government for themselves and their children!"[5] Less than a month before Independence, Adams wrote from Philadelphia, where the Continental Congress was in session, "Objects of the most stupendous magnitude, and measures in which the lives and liberties of millions yet unborn are intimately interested, are now before us. We are in the very midst of a revolution, the most complete, unexpected, and remarkable, of any in the history of nations. . . . When these things are once completed, I shall think that I have answered the end of my creation, and sing my *nunc dimittis*." Myth taking shape before one's eyes is a disconcerting experience, however, as we see from Adams' comments of 1777 when, in the face of Washington's ascension, adulation veered toward idolatry. "Now we can allow a certain citizen to be wise, virtuous, and good, without thinking him a deity or saviour," he wrote Abigail. And some months earlier he had said to Benjamin Rush, "I have been distressed to see some of our members disposed to idolize an image which their own hands have molten. I speak of the superstitious veneration which is paid to General Washington."[6] In the following year Washington was, for the first time, indeed proclaimed "Father of his Country" in Francis Bailey Lancaster's 1778 *Almanac*.[7] Adams' irritation and misgivings were patent. They grew from his historical awareness of the danger to liberty and republican institutions posed by charismatic military leaders and the opinion that, as

5. John Adams to John Penn, Jan. 1776, in C. F. Adams (ed.), *Works of John Adams*, IV, 203.

6. John Adams to William Cushing, June 9, 1776, *ibid.*, IX, 391; John Adams to Abigail Adams, Oct. 26, 1777, in C. F. Adams (ed.), *Letters of John Adams*, II, 14. Rush's account of Adams' views is given *ibid.*, 15–16.

7. Jürgen Gebhardt, *Die Krise des Amerikanismus: Revolutionäre Ordnung und gessel-schaftliches Selbstverständnis in der amerikanischen Republik* (Stuttgart, 1976), 46. Translation in press as Gebhardt, *Americanism: Revolutionary Order and Social Self-Understanding in the American Republic*, at Louisiana State University Press. This is the best study of Americanism I have found.

worthy as Washington truly was, "in this house [*i.e.*, Congress], I feel myself his superior"—views that very nearly implicated him in the popular mind in an unsavory intrigue against the emergent legendary Father of his Country.[8]

It is with some further irony, then, that in Adams' preface to the first volume of *A Defence of the Constitutions of the United States of America Against the Attack of M. Turgot . . .* (1787) he points out that, while it "was the general opinion of ancient nations, that Divinity alone was adequate to the important office of giving laws to men," in the United States of America "it will never be pretended that any persons employed in that service had interviews with the gods, or were in any degree under the inspiration of Heaven," since "men are now sufficiently enlightened to disabuse themselves of artifice, imposture, hypocrisy, and superstition."[9] This was partly, no doubt, a swipe at the burgeoning Washington cult born of envy, perhaps, but also of the distasteful recollection that King James I and Oliver Cromwell each had been lauded as Father of his Country (*parens patriae; pater patriae*). It was also a counter to Turgot, meant to assure the enlightened *philosophe* that American lawgivers were as rational as he and relied upon "the simple principles of nature . . . reason and the senses" in contriving their new governments.[10] Still, Adams celebrated the "divine science of politics."[11]

By 1790, Adams' irritation with the myth of Washington at large in the country hatched a fleeting Swiftian satire as he sketched a "fable plot." "The essence of the whole will be that Dr. Franklin's electrical rod smote the earth and out sprung General Washington. That Franklin electrified him with his rod—and thence forward these two concluded the policy, negotiations, and war." The myth took its scientistic turn in the inevitable direction of Newtonian physics in this parody of the country's "Saviour, Deliverer, and Founder."[12] Two decades later, long after Washington's death, Adams still ridi-

---

8. C. F. Adams (ed.), *Letters of John Adams*, II, 16n.

9. C. F. Adams (ed.), *Works of John Adams*, IV, 291–92. Cf. *Federalist No. 38*.

10. C. F. Adams, *Works of John Adams*, IV, 292; and Gebhardt, *Amerikanismus*, 45–46.

11. John Adams to James Warren, June 17, 1782, C. F. Adams (ed.), *Works of John Adams*, IX, 512.

12. John Adams to Benjamin Rush, April 4, 1790, quoted from Gebhardt, *Amerikanismus*, 22.

culed the "hypocritical cult" that idolized "*divus* Washington, *sancte* Washington, *ora pro nobis!*" And he implored another correspondent, Dr. Benjamin Waterhouse, "Do not however, I pray you, call me 'the godlike Adams,' 'the sainted Adams,' 'Our Saviour Adams,' 'Our Redeemer Adams.'"[13] Recoil as he might from the rhetoric of myth, Adams jocularly stated in private correspondence what he had really long since soberly concluded. If, come what may, there is to be a Father of the Country, then his own credentials were as good as anybody's. He wrote to William Cunningham: "They called me venerable Father of New England. I resented that, because if there was any pretence for calling me Father of New England, there was equal pretence for calling me Father of Kentucky and Tennessee. I was therefore willing to be thought the Father of the Nation."[14]

In truth, the matter was settled long before July 4, 1826, and long before Adams staked his own claim in the letter of 1809 to Cunningham. To be sure, John Adams would have to settle for the merely collective immortality of the founding fathers, as befitted an underworkman, but this already had been achieved. One example must suffice. In *The United States Elevated to Glory and Honor,* the election sermon preached in 1783 by President Ezra Stiles of Yale College (mentioned earlier), Washington, Jefferson, Adams, and others of the national pantheon were mustered in a mighty "discourse upon the political welfare of God's American Israel . . . allusively prophetick [*sic*] of the future prosperity and splendour of the United States." Stiles exclaimed: "Already does the new constellation of the United States begin to realize this glory. . . . And we have reason to hope, and I believe to expect, that God has still greater blessings in store for this vine which his own right hand hath planted, and to make us 'high among the nations in praise, and in name, and in honour,'" quoting Deuteronomy 26:19, his text for the occasion.[15] God's wrath abated, and the Revolution ended in victory and secure independence for the American Israel, so "does it not become us to reflect how wonderful, how gracious, how glorious has been the good hand of our God upon

13. John Adams to Benjamin Rush, Feb. 25, 1808, and John Adams to Benjamin Waterhouse, Aug. 16, 1812, quoted *ibid.*, 21.
14. John Adams to William Cunningham, April 24, 1809, quoted *ibid.*, 9.
15. Stiles quoted from Cherry (ed.), *God's New Israel,* 83–84.

us in carrying us through so tremendous a warfare!" Washington, true to Adams's grumblings, is lauded above all others as the leader

Congress put at the head of [its] spirited army [as] the only man on whom the eyes of all Israel were placed. Posterity . . . inconsiderate and incredulous as they may be of the dominion of heaven, will yet do so much justice to the divine moral government as to acknowledge that this American Joshua was raised up by God and divinely formed by a peculiar influence of the Sovereign of the Universe for the great work of leading the armies of this American Joseph (now separated from his brethren) and conducting this people through the severe, the arduous conflict, to Liberty and Independence.[16]

Stiles, in common with other preachers of the period and even with Tom Paine (in the *Crisis Papers*), characterizes the Revolution as a Just War, retold as a heroic tale in the rhetoric of an Old Testament parable. Washington is greater than Cyrus or Caesar, and others even compared him to Jesus Christ! Jefferson, Stiles continues, "poured the soul of the continent into the monumental act of Independence," and Franklin, Adams, Jay, and others "resolutely and nobly dared to sign the glorious act," thereby meriting the immortality of fame. Adams is eulogized as "that great civilian" and quoted as expressing his faith that the Revolution served the purposes of divine Providence, accelerating by centuries the progress of society toward the millennium. The language becomes apocalyptical as America's messianic destiny is meditated to the point where the "collective body of the United States" is evoked in close analogy to the mystical body of Christ ordained to "illume the world with TRUTH and LIBERTY." Unique to the new dispensation is that it "will embosom all the religious sects or denominations in Christendom. Here they may all enjoy their whole respective systems of worship and church government complete." Thereby, America's true republicanism and steadfast faithfulness may providentially conspire to attain "a singular superiority—with the ultimate subserviency to the glory of God, in converting the world" to Christianity.[17]

16. *Ibid.,* 85.
17. *Ibid.,* 87, 90, 91, 92. Additional material interpolated and quoted from the text of Stiles' sermon as printed in Thornton (ed.), *Pulpit of the American Revolution,* 452–65. See Edmund S. Morgan, *Gentle Puritan: A Life of Ezra Stiles, 1727–1795* (New Haven, Conn., 1962), 453–55 (for the quoted sermon), 447 (as a student of mysticism, esp. of Pseudo-Dionysius the Areopagite).

It can readily be seen from Stiles' sermon how the mythopoeic imagination of Americans of the formative period translated for general consumption the great events of the time into the genre of a sacred history augmenting that provided in the Bible. For all the theoretical acuity and up-to-date rationalism of the intellectual leadership of America—including Ezra Stiles himself—the controlling self-interpretation of the founding lay in the mode of articulation just illustrated, and it remained substantially controlling as the basis of Americanism, the common sense of the nation. In Perry Miller's summary, the preachers of the time were not selling a Revolution to a people sluggish to buy by providing a religious interpretation of events. They were explaining matters as they truly believed them to be.

Nor were they distracted by worries about the probability that Jefferson held all their constructions to be nonsense. A pure rationalism such as his might have declared the independence of these folk, but it could never have inspired them to fight for it. . . .

The American situation was not what Paine presented in *Common Sense*— a community of hard-working, rational creatures being put upon by an irrational tyrant—but more like the recurrent predicament of the chosen people in the Bible. The Jews originally were a free republic founded on a covenant over which God "in peculiar favor to that people, was pleased to preside." When they offended Him, He punished them by destroying their republic, subjecting them to a king. Hence when we angered our God, a king was also inflicted upon us; happily, Americans have succeeded, where the Jews did not, in recovering something of pristine virtue, whereupon Heaven redressed America's earthly grievances.[18]

Due to secularization during the past two centuries, pains must be taken to supply the experiential context that makes the foundation myth plausible and intelligible. To be sure, the mythic quality of the Declaration and Constitution is apparent to some degree. The atmosphere in which founding fathers of such heroic dimension proclaim self-evident truths respecting the creation and creatures therein, and contrive out of more than merely mortal wisdom a matchless instrument for the ordering of the lives of all future generations of Americans (a model for mankind itself) is plainly a world of mythopoeic

---

18. Miller, "From Covenant to Revival," in *Religion in American Life*, eds. Smith and Jamison, I, 342–43.

contrivance. Yet the verdant foliage of the people's myth, told in the parlance of a popular consciousness formed by Scripture, is missing. While complete on principle and aimed toward magistrates and the enlightened urbane of America and the world, the official, secular version is deficient in the pathos of which it is an intellectualized expression. The myth that arises from the experience of America as New Israel, a land apart, of Americans as a Chosen People whose destiny lies among the stars of the heavenly firmament, and of a providentially ordained history tending inexorably toward the kingdom of God is only hinted in the state papers. The decisive context must be sought elsewhere in contemporary sources. The sense of divine election and messianic purpose that crowns Ezra Stiles' political faith, as we glimpse it in his 1783 sermon, composes a vital dimension of Americanism that need not be left to supposition.

The outlook of the founders is well suggested and permanently symbolized by the inclusion on the reverse of the Great Seal of the United States (conceived and designed between 1776 and 1782) of the "Eye of Providence in a radiant Triangle" placed above a "pyramid unfinished" on the base of which appears the "Annuit Coeptis MDCCLXXVI" and "underneath the following motto, '*Novus Ordo Seclorum*.'"[19] As the symbols indicate, divine Providence presides over the establishment of the New Order of the Ages by its anointed people, America. Adams, Jefferson, and Charles Thomson explained it to Congress in these words in 1782: "The pyramid signifies Strength and Duration: The Eye over it and the Motto allude to the many signal interpositions of Providence in favour of the American cause. The date underneath is that of the Declaration of Independence and the words under it signify the beginning of the new American Aera [*sic*], which commences from that date."[20]

When Washington was inaugurated first president of the United States in New York City on April 30, 1789, the Bible was opened to

19. Quotations from official reports dated August 20, 1776, and June 20, 1782, as given in Gaillard Hunt, *History of the Seal of the United States* (Washington, D.C., 1909), 11, 41–42. See the reproduction on the one-dollar bill! The reverse of the seal, uncut since 1884, is in disuse for any other purpose (except as a decoration on some federal buildings) because it is regarded to be "spiritless, prosaic, heavy, and inappropriate" (*ibid.*).

20. *Ibid.*, 42. The mottoes are from Virgil: "Audacibus annue coeptis" (favor my daring undertaking), *Aeneid*, Bk. IX, Ver. 625; *cf. Georgics* I. 40; and "Magnus ab integro seclorum nascitur ordo" (the great series of ages begins anew) from the *Fourth Eclogue*, Ver. 5 (*ibid.*, 34).

the forty-ninth chapter of Genesis for the administration of the oath of office. He laid his hand upon verses 13 to 33, which recount Jacob's blessing of Joseph as the prince of his brethren.[21]

II

The authority of the founders (attested by the spontaneous emergence of the public cult around them that viewed them as heroic figures) rested on the conviction of the American community that their words and deeds served liberty, truth, justice, and reason. The vindication of this conviction through the success of both the Revolution militarily and the transition from colonial status to sovereign nationhood—marked by the framing of the Constitution, its ratification, inauguration of the president, convening of the Congress, and adoption of the Bill of Rights during a decade and a half—profoundly secured the concord of the people and durably institutionalized their vision of public order. These achievements are no less remarkable politically because of their familiarity to us two centuries later, or because we so easily concede the wisdom and good luck of the generation of '76 of whom we are beneficiaries.

The creation of a society organized for action in history is no merely pragmatic achievement, important as the practicalities indeed are. Mere utility does not evoke the passion for liberty and justice commonplace in the utterances of the period. The small politics of mutual accommodation and self-aggrandizement (always present) cannot account fully for great political achievement. However much the high achiever may be driven to attain fame and glory, and rightly claim them when they are his due, persons as well educated as Adams, Jefferson, Madison, and other leaders of the founding knew (whatever Machiavelli and Bacon had said) that the timocratic men were not the true *aristoi*, noble though they might be.[22] Rather, at the pinnacle of worthy achievement of the order encountered in the American founding, we must look to vision and virtue for primary explana-

21. *Christian Science Monitor*, Oct. 16, 1952.
22. Aristotle *Nicomachean Ethics* I. 5. 4–7. 1095b23–1096a6. See the remarkable exchange of letters between the second and third presidents of the United States during the summer and fall of 1813 in Cappon (ed.), *Adams-Jefferson Letters*, II, 335–413. *Cf.* Douglass Adair, *Fame and the Founding Fathers*, ed. Trevor Colbourn (New York, 1974).

tion. And as we look, we should not forget that humble Socrates himself laid just claim to the highest honor Athens could bestow (*Apology* 36A–37A).

If it is true that the order of a society not only has a pragmatic dimension but also a theoretical one, and that it represents not only a self-contained parochial truth of a conventional sort but also existential and transcendental truth that relates the society and its citizenry to nature and the Ground of being to assert the claim of universal validity, then the ultimate theoretical moorings of the American mind may properly be sought. They can be found, I have suggested, in philosophy and Christianity.[23] What this ultimate horizon of reality comes to in certain central aspects is concisely stated by John H. Hallowell.

The Hebraic-Greek-Christian tradition teaches us . . . that the ultimate reality behind nature and history is a creative, rational, moral, loving Will and that man, since he is created in the image and likeness of God, achieves the perfection of his being in willing submission to the Reason and Will of Him that governs the universe. Men may resist that will or submit to it, but they cannot change it. The ultimate reality cannot be made over to conform to our desires—it is not something we can make or manipulate but something to which ultimately we must conform. Ultimately, all our actions will be judged by a standard which is not our own but God's.[24]

Since we have come so far with John Adams, perhaps the deepest thinker among the founders, it will serve to go yet a little farther with him to ascertain the character of American concord (or *homonoia*) that made it a community bound together by affection and mutual conviction. He is a fit spokesman. "I have hitherto had the happiness to find that my pulse beat in exact union with those of my Countrymen," he wrote in 1778.[25] In Adams' view, the substance of the community consisted of Christianity, moral and intellectual virtue, and love of liberty, that is, "governments . . . founded on the natural authority of the people . . . authority in magistrates and obedience of citizens . . . grounded on reason, morality, and the Christian reli-

23. *Cf.* Voegelin, *New Science of Politics*, Chaps. 2–3; *cf.* the analysis in Sandoz, *Voegelinian Revolution*, 90–115.
24. John H. Hallowell, *Moral Foundation of Democracy* (Chicago, 1954), 98–100.
25. John Adams to James Warren, Aug. 4, 1778, quoted from Gebhardt, *Amerikanismus*, 37.

gion."[26] The "divine science of politics" of the founders presupposed a virtuous citizenry, true religion, and honest and able leaders. That some such community actually existed is acknowledged by John Jay in *Federalist No. 2*, and James Madison reported that the people were "knit together . . . by . . . many chords of affection." Thomas Jefferson, writing toward the end of his life, believed that he and Adams and the other authors of the Declaration of Independence had spoken nearly fifty years earlier for a unified community by merely stating "the common sense of the subject . . . [as] an expression of the American mind. . . . All its authority rests then on the harmonizing sentiments of the day." "[T]here was but one opinion on this side of the water. All American Whigs thought alike on these subjects."[27]

The founders' political science embraces a "true map of man" that delineates "the dignity of his nature, and the noble rank he holds among the works of God," that lays it down "that consenting to slavery is a sacrilegious breach of trust as offensive in the sight of God as it is derogatory from our own honor or interest in happiness," and that acknowledges "that God Almighty has promulgated from heaven, liberty, peace, and good-will to man!"[28] With customary power, Adams reaffirmed his views long years after the founding. After quoting from an old pamphlet entitled "Address of the Young men of the City of Philadelphia," to which he had responded while president ("We regard our Liberty and Independence, as the richest portion given Us by our Ancestors"), Adams asks Jefferson:

And who were these Ancestors? Among them were Thomas Jefferson and John Adams. And I very cooly believe that no two Men among those Ancestors did more toward it than those two. . . . The *general Principles,* on which the Fathers achieved Independence, were the only Principles in which that beautiful Assembly of young Gentlemen [representing the numerous religious denominations of the country at the time of the Revolution] could Unite. . . . And what were these *general Principles?* I answer, the general Principles of Christianity, in which all those Sects were United: And the *general Principles* of English and American Liberty, in which all those young

26. C. F. Adams (ed.), *Works of John Adams*, IV, 293.
27. Cooke (ed.), *Federalist*, 9 (No. 2) and 88 (No. 14). Thomas Jefferson to Henry Lee, May 8, 1825, in Adrienne Koch and William Peden (eds.), *Life and Selected Writings of Thomas Jefferson* (New York, 1944), 719.
28. C. F. Adams (ed.), *Works of John Adams*, III, 463.

Men United, and which has United all Parties in America, in Majorities sufficient to assert and maintain her Independence.

Now I will avow, that I then believed, and now believe, that those general Principles of Christianity, are as eternal and immutable, as the Existence and Attributes of God; and that those Principles of Liberty, are as unalterable as human Nature and our terrestrial, mundane System.[29]

III

Space does not permit a full synopsis of the founders' divine science of politics, yet it is vital to appreciate the breadth and depth of the vision that their work as lawgivers, philosophers, and statesmen in fact reflects. In discharge of their pragmatic tasks, they moved in full awareness of the Western political tradition and sought to establish, in the wake of the Revolution, the best governments—for the states and through the Constitution, for the nation—that the nature of man and the force of circumstances would allow. For this purpose they had full recourse to the differentiated thought of ancient and modern philosophers, and the spiritual insight of the Christian faith into the reality of human existence, no less than to the science of government and to extensive experience in practical politics. They knew that the happiness of men is the end of politics and their blessedness the goal of faith: *salus populi suprema lex esto.* They believed that the laws of nature and nature's God represented the objective Truth of Being and, therefore, provided the foundation of positive law and of the liberties inherent to themselves as men, and thus were inalienable.

Blackstone, on the eve of the Revolution, had confirmed the traditional view that the law of nature was "coeval with mankind, and dictated by God himself," and was universally obligatory, so that no laws were binding that did not conform to it. In this he was repeating Coke, who had anointed Aristotle "nature's Secretary" in tracing the truth of order. Behind John Locke's powerful rationalistic summary lay the unfolding of the Whig interpretation of politics and history. That interpretation subtly blended the constitutional order of England and the legacy of the common law back to Magna Carta and

29. John Adams to Thomas Jefferson, June 28, 1813, in Cappon (ed.), *Adams-Jefferson Letters*, II, 339–40. *Cf.* C. F. Adams (ed.), *Works of John Adams*, IX, 187–88, for President Adams' response to the Philadelphians, dated May 7, 1798.

immemorial usage with the higher law guaranteed by right reason and "written with the finger of God in the heart of man."[30] At the core of this extensive body of thought lay the notions of government by consent (popular sovereignty) and the sanctity of the fundamental law limiting government's authority, whose kernel of protected liberties unfolded especially from Article 39 of Magna Carta (1215 A.D.).

As early as 1646 in America, John Winthrop recited the so-called Lockean formula that government primarily exists to protect men's "lives, liberties, and estates, etc., according to their due natural rights, as freeborn English, etc. [*sic*]"[31] This phrase was made famous in 1689 when Locke rendered it as equivalent to "Property," a way station on its long passage from Magna Carta to Declaration to the Fifth and Fourteenth Amendments' Due Process clauses as a part of the supreme law of the land's fundamental liberty. James Madison and the other framers completely understood that their handiwork rested on "the transcendent law of nature and of nature's God, which declares that the safety and happiness of society are the objects at which all political institutions aim, and to which all such institutions must be sacrificed."[32] In the founders' ransacking of the sources of political wisdom to establish optimally a free government of laws and not of men—government dedicated to the good of man through efficacious order and the preservation of individual liberties prized as

30. Blackstone, *Commentaries*, I, 40–41; Sir Edward Coke, *Seventh Reports*, at 12a–12b, *Calvin's Case* (1610), quoted from Corwin, *"Higher Law" Background of American Constitutional Law*, 46.

31. Not with approval, however. See James K. Hosmer (ed.), *Winthrop's Journal: History of New England, 1630–1649* (New York, 1908), II, 301. Quoted by John Winthrop as the claim of one Dr. Robert Child, with whom the colony was in serious conflict. *Cf.* Locke, *Second Treatise of Government*, Sec. 123, where he calls the three terms together *Property*. The earliest use of the formula "lives, liberties, and estates" that I have found occurs in the unfortunate notice from Charles I of the impeachment of Lord Kimbolton and the five members of the House of Commons (Hampden, Pym, et al.) of Jan. 3, 1642; see S. R. Gardiner (ed.), *Constitutional Documents of the Puritan Revolution, 1625–1660* (3rd ed., rev.; Oxford, 1906), 236; see also J. W. Gough, *Fundamental Law in English Constitutional History* (Cor. ed.; Oxford, England, 1961), 78.

32. Cooke (ed.), *Federalist*, 297 (No. 43), a view confirmed by Madison forty years later and, again, at the very end of his life. *Cf.* James Madison to N. P. Trist, April 1827, and James Madison to C. Caldwell, Sept. 20, Nov. 23, 1826, in Irving Brant, *James Madison* (Indianapolis, 1941–61), VI, 445–46; see also James Madison, "The Nature of the Union: A Final Reckoning," (dated 1835–36) in *Mind of the Founder: Sources of the Political Thought of James Madison*, ed. Marvin Meyers (Indianapolis, 1973), 567. On the role of "higher law" jurisprudence in modern American constitutional law more generally see Ellis Sandoz, *Conceived In Liberty: American Individual Rights Today* (North Scituate, Mass., 1978).

antecedent to government and enhanced by sound institutional design, yet ultimately dependent upon the people as the supreme human authority—they knew that the virtue of the citizenry was no less essential simply because selfish passion tends to overwhelm ennobling reason and its offspring, law. The sum of all their testimony attests that the founders emphatically agreed with the "Judicious" Hooker.

Two foundations there are which bear up public societies; the one a natural inclination, whereby all men desire sociable life and fellowship; the other, an order expressly or secretly agreed upon touching the manner of their union in living together. The latter is that which we call the Law of a Commonweal, the very soul of a politic body, the parts whereof are by law animated, held together, and set on work in such actions, as the common good requireth. Laws politic, ordained for external order and regiment amongst men, are never framed as they should be, unless presuming the will of man to be inwardly obstinate, rebellious, and averse from all obedience unto the sacred laws of his nature; in a word, unless presuming man to be in regard of his depraved mind little better than a wild beast, they do accordingly provide notwithstanding unto the common good for which societies are instituted; unless they do this, they are not perfect. . . . All men desire to lead in this world a happy life. That life is led most happily, wherein all virtue is exercised without impediment or let.[33]

The theory of the Constitution's most famous innovation, the separation of powers and system of checks and balances, is predicated on the classical and Christian conceptions of man and law succinctly expressed by Hooker. Justice no less than reason is a divine trait of man's nature and not, as in "Hobbes . . . founded in contract solely." Rather, it is "instinct, and innate, [embedded in] the moral sense [that] is as much a part of our constitution as . . . feeling, seeing, or hearing," the gift of "a wise Creator [who] must have seen [it] to be necessary in an animal destined to live in society" virtuously and happily. Because all men enjoy equality of nature, laws—including constitutions—must not only embody justice but also rest upon the consent of the people. Hence, on the one side, an unjust law is a nullity, and on the other side, "Laws they are not therefore which public

33. Hooker, *Ecclesiastical Polity*, I, 188 (Bk. I., Chap. 10, para. 1, first published in 1593). *Cf.* Aristotle *Politics* I. 1. 8–12. 1252b28–53a40; III. 11. 4. 1287a29–35.

approbation hath not made so."[34] In the language of the *Federalist,* "A good government implies two things; first, fidelity to the object of government, which is the happiness of the people; secondly, a knowledge of the means by which that object can best be attained."[35] *Primary* reliance for the securing of a just regime, one conducive to the liberty, well-being and happiness of the   untry, must ever rest on "the virtue and intelligence of the people ot America."[36]

Everyone understood, as the debate over the Bill of Rights showed, that if "the great mass of the people shou'd become *Corrupt!* ignorant of their Birthrite—and regardless of their posterity . . . it will not be in the power of Folios of Bills of rights to maintain their Liberties. The rights of Freemen are only to be maintain'd by Freemen."[37] It is essential, however, to cope with the factious, self-serving, passionate inclinations of men (as vividly known to Aristotle and Hooker as to Hobbes) by supplementing the primary "dependence on the people" for good government in a republic with the "auxiliary precautions" of the familiar institutional system of checks and balances resting on rival ambitions (Madison), thereby securing balance and equipoise by managing man's universal desire for emulation (Adams). Therewith, as Dudley Digges quaintly said in 1644, "charity to our neighbor, and love of our selves, doe sweetly kisse each other."[38]

Madison's elegant explanation in *Federalist No. 51* is familiar

34. Thomas Jefferson to John Adams, Oct. 14, 1816, and John Adams to Thomas Jefferson, Nov. 4, 1816, in Cappon (ed.), *Adams-Jefferson Letters,* II, 492, 494. Hooker, *Ecclesiastical Polity,* 194; quoted by Locke, *Second Treatise of Government,* Sec. 134n.

35. Cooke (ed.), Madison, *Federalist,* 419 (No. 62); *cf.* Adams, "Thoughts on Government" (1776), in C. F. Adams (ed.), *Works of John Adams,* IV, 193: "We ought to consider what is the end of government, before we determine which is the best form. Upon this point all speculative politicians will agree, that the happiness of society is the end of government, as all divines and moral philosophers will agree that the happiness of the individual is the end of man." A similar passage in a letter from Adams to John Penn (dated Jan. 1776) continues: "For the true idea of a republic is an empire of laws, and not of men; and, therefore, as a republic is the best of governments, so that particular combination of power which is best contrived for a faithful execution of the laws, is the best of republics" (*ibid.,* 204).

36. Cooke (ed.), *Federalist,* 341 (No. 49); *cf.* 315 and editor's note (No. 46) and 349 (No. 51).

37. George Lee Turbeville to James Madison, April 6, 1788, in William T. Hutchinson, et al. (eds.), *Papers of James Madison* (Chicago, 1962–67; Charlottesville, 1968–), XI, 24.

38. Cooke (ed.), *Federalist,* 349 (No. 51); C. F. Adams (ed.), *Works of John Adams,* VI, 279 and *passim.* Digges quoted from Richard Tuck, *Natural Rights Theories: Their Origin and Development* (Cambridge, England, 1979), 106.

to all. Adams theorized the problem exhaustively in the *Defence of the Constitutions* and elsewhere, although everyone was familar with the general theory of the balanced constitution from Blackstone, Montesquieu, and Charles I's classic statement in his *Answer to the XIX Propositions* (1642).[39] Americans, however, do not view ambition or emulation as utterly depraved *amor sui* (in Augustine's sense), and the system of checks and balances upon which it is predicated is at once the most ingenious feature of our government and the rock upon which the Constitution stands. As Adams remarks in discussing this crowning feature of the divine science of politics, the passion of emulation is as central to human institutions as gravity is to the motions of the heavenly bodies. Both are rooted in nature, the desire for emulation "implanted in the human heart for the wisest and best purposes [by] God and nature. Democratic and aristocratic states are not in their own nature free. Political liberty is to be found only in moderate governments. . . . It is there only when there is no abuse of power. But constant experience shows us that every man invested with power is apt to abuse it, and to carry his authority as far as it will go. . . . To prevent this abuse, it is necessary from the very nature of things that power should be a check to power." The rule of law and its equivalent, reason, is only possible by pitting desire against desire, so "that [the] balance of passions and interests" is achieved "which alone can give authority to reason" in human affairs.

In practice, this requires the separating and checking of "three different orders of men *in equilibrio*." This theory applies the principle of a parallelogram of forces drawn from Newton's second law of motion to the institutionalization of governmental power, government then being conceived as operating in analogy to the solar system and ruled by intrinsic psychological forces like the physical forces that regulate celestial mechanics.[40]

By such fascinatingly scientific means, government can attain moderation and prudence in normal operations, and men can more surely

39. *Cf.* Montesquieu, *Spirit of Laws*, Bk. IX; Blackstone, *Commentaries*, 1:154–55; Weston, "Beginnings of the Classical Theory of the English Constitution," 133–44.

40. C. F. Adams (ed.), *Works of John Adams*, VI, 10, 40, 234–98, 397–99, 488; IV, 391, 408, 436. *Cf.* the discussion in Walsh, *Political Science of John Adams*, 233 and *passim*. On *amor sui* and *amor Dei* in Augustine see *City of God* XIV. 28, XV. 1–8.

progress toward the justice and happiness that are their natural ends. "So far from believing in the total and universal depravity of human Nature," Adams stresses in 1817, "I believe there is no Individual totally depraved. The most abandoned scoundrel who ever existed, never Yet Wholly extinguished his Conscience, and while Conscience remains there is some Religion."[41] With men being neither gods nor beasts, and being capable of virtue but inclined to vice, the means whereby the good polity can be approximated is a properly ordered free government; and "the essence of free government consists in an effectual control of rivalries. . . . The nation which will not adopt an equilibrium of power must adopt a despotism. There is no alternative."[42]

IV

Power and spirit do not polarize in the founders' divine science of politics, despite their great stress on religious liberty and on the division of church and state in the institutional pattern. They never in their wildest flights dreamed of a system so perfect that the people would not need to be good.[43] To the contrary, they knew that good government presupposes good people—good, not perfect. All their aspirations and hopes utterly depend on the maintenance of the integrity of the community as the basis of the intricate constitutional system of their inspired design. Good morals and virtuous people depend, in turn, on true religion. "Patriotism without piety is mere grimace," a minister exclaimed in 1775.[44] In reflecting on the quality of the Constitution and the astonishing unity of the nation in support of it ratification, Madison in *Federalist No. 37* remarks, "It is impossible for the man of pious reflection not to perceive in it, a finger of

41. John Adams to Thomas Jefferson, April 19, 1817, in Cappon (ed.), *Adams-Jefferson Letters*, II, 509.
42. Adams, "Discourses on Davila" (1790), in C. F. Adams (ed.), *Works of John Adams*, VI, 280. *Cf.* Zoltan Haraszti, *John Adams and the Prophets of Progress* (1952; rpr. New York, 1964), 165–79; John R. Howe, Jr., *Changing Political Thought of John Adams* (Princeton, 1966), 28–58.
43. *Cf.* T. S. Eliot, "Choruses from 'The Rock,'" in *Complete Poems and Plays, 1909–1950* (New York, 1971), 106.
44. Rev. Thomas Coombe, quoted in Miller, "From Covenant to Revival," 329.

the Almighty hand which has been so frequently and signally extended to our relief in the critical stages of the revolution."[45] Human affairs are embedded in the natural order conceived on the pattern of creation and Creator. Later expositors of the mind of the founders sometimes share the affliction noted by Jefferson: "They wish it to be believed that he can have no religion who advocates it's [sic] freedom."[46]

Indeed, the founders did advocate freedom of conscience, including religious freedom. They did so for several reasons. Most compelling was the one noticed in Adams' letter of June 28, 1813, previously quoted. The common ground of Christianity united the country, but to prefer one sect or denomination over another would have torn the community apart. Religious liberty was the only feasible policy in pragmatic terms, one well considered when viewed against two centuries of the "madness" of religious strife, civil wars, fanaticism, and persecution.[47] The founders sought to end the dogmatomachy by protecting liberty and institutionalizing separate spheres of action for political and religious communities. This solution ranks without question as one of the greatest achievements of the entire founding, deserving comparison with the theocratic solutions of Plato in antiquity and of Gelasius' "Doctrine of Two Swords," basic to the *Christianitas* of the Middle Ages.

The force of reason and justice could prevail, by the founders' calculations, only to the degree that passion was minimized in the conduct of public affairs. We have noticed this familiar strand of argumentation in Madison's and Adams' exegesis of the Constitution.

45. Cooke (ed.), *Federalist*, 238.

46. Thomas Jefferson to John Adams, June 15, 1813, in Cappon (ed.), *Adams-Jefferson Letters*, II, 331. On Jefferson's religion see the useful survey in Charles B. Sanford, *Thomas Jefferson and His Library* (Hamden, Conn., 1977), Chap. 4. Of great importance is the editor's introduction in Dixon W. Adams (ed.), *Jefferson's Extracts from the Gospels: "The Philosophy of Jesus" and "The Life and Morals of Jesus"* (Princeton, 1983). See the discussion in Chap. 5 at pp. 147–49 herein.

47. *Cf.* the material cited in n. 29 earlier in this chapter. For a characteristic view of the "religious madness called enthusiasm" see John Trenchard and Thomas Gordon, *Cato's Letters: or, Essays on Liberty, Civil and Religious* (6th ed.; 1755; rpr. New York, 1971), IV, 143–52 and *passim*. Originally published in England in the early 1720s, these essays by Trenchard and Gordon were widely circulated in America as staples of Old Whig politics as the rift with Britain widened.

The great source of chaos in political life from the sixteenth to the eighteenth century was religious passion. Every political writer of consequence, from Bodin and Hooker to Rousseau, considered the "madness of enthusiasm" and its cures. Short of Leviathan, no universal orthodoxy was practicable in the modern context and, indeed, there has been no dearth of Leviathans in the twentieth century. For the founders, however, solution lay in the espousal of toleration and a tacit minimum dogma. Religious liberty that includes toleration and disestablishment was justified *either* on the faith that the truth will prevail and therefore divergent views in religion, as in other subjects, ought to be allowed full expression (so long as public peace were not disrupted); *or* on the faith that Christ's kingdom is not of this world, that God and Caesar are therefore entitled to their separate due, and that spiritual truth can only be fostered by spiritual means. A man might embrace liberty reasonably on the first grounds and piously on the second.

The American mixture of toleration and a minimum dogma at the founding turns on the understanding that basic agreement on the principles of Christianity is an essential element of the moral foundation of the society. That agreement is negatively hedged in by distrust of "popery and prelacy" as defining the outer limit of toleration. Adams and Jefferson profoundly feared the inquisitorial spirit to which every denomination was susceptible. The great history of opposing Catholicism and the establishment of an Anglican bishopric in America powerfully fueled the fears and distrust of these churches and their political schemes in the minds of even the most enlightened Americans of the time.

Americanism itself, then, serves as a kind of commonsense and civil theology based on nonsectarian Christianity and on the reasoned faith that men are more than mere fireflies; that this all is, indeed, not without a father.[48] Into this context step the Argonauts of the Heroic Age of our founding and its myth, reluctantly and rather self-consciously, to be sure; yet step they do nonetheless. The philosopher does not need the dogmas of the public *cultus* to secure his personal

---

48. *Cf.* C. F. Adams (ed.), *Works of John Adams*, VI, 281.

order and happiness, but a nation cannot do without them. And it is nobler to secure happiness for a nation than for merely one or a few men. Such is the divine science of politics.

The question nonetheless remains of the specific contours of the faith of the founders and its implicates for creation of the American republic. The following chapter directly undertakes to explore these matters, with the result of disclosing metaphysical depths of the American mind seldom glimpsed in conventional accounts of the founding.

CHAPTER 5 Reflections on Spiritual Aspects

of the American Founding

To speak of the American founding is to speak of great things, a great conspiracy of faith and reason. A glorious cause wins the day, an epoch ends, and a new order of the ages is proclaimed.

What is the role of religion in this remarkable drama? My concern with that subject here should not be misunderstood. Any attempt to reduce the event into this or that influence or element is patently defective and fallacious. Neither a single human life, nor a social entity, nor a passage of history, nor the comprehending reality itself is monistic, and merely to raise the possibility carries the refutation of self-evidence. We live, as William James clearly saw, in a pluralistic universe, a differentiated reality of transcendence and immanence that invites exploration of its richness in the open and generous spirit of wonder, awe, and the humility of the reflective part confronting the intelligible Whole in search of meaning and truth.

These elementary verities are intended to modulate the discussion of spiritual aspects of the American founding to portray it as reflections on the highly stratified, richly textured historical reality of the birth of the nation, with the Constitution as the focal point. Narrowly put, then, what role did things spiritual—the Bible, Christianity, the perspectives of transcendental faith and reason—play in the framing of the United States Constitution? Perhaps I should add, "if any," since the framing is widely regarded as being a purely secular enterprise. Proof positive for this enlightened conclusion is the celebrated proposal of Benjamin Franklin (evidently in his dotage) that the Convention turn to prayer to break the weeks-long impasse that threatened the entire endeavor. The proposal was turned aside without a vote, and Franklin noted on his manuscript, "The Convention, except three or four persons, thought Prayers unnecessary."[1] Moreover, despite the existence of established churches in several states and religious tests for holding office, the framers determined that officials "shall be bound by Oath or Affirmation, to support this Constitution; but no religious Test shall ever be required as a Qualification to any Office of public Trust under the United States" (Art. VI, Sec. 3), and by 1791 the First Amendment had been ratified, the opening clause of which reads, "Congress shall make no law respecting an establishment of religion, or prohibiting the free exercise thereof."

Despite these facts, I suggest that the Constitution owes a great debt to the spiritual convictions of the country and to its Christian traditions. It may not be entirely amiss to notice that the Convention was occasioned by acute political problems which, if unresolved, might undermine the very nation itself. It was a *political* event of a highly pragmatic sort, not a religious convocation or camp meeting. The business before it was a political emergency engendered by ineffectual government under the Articles of Confederation. The task at hand was to design a workable form of government in the setting of the new American nation.[2] It is primarily in terms of contextual factors that the spiritual aspects of the Constitution are to be sought. The emendations made by the Convention had to meet the satisfaction of the country. Of course, the emendations became an entirely new plan of government. Yet acceptability to a diverse and divided people organized into thirteen separate states, each of which thought of itself as (in some sense) sovereign, was the challenge which all the delegates knew to be critically important. While the familiar

1. Farrand (ed.), *Records of the Federal Convention of 1787*, I, 452n.
2. For a discussion of the acute crisis that precipitated the Federal Convention see Jack N. Rakove, *Beginnings of National Politics: An Interpretative History of the Continental Congress* (New York, 1979), Chap. 14. Rakove writes: "When in 1786 and 1787 Madison committed himself to a study of the history and theory of federal government, his motives were intensely and consciously pragmatic," *ibid.*, 379–80.

issues leading to the Great Compromises and the general design of the government reflect the Convention's sensitivity to sectional, demographic, economic, and political issues as components of the people's views, can there be any doubt that they knew the proposed Constitution would also be tested by the public's fundamental intellectual and spiritual convictions?

Religious liberty was the Constitution's answer to this central concern of public opinion. As James Iredell (later U.S. Supreme Court Associate Justice) said in the North Carolina ratifying convention, "Is there any power given to Congress in matters of religion? Can they pass a single act to impair our religious liberties? If they could, it would be a just cause of alarm. If they could, sir, no man would have more horror against it than myself."[3] Despite what *may* have been a decline in religion during and just after the Revolution, what Carl Bridenbaugh emphasizes about Americans of 1776 still held true a decade later, as Iredell's language implies and as North Carolina proved when it refused to ratify the Constitution until liberty was more clearly assured: "Who can deny that for them the very core of existence was their relation to God?"[4] In order to win his race for Representative in the first Congress, James Madison was compelled to come out for amendments to a Constitution that he initially thought needed none. He wrote to the Baptist minister and his supporter, Rev. George Eve, to remind him of his devotion to "religious liberty."

3. Farrand (ed.), *Records of the Federal Convention of 1787*, I, 125; Jonathan Elliott (ed.), *Debates in the Several State Conventions on the Adoption of the Federal Constitution* (2nd ed.; 1937; rpr. New York, 1974), IV, 194. For a distressing critique of the reliability of our key sources for understanding the formation of the United States (including *Madison's Notes* and *Elliott's Debates*), see James H. Hutson, "The Creation of the Constitution: The Integrity of the Documentary Record," *Texas Law Review*, LXV (1986), 1–39.

4. Bridenbaugh, *Spirit of '76*, 118. The received view of a general decline in religion during and following the Revolution is typically expressed by Sydney E. Ahlstrom, *A Religious History of the American People* (New Haven, 1972), 365. Recent scholarship strongly challenges this orthodoxy; see Patricia U. Bonomi and Peter R. Eisenstadt, "Church Adherence in the Eighteenth-Century British American Colonies," *William and Mary Quarterly*, 3rd ser., XXXIX (1982), 245–76, who conclude that 59 percent of the population were church members in 1780 and that number enormously expanded after 1790 with the Second Great Awakening (p. 274). See also Douglas H. Sweet, "Church Vitality and the American Revolution: Historiographical Consensus and Thoughts Towards a New Perspective," *Church History*, XLV (1976), 341–57. North Carolina finally ratified the Constitution on Nov. 21, 1789, the last state to do so, save only Rhode Island.

Now that eleven states had ratified the Constitution, Madison expressed his "sincere opinion that the Constitution ought to be revised, and that the First Congress meeting under it ought to prepare and recommend to the States for ratification the most satisfactory provisions for all essential rights, particularly the rights of conscience in the fullest latitude, the freedom of the press, trials by jury, security against general warrants, & c."[5]

To provide an empirical basis for the discussion, the argument here will proceed by first surveying learned opinion of the significance of things religious for the founders and their generation. Then I shall turn to contemporary evidence showing the nature and depth of religious views at the time, paying detailed attention to such representative documents as the Continental and Confederation Congress' official proclamations, to the texts of the sermons preached by leading churchmen, and to some of the other pamphlet literature. On the basis of this defining context, I shall then suggest the appeal to the spiritual order of the Constitution's central structures of assuring *liberty under law,* thereby arguing that this is the ultimate theoretical grounding in American consciousness of these salients. The purpose of this presentation is to provide evidence for the *fact* of a substantial spiritual dimension to our founding and to sketch the *character* of the debt of the Constitution and its order to that dimension. While the argument does not contend that the framers established a Christian Republic, it does challenge the view that they established a purely secular state. Their lodestar in this respect was the pronouncement from the New Testament—"My kingdom is not of this world" (John 18:36)—a verity whose acknowledgment is charged with spirituality.

I

The concern for religious liberty is the thread to follow in unraveling the framers' debt to the Bible and Christianity. This sort of inquiry, however, cannot be as successful, much less as persuasive as it is in-

5. James Madison to George Eve, Jan. 2, 1789, in C. F. Adams (ed.), *Letters and Other Writings of James Madison* (Philadelphia, 1865), I, 447; Bernard Schwartz, *Great Rights of Mankind: A History of the American Bill of Rights* (New York, 1977), 160–61.

tended to be unless we first take stock of the broader vistas surrounding our discussion. To begin with, there is the ubiquity of the Bible in early America. In George Trevelyan's words: "The effect of the continual domestic study of the book (*i.e.*, the Bible) upon the national character, imagination, and intelligence for three centuries—was greater than that of any literary movement in the annals, or any religious movement since St. Augustine."[6] Alexis de Tocqueville writes in the 1830s of his visits to the log cabins on the American frontier, finding there the typical pioneer in rustic isolation yet, astonishingly enough, "aware of the past, curious about the future, and ready to argue about the present; he is a very civilized man prepared for a time to face life in the forest, plunging into the wildernesses of the New World with his Bible, ax, and newspapers." As Donald S. Lutz shows, Bible reading persisted unabated throughout the entire formative period (1760–1805), with a full one-third of *all* citations in the enormous pamphlet literature produced in that forty-five-year period being to that book.[7]

The political significance is vast. Alice Baldwin concludes from a study of clergy in Virginia and North Carolina during and after the Great Awakening (roughly 1740–1770) that the

southern Presbyterian ministers based their political concepts on the Bible. The idea of a fundamental constitution based on law, of inalienable rights which were God-given and therefore natural, of government as a binding compact made between rulers and peoples, of the right of the people to hold their rulers to account and to defend their rights against oppression, these seem to have been doctrines taught by them all. . . . In the South as in New England, the clergy helped in making familiar to the common people the basic principles on which the Revolution was fought, our constitutional conventions held, our Bills of Rights written and our state and national constitutions founded.

She also quotes John Adams' letter of June 1776 to James Warren. "I am amazed," writes Adams, "to find an inclination so prevalent

---

6. Quoted by H. Richard Niebuhr, "The Idea of Covenant and American Democracy," *Church History* XXII (1954), 130.

7. Tocqueville, *Democracy in America*, ed. Mayer, I, 302. Donald S. Lutz, "Relative Influence of European Writers on Late Eighteenth-Century American Political Thought," *American Political Science Review*, LXXVIII (1984), 189–97.

throughout all the southern colonies, to adopt plans so nearly resembling that in the *Thoughts on Government*. I assure you, until the experiment was made, I had no conception of it."[8]

Sydney Ahlstrom discerns a "longterm American Revolution, 1607– 1776. This was the revolution in men's hearts to which, in John Adams' view, the Declaration of 1776 gave only belated expression. And the source of its strength lay in the religious substratum, which was always Nonconformist, Dissenting, and Puritan in its basic disposition." For this reason the Old Whig or Commonwealthman writers were so much more popular in eighteenth-century America than in England. Not only political antipathy and a desire for independence resulted in America, Ahlstrom continues, but also a "new conception of freedom and equality took shape, involving conceptions of God, man, human rights, the state, and history, which became inseparable from the [American] Enlightenment's outlook on reality. On 4 July 1776, these conceptions became a cornerstone of the American political tradition; during this period they were given further embodiment in state constitutions (and in due course in the federal Constitution)."[9]

In reflecting on Bernard Bailyn's and others' thesis about the decisive role played by the Old Whig political ideology in the origins of American politics and in the Revolution, Robert Middlekauff writes to similar effect.

Radical Whig perceptions of politics attracted widespread support in America because they revived the traditional concerns of a Protestant culture that had always verged on Puritanism. That moral decay threatened free government could not come as a surprise to a people whose fathers had fled England to escape sin. The importance of virtue, frugality, industry, and calling was at the heart of their moral code. . . . The generation that made the Revolution were the children of the twice-born, the heirs of this seventeenth-century religious tradition. George Washington, Thomas Jefferson, John Adams, Benjamin Franklin . . . may not have been men moved by religious

---

8. Alice M. Baldwin, "Sowers of Sedition: The Political Theories of the New Light Presbyterian Clergy of Virginia and North Carolina," *William and Mary Quarterly*, 3rd ser., V (1948), 76; C. F. Adams (ed.), *Works of John Adams*, IX, 398. See also Alice M. Baldwin, *New England Clergy and the American Revolution* (Durham, N.C., 1928).

9. Ahlstrom, *Religious History*, 362.

passions. But all had been marked by the moral dispositions of a passionate Protestantism. They could not escape this culture; nor did they try. They were imbued with an American moralism that colored their perceptions of politics. . . . Their responses—the actions of men who felt that Providence had set them apart for great purposes—gave the Revolution much of its intensity and much of its idealism.[10]

Middlekauff elsewhere remarks that "religion is supremely important" for understanding American history, not only through the Revolution but also through the Civil War and later. Understanding religion is at least as vital to a comprehension of these earlier centuries as understanding economics is to comprehending the twentieth century. "This is a terribly rough equation," Middlekauff says, "but Calvin is to the 17th and maybe the 18th century what John Maynard Keynes is to the 20th century."[11] He might better have substituted *Bible* for *Calvin*, but the point is made and it is sound. However diligently they studied Calvin, Americans' daily and pervasive converse with the Bible far eclipsed every other literary source.

II

The foregoing statements reflect the understanding that the Declaration of Independence, Revolutionary War, framing of the Constitution, ratification and adoption of the Bill of Rights, and transformation of the thirteen British colonies in North America into the new United States compose the unit of meaning we are studying and symbolize as the *founding*. And such is the seamless web of history that even this broad sweep is palpably inadequate for a rounded comprehension of our subject matter, particularly in its more theoretical aspects. If the American public in 1786 responded when Dr. Benjamin Rush of Philadelphia urged them "not to confound the terms of the American revolution with those of the late American war," they also

10. Robert Middlekauff, *Glorious Cause: The American Revolution, 1763–1789* (New York, 1982), 48. *Cf.* Bailyn, *Ideological Origins of the American Revolution;* Bernard Bailyn, *Origins of American Politics* (New York, 1969).

11. "Is America Still a Glorious Cause? A Conversation with Historian Robert Middlekauff," *Claremont Review of Books,* Dec. 1983, p. 10.

concurred with him that "nothing but the first act of the great drama is closed. It remains yet to establish and perfect our new forms of government, and to prepare the principles, morals, and manners of our citizens, for these forms of government, after they are established and brought to perfection." [12] There also was wide agreement with some of Rush's further notions.

The only foundation for a useful education in a republic is to be laid in RELIGION. Without this, there can be no virtue, and without virtue there can be no liberty, and liberty is the object and life of all republican governments. . . . The religion I mean to recommend in this place is the religion of JESUS CHRIST. . . . A Christian cannot fail of being a republican. The history of the creation of man and the relation of our species to each other by birth, which is recorded in the Old Testament, is the best refutation that can be given to the divine right of kings and the strongest argument that can be used in favor of the original and natural equality of all mankind. A Christian, I say again, cannot fail of being a republican, for every precept of the Gospel inculcates those degrees of humility, self-denial, and brotherly kindness which are directly opposed to the pride of monarchy and the pageantry of a court. A Christian cannot fail of being useful to the republic, for his religion teacheth him that no man 'liveth to himself.' And lastly, a Christian cannot fail of being wholly inoffensive, for his religion teacheth him in all things to do to others what he would wish, in like circumstances, they should do to him. [13]

A strong consensus supported Rush's views, which can be taken as representative before, during, and after the founding and might be endlessly illustrated. In 1804, for instance, Rev. Samuel Kendal preached an election sermon entitled *Religion the Only Sure Basis of Free Government* in Weston, Massachusetts, partly to combat the anti-clericalism that accompanied American reaction to the ideology of the French *philosophes,* their Revolution, and Jeffersonian democ-

---

12. Quoted by Rakove, *Beginnings of National Politics,* 388.

13. Benjamin Rush, *A Plan for the Establishment of Schools . . . Thoughts Upon the Mode of Education Proper in a Republic* (Philadelphia, 1786), in Charles S. Hyneman and Donald S. Lutz (eds.), *American Political Writing During the Founding Era, 1760–1805* (Indianapolis, 1983), I, 681–82. See Donald J. D'Elia, "The Republican Theology of Benjamin Rush," *Pennsylvania History,* XXXIII (1966), 187–202; see also Eugene F. Miller, "On the American Founders' Defense of Liberal Education in a Republic," *Review of Politics,* XLVI (1984), 71–74.

racy—intertwined phenomena to the clergy who were ever vigilant in fighting Satan's minions and who were in full cry by this time with the Second Great Awakening reviving the country. Yet Kendal's large and timeless purpose, he said, was "to illustrate this general truth. . . . That religion, and the moral and social virtues, of which *that* is the great spring, are, under God, the life and security of a free people." [14] The scare over Jefferson's "Jacobinism" eventually dissipated. That the consensus held is evidenced a generation later by the reports of Tocqueville, who confirmed Rush's logic as essentially correct and who anguished that his own countrymen were so devoid of such understanding as to split the nation because of it: "Liberty cannot be established without morality, nor morality without faith." [15]

Anglo-American civilization, Tocqueville found to his astonishment, is the product of "two perfectly distinct elements which elsewhere have often been at war with one another but which in America it was somehow possible to incorporate into each other, forming a marvelous combination. I mean the *spirit of religion* and the *spirit of freedom.*" This feat was possible because the English colonists

brought to the New World a Christianity which I can only describe as democratic and republican. . . . There is not a single religious doctrine hostile to democratic and republican institutions. . . . America is . . . the place where the Christian religion has kept the greatest real power over men's souls; and nothing better demonstrates how useful and natural it is to man, since the country where it now has widest sway is both the most enlightened and the freest. . . . It was religion that gave birth to the English colonies in America. One must never forget that. In the United States religion is mingled with all the national customs and all those feelings which the word fatherland evokes. For that reason it has peculiar power. . . . Christianity has kept a strong hold over the minds of Americans, and . . . its power is not just that of a philosophy which has been examined and accepted, but that of religion believed in without discussion. . . . Christianity itself is an established and irresistible fact which no one seeks to attack or to defend. [16]

14. For Kendal's sermon see Hyneman and Lutz (eds.), *American Political Writing*, II, 1242–63 at 1243.

15. Tocqueville, *Democracy in America*, ed. Mayer, I, 17; quoted from Alexis de Tocqueville, *Democracy in America*, ed. Richard D. Heffner (New York, 1956), 34.

16. Tocqueville, *Democracy in America*, ed. Mayer, I, 46–47, 288, 289, 291, II, 432.

Of course, Tocqueville is also uniquely astute in recognizing that the spiritual dimensions of human existence do not vanish simply because men become atheistic and rebellious. He brilliantly analyzed the ideology of the French Revolution as an *Ersatz* religion aiming at "nothing short of a regeneration of the whole human race. . . . This strange religion has, like Islam, overrun the whole world with its apostles, militants, and martyrs."[17]

Since no more than an illustrative analysis of our complex theme can be attempted here, perhaps enough has been said to disperse some of the "obtuse secularism" Perry Miller decries in those who approach the founding as a merely rationalistic enterprise of men preoccupied with the European Enlightenment's progressive notions and contemptuous of traditional religion. Reason and faith were readily reconciled on the American side of the Atlantic throughout the debates of the founding period, and John Locke and the Bible often were quoted as spokesmen of the same eternal verities in a single sentence. However analytically cogent the modern analysis may or may not be, to polarize as incompatible the politics of Locke's *Second Treatise* and the theology and cosmology of the Old and New Testaments was simply unthinkable to the American founders.[18]

Seventy-five years ago, when C. H. van Tyne ventured to suspect that Charles Beard's economic interpretation had become the historical muse's "golden calf" and that religion may have had something to do with the American Revolution, he was quick to say (in his second sentence), "This is not to argue that the Revolution was a holy war."[19] The most persuasive writer on our subject, Perry Miller, makes it out as very nearly just that in a seminal essay published in 1961. "The

17. Alexis de Tocqueville, *Old Regime and the French Revolution*, trans. Stuart Gilbert (Garden City, N.Y., 1955), 13. *L'Ancien regime et la revolution* first appeared in 1856.

18. *Cf.* Strauss, *Natural Right and History*, 215–21; for the continuing and sometimes vitriolic debate in this mode see Harry V. Jaffa, "Were the Founding Fathers Christian?" with a "Reply" by Walter Berns, *This World*, VIII (Spring/Summer 1984), 3–12. The enormous literature devoted to Locke includes all possible interpretations, including the notion that Locke was, after all, a Christian philosopher (John Dunn, see p. 191*n* herein). The complexity of the subject is suggested by our treatment of some of its aspects herein, esp. in the introduction, Chap. 2, and Chap. 6 herein. See also Henry F. May, *Enlightenment in America* (New York, 1976), esp. 10–15, 153–64.

19. Claude H. van Tyne, "Influence of the Clergy, and of the Religious and Sectarian Forces, on the American Revolution," *American Historical Review*, XIX (1913/1914), 44–64.

basic fact is that the Revolution had been preached to the masses as a religious revival, and had the astounding fortune to succeed." [20]

The American situation, as the preachers saw it, was not what Paine presented in *Common Sense*—a community of hard-working, rational creatures being put upon by an irrational tyrant—but was more like the recurrent predicament of the chosen people in the Bible. As Samuel Cooper declared on October 25, 1780, upon the inauguration of the Constitution of Massachusetts, America was a new Israel, selected to be "a theatre for the display of some of the most astonishing dispensations of His Providence." When they offended Him, He punished them by destroying their republic, subjecting them to a king. Thus while we today need no revelation to inform us that we are all born free and equal and that sovereignty resides in the people—"these are the plain dictates of that reason and common sense with which the common parent has informed the human bosom"—still Scripture makes these truths explicit. Hence, when we angered our God, a king was inflicted upon us; happily, Americans have succeeded, where the Jews did not, in recovering something of pristine virtue, whereupon Heaven redressed America's earthly grievances. Only as we today appreciate the formal unity of the two cosmologies, the rational and Biblical, do we take in the full import of Cooper's closing salute to the new [Massachusetts] Constitution: "How nicely it poises the powers of government, in order to render them as

20. Perry Miller, "From the Covenant to the Revival," in John M. Mulder and John F. Wilson (eds.), *Religion in American History: Interpretive Essays* (Englewood Cliffs, N.J., 1978), 145–61 at 157; originally published in Smith and Jamison (eds.), *Religion in American Life*, I, 322–68. References hereinafter are to the (abridged) 1978 edition unless otherwise indicated. "Obtuse secularism" is applied by Miller (*ibid.*, 160) to Clinton Rossiter, *Seedtime of the Republic* (New York, 1953). That the Revolution was a new outbreak of the religious wars was self-evident to such contemporary observers as Ambrose Searle, who represented Lord Dartmouth in New York and called it "very much a religious war." He especially attributed the whole affair to the Presbyterians and to the old grudges the Scots held against the English. See Martin E. Marty, *Pilgrims in Their Own Land: 500 Years of Religion in America* (Boston, 1984), 138. Substantial contemporary opinion placed blame for the Revolution on the shoulders of the Scottish Presbyterians, including no less a figure than Ezra Stiles, president of Yale and Congregationalist, who saw in the "only two Scotchmen in Congress, *viz.,* Dr. [John] Witherspoon Presidt [*sic*] of Jersey College [Princeton], & Mr. [James] Wilson, Pennsylva [*sic*], a Lawyer" the core of the drive for independence in America as it appeared to him in July 1777. Stiles further noted in his diary: "Let us boldly say, for History will say it, that the whole of the War is so far chargeable to the Scotch Councils, & to the Scotch as a Nation (for they have nationally come into it) as that had it not been for them, this Quarrel had never happened." Quoted in Varnum Lansing Collins, *President Witherspoon: A Biography* (1925; rpr. New York, 1969), II, 188–89, quoting Stiles, *Literary Diary*, II, 184. For a study of the Celtic population of America during the founding see Forrest McDonald and Ellen Shapiro McDonald, "The Ethnic Origins of the American People, 1790," *William and Mary Quarterly*, 3rd ser., XXXVII (1980), 179–99, which concludes that some of the political polarizations of the time "may have reflected ethnic differences rather than ideology or economic circumstances," p. 199.

far as human foresight can, what God ever designed they should be, power only to do good."

Once this light is allowed to play on the scene, we perceive the shallowness of that view which would treat the religious appeal as a calculated propaganda maneuver. The ministers did not have to "sell" the Revolution to a public sluggish to "buy." They were spelling out what both they and the people sincerely believed, nor were they distracted by worries about the probability that Jefferson held all their constructions to be nonsense. A pure rationalism such as his might have declared the independence of these folk, but it could never have inspired them to fight for it.[21]

III

The outpourings from the pulpits of the country were not merely spontaneous but came on at least sixteen occasions upon request of the Continental Congress, which called for various days of public fasting, humiliation, and thanksgiving throughout the Revolutionary War. These kinds of observances had been a practice of the colonies prior to the reign of King George III and had been practiced in England and Scotland as well in previous centuries. They were continued in the administrations of Washington and Adams, spurned by Jefferson, and reluctantly reinstated by Madison amidst the troubles of the War of 1812.[22] Such official expression of religious interest by the American political elite is indicative of the fact, to be further considered, that a common bond of fundamental conviction in things spiritual united the people and their leadership in like-mindedness (*homonoia*) during the founding. The leadership throughout the period from 1775 to 1791 was highly homogeneous. "The Founding Fathers were so similar to the broader elite of Revolutionary executive officeholders as to be indistinguishable from them."[23]

21. Miller, "From the Covenant to the Revival," 152–53.
22. See Gardiner (ed.), *Constitutional Documents of the Puritan Revolution*, liii, 392; Anson P. Stokes, *Church and State in the United States* (New York, 1950), I, Chaps. 6 and 7.
23. Richard D. Brown, "Founding Fathers of 1776 and 1787: A Collective View," *William and Mary Quarterly*, 3rd ser., XXXIII (1976), 466; see James K. Martin, *Men in Rebellion: High Governmental Leaders and the Coming of the American Revolution* (New Brunswick, N.J., 1973), 126–51. There is evidence to counter the recent (Marx induced?) presumption that religion was primarily an affair of the masses in eighteenth-century America. That it was primarily an affair of the educated upper classes can be surmised from the demanding intellectual

The power of religious symbolism can be seen from a glance at some of Congress' resolutions. The Resolution of June 12, 1775, reads as follows:

As the great Governor of the World, by his supreme and universal Providence, not only conducts the course of nature with unerring wisdom and rectitude, but frequently influences the minds of men to serve the wise and gracious purposes of his providential government; and it being, at all times, our indispensable duty devoutly to acknowledge his superintending providence, especially in times of impending danger and public calamity, to reverence and adore his immutable justice as well as to implore his merciful interposition for our deliverance: [Congress recommended that July 20] be observed, by the inhabitants of all the English colonies on this continent, as a day of public humiliation, fasting and prayer; that we may, with united hearts and voices, unfeignedly confess and deplore our many sins; and offer up our joint supplications to the all-wise, omnipotent, and merciful Disposer of all events; humbly beseeching him to forgive our iniquities, to remove our present calamities, to avert those desolating judgments, with which we are threatened, and to bless our rightful sovereign, King George the third, and inspire him with wisdom to discern and pursue the true interest of all his subjects, that a speedy end may be put to the civil discord between Great Britain and the American colonies without further effusion of blood. . . . That virtue and true religion may revive and flourish throughout our land; And that all America may soon behold a gracious interposition of Heaven, for the redress of her many grievances, the restoration of her invaded rights, a reconciliation with the parent state, on terms constitutional and honorable to both; And that her civil and religious priviledges [*sic*] may be secured to the latest posterity.

And it is recommended to Christians, of all denominations, to assemble

---

content of the sermons that have come down from the late eighteenth century. *Cf.* Marty, *Pilgrims in Their Own Land*, 123. This situation of the unchurched multitudes, if accurately assessed, would help explain Americans' receptiveness to evangelism as expressed in the great waves of revivalism that swept the country. These were led by George Whitefield during seven trips to America between the 1730s and 1770 in the Great Awakening and its aftermath. Widespread revivalism later reappeared in the resurgence sparked by the frontier challenge and the threat of satanic Jacobinism perceived in the ideology of the French revolutionaries and their American followers. This is called the Second Great Awakening, dating from the 1780s through the 1820s.

As to the intellectual demands of Calvinist teaching, Ahlstrom writes: "Doctrine . . . was almost always felt to stand in need of support from both philosophical reason and common experience. Puritanism, in short, is generally marked by careful thought; it is an intellectual tradition of great profundity." Ahlstrom, *Religious History*, 130. But, then, John Adams claimed all Americans were philosophers! See C. F. Adams (ed.), *Works of John Adams*, III, 456.

for public worship, and to abstain from servile labour and recreations on said day.[24]

Language and form remained much the same through all these resolutions and proclamations, the chief point being simultaneously to bring together the entire country as *one* moral and religious community—despite denominationalism, it should be noted—in covenant with their God, individually and collectively. There the nation should prostrate itself in repentence of sin and pray for forgiveness, confessing its iniquities and corruptions, and seeking God's loving mercy as the fruit of faith restored and made whole again. The Americans, then, here represented their plight as indeed being that of a people in the hands of an angry God whose Providence must be reckoned with and whose sovereignty cannot be doubted. The one hope for the community is a restoration to divine grace so that God's wrath will abate. Out of the cleansing of the sinful hearts of the persons composing the national community, forgiveness can ensue and concord be restored with heaven and peace on earth.

Thus, another call in urgent language went out on March 16, 1776, for the nation to do "its indispensable duty" and "with true penitence of heart, and the most reverant devotion, publicly to acknowledge the over ruling providence of God; to confess and deplore our offences against him; and to supplicate his interposition for averting the threatened danger." May 17 is recommended as "a day of humiliation, fasting, and prayer; that we may with united hearts, confess and bewail our manifold sins and transgressions, and by a sincere repentance and amendment of life, appease his righteous displeasure, and, through the merits and meditations of Jesus Christ, obtain his pardon and forgiveness," so that God will then soften the hearts of the English. If this is not to be, *then* "may it please the Lord of Hosts, the God of Armies, to animate our officers and soldiers with invincible fortitude . . . and to crown [them] . . . with victory and success." The resolution also asks God's blessing on the land and its people and leaders, and that he "grant that a spirit of incorruptible patriotism, and of pure undefiled religion, may universally prevail."[25] Another

24. Worthington C. Ford, et al. (eds.), *Journals of the Continental Congress* (Washington, D.C., 1904–1937), II, 87–88.
25. *Ibid.*, IV, 208–209.

appeal is made on December 11, 1776, "to reverence the Providence of God, and look up to him as the supreme disposer of all events, and the arbiter of the fate of nations" so that the nation by request of Congress and each of the states "beg the countenance of his Providence in the prosecution of the present *just and necessary war*." It is of particular importance for the members of the army to observe strictly the regulation "which forbids profane swearing, and all immorality, of which all such officers are desired to take note."[26] The Revolution again is characterized as a "just and necessary war" in the calling of a day of Thanksgiving (written in the hand of Sam Adams) by Congress on November 1, 1777. Here, too, confession of sins and forgiveness are begged "that it may please God, through the merits of Jesus Christ, mercifully to forgive and blot them out of remembrance . . . [and] under the providence of Almighty God, to secure for these United States the greatest of all human blessings, independence and peace . . . to prosper the means of religion for the promotion and enlargement of that kingdom which consisteth 'in righteousness, peace and joy in the Holy Ghost.'"[27]

As the Revolution neared its end, a more cheerful and self-confident note entered the proclamations, the turning point being France's entry into the conflict. The rhetoric is instructive for the prevailing categories of thought it displays. The founding is a conspiracy of faith and reason, we have said, and enlightenment and devotion are inseparable in the thinking of the Americans of the time. Thus, in the spring of 1782 another "Proclamation" is prepared by Congress.

The goodness of the Supreme Being to all his rational creatures demands their acknowledgements of gratitude and love; his absolute government of this world dictates, that it is the interest of every nation and people ardently to suplicate his ~~mercy~~ [sic] favor and implore his protection. When the lust for dominion or lawless ambition excites arbitrary power to invade the rights, or endeavor to ~~wrench~~ [sic] wrest from a people their sacred and ~~unalienable~~ [sic] invaluable privileges, and compels them, in defense of the same, to encounter all the horrors and calamities of a bloody and vindicative war; then is that people loudly called upon to fly unto that God for protection, who hears the cries of the distressed, and will not turn a deaf ear to the supplication of the oppressed.

26. *Ibid.*, VI, 1022. *Emphasis added.*
27. *Ibid.*, IX, 854–55.

A day of public fasting, prayer, and humiliation is called so "our joint supplications may then ascend to the throne of the Ruler of the Universe, beseeching Him . . . to diffuse a spirit of universal reformation among all ranks and degrees of our citizens; and make us a holy, that so we may be an happy people. . . . That He would incline the hearts of all men to peace, and fill them with universal charity and benevolence, and that the religion of our Divine Redeemer, with all its benign influences, may cover the earth as the waters cover the seas."[28]

These sentiments seem restrained enough for a people who have achieved victory over a mighty imperial power after eight years of warfare. The Thanksgiving proclamations for 1783 and 1784 attribute "the progress of a contest on which the most essential rights of human nature depended" to the "interposition of Divine Providence in our favour." Therefore, there is every reason "for praise and gratitude to the God of their salvation . . . and above all, that he hath been pleased to continue to us the light of the blessed gospel, and secured to us in the fullest extent the rights of conscience in faith and worship." It is prayed that God "smile upon our seminaries and means of education, to cause pure religion and virtue to flourish, to give peace to all nations, and to fill the world with his glory."[29] The signing of the Treaty of Paris on September 3, 1783, is observed the following year with a Thanksgiving Proclamation offering gratitude that "the freedom, sovereignty and independence of these states" is "fully and compleately [*sic*] established . . . and . . . the dearest and most essential rights of human nature" secured through the "benign interposition of Divine Providence," as that has "been most miraculously and abundantly manifested." Hence, "the citizens of the United States have the greatest reason to return their most hearty and sincere praises and thanksgiving to the God of their deliverance. . . . And above all

28. Proclamation of March 19, 1782, *ibid.*, XXII, 137–38. For the Thanksgiving Proclamation adopted shortly after Cornwallis' surrender at Yorktown on October 19, 1781, see the proceedings for October 26, 1781, *ibid.*, XXI, 1074–76, which begins: "Whereas, it hath pleased Almighty God, father of mercies, remarkably to assist and support the United States of America in their important struggle for liberty, against the long continued efforts of a powerful nation: it is the duty of all ranks to observe and thankfully acknowledge the interpositions of his Providence in their behalf. Through the whole of the contest, from its first rise to this time, the influence of divine Providence may be clearly perceived in many signal instances, of which we mention but a few."

29. *Ibid.*, XXV, 699–700.

[because], . . . he hath been pleased to continue to us the light of gospel truths, and secured to us, in the fullest manner, the rights of conscience in faith and worship." [30]

IV

How all this official piety looked to the other side is hinted by a fervent English friend of the American Revolution, Richard Price, who contrasted America's virtue with England's corruption in 1776 in these words: "From one end of *North America* to the other, they are FASTING and PRAYING. But what are we doing?—Shocking thought! we are ridiculing them as *Fanatics,* and scoffing at religion— We are running wild after pleasure, and forgetting every thing serious and decent at *Masquerades*—We are gambling in gaming houses; trafficking for Boroughs; perjuring ourselves at Elections; and selling ourselves for places—Which side then is Providence likely to favour?" [31] At home and in retrospect, John Quincy Adams believed that the "highest glory of the American Revolution . . . was this: *it connected, in one indissoluble bond, the principles of civil government with the principles of Christianity.*" [32]

There obviously is some truth in the assertion that the Bible was the chief "textbook of the fathers of the Republic." [33] The relative neglect of these themes by our secular age, despite the good work especially of Alice Baldwin, Carl Bridenbaugh, and Perry Miller, and the tendency to read religious history as indicative of political concerns, lends weight to John M. Murrin's whimsical query at the close of a study of the Court and Country ideologies during the developing politics of America's early national period—"In the United States has politics instead of religion been the true 'opiate of the people'—and of their historians?" [34] Perhaps so, yet neither the people nor their his-

30. *Ibid.,* XXVII, 627–29.

31. Richard Price as quoted by May, *Enlightenment in America,* 158–59. Emphasis as in original.

32. Thornton (ed.), *Pulpit of the American Revolution,* xxix. Emphasis as in original. (The [facsimile] reprint edition is cited hereinafter unless otherwise indicated.)

33. *Ibid.,* 262.

34. John M. Murrin, "Great Inversion, or Court versus Country: A Comparison of the Revolution Settlements in England (1688–1721) and America (1776–1816)," in J. G. A. Pocock (ed.), *Three British Revolutions: 1641, 1688, 1776* (Princeton, 1980), 368–430 at 430.

torians are entirely to blame, nor is the problem peculiarly American as Samuel, last of the Judges, readily informs us.

In New England, John Cotton founded the Boston Thursday Lecture in 1633 at which time social and political matters were discussed and combined with a "market day." With nearly a century and a half of precedent to rely on, the Rev. William Gordon's Thanksgiving Sermon of 1774, dedicated to the political crisis of America, opens with a reminder we are prone to ignore. "The pulpit is devoted, in general, to more important purposes than the fate of kingdoms, or the civil rights of human nature, being intended to recover men from the slavery of sin and Satan, to point out their escape from future misery through faith in a crucified Jesus, and to assist them in their preparations for an eternal blessedness. But still there are special times and seasons when it may treat of politics."[35] The fundamental tension of reality, and man's existence in the In-Between of immanence and transcendence, is nicely expressed by the Rev. Gordon's preamble as the true source of the misgiving Professor Murrin senses in the people's and historians' preoccupation with merely secular politics as the final resting point of intellectual and spiritual concern. The Marxian metaphor, of course, obfuscates the existential issue by denigrating both religion and politics—a consequence of its author's metaphysical rebellion, as Camus called it. Yet Rev. Gordon is clear that politics does *not* exhaust human reality, since men are destined for eternal Blessedness through Christ as the hoped-for homecoming of the prodigal sons of men. By this accounting, the historians and the people they chronicle may indeed be wandering in the wilderness, venerating now one golden calf and then another.

The flavor of the founders' theology as they grappled with the great temporal crises of the period needs to be kept in mind as we explore our subject. President Samuel Langdon of Harvard College preached an election sermon in the spring of 1775 based on Isaiah 1:26. "And I will restore thy judges as at the first, and thy counsellors as at the beginning; afterward thou shalt be called the city of righteousness, the faithful city." An election sermon, of course, was in any event a political occasion, and this one was preached in the neighborhood of

35. Thornton (ed.), *Pulpit of the American Revolution*, 188, 197.

Lexington and Concord (of necessity, at Watertown) six weeks after the famous events of April 19. "We must," Dr. Langdon says, "keep our eyes fixed on the supreme government of the Eternal King, as directing all events. . . . For the sins of a people God may suffer the best government to be corrupted or dissolved, and . . . nothing but a general reformation can give good ground to hope that the public happiness will be restored." After recounting the circumstances of Isaiah's prophecy and the vicissitudes of the Chosen People through the Babylonian exile, Dr. Langdon continues:

The Jewish government, according to the original constitution which was divinely established, if considered merely in a civil view, was a perfect republic. The heads of their tribes and elders of their cities were their counsellors and judges. They called the people together in more general or particular assemblies,—took their opinions, gave advice, and managed the public affairs according to the general voice. Counsellors and judges comprehend all the powers of that government; for there was no such thing as legislative authority belonging to it,—their complete code of laws being given immediately from God by the hand of Moses. And let them who cry up the divine right of kings consider that the only form of government which had a proper claim to a divine establishment was so far from including the idea of a king, that it was a high crime for Israel to ask to be in this respect like other nations; and when they were gratified, it was rather as just punishment of their folly.

The trouble at hand has one main cause: "We have rebelled against God. We have lost the true spirit of Christianity, though we retain the outward profession and form of it. We have neglected and set light by the glorious gospel of our Lord Jesus Christ, and his holy commands and institutions." The prevailing moral philosophy is a corruption "little better than ancient Platonism." The excellent British constitution is a "mere shadow of its ancient" splendor. The "sins of America, and of New England in particular" have brought "down upon us the righteous judgment of Heaven." The punishment must be doubly severe. Since America is so favored of God, it "will receive more speedy and signal punishment; as God says of Israel: 'You only have I known of all the families of the earth, therefore will I punish you for all your iniquities'" (Amos 3:2). In his peroration Dr. Langdon does not fail to proclaim, "If God be for us, who can be against us? [Romans 8:31]. The enemy has reproached us for calling on his name, and professing our trust in him. They have made mock of our solemn fasts, and every appearance of serious Christianity in the land. . . . May we be truly a holy people, and all our towns cities of righteousness! Then the Lord will be our refuge and strength." [36]

The Reverend Samuel West, preaching in Boston a year later (May 29, 1776), concentrates on a common theme of these sermons, that resistance to tyranny is a sacred obligation. Dr. Langdon quoted Proverbs 28:15 as the epigraph of his sermon: "As a roaring lion and a ranging bear; so *is* a wicked ruler over the poor people." In preaching on Titus 3:1 ("Put them in mind to be subject to principalities and powers, to obey magistrates, to be ready to every good work"), Rev. West finds that neither the Old Testament nor the New requires obedience to evil rulers. Whoever imposes evil government

has degraded himself below the rank and dignity of a man, and deserves to be classed with the lower creation. Hence we find that wise and good men, of all nations and religions, have ever inculcated subjection to good government and have borne their testimony against the licentious disturbers of the public peace. Nor has Christianity been deficient on this capital point.

After reconciling the Bible and Locke, Rev. West asserts that

the law of nature gives men no right to do anything that is immoral, or contrary to the will of God, and injurious to their fellow-creatures; for a state of nature is properly a state of law and government, even a government founded upon the unchangeable nature of the Deity, and a law resulting from the eternal fitness of things. . . . This law is as unchangeable as the Deity himself, being a transcript of his moral perfections. A revelation, pretending to be from God, that contradicts any part of natural law, ought immediately to be rejected as an imposture; for Deity cannot make a law contrary to the law of nature without acting contrary to himself,—a thing in the strictest sense impossible, for that which implies contradiction is not an object of the divine power. . . . The doctrine of non-resistance and unlimited passive obedience to the worst of tyrants could never have found credit among mankind had the voice of reason been hearkened [sic] to for a guide, because such a doctrine would immediately have been discerned to be contrary to natural law. . . . The most perfect freedom consists in obeying the dictates of right reason. . . . Where licentiousness begins, liberty ends.

The obligation of obedience to the powers that be, as ordained of God, means an obedience to lawful magistrates. "Those only are to

36. *Ibid.*, 227–57.

be esteemed lawful magistrates, and ordained of God, who pursue the public good by honoring and encouraging those that do well and punishing all that do evil. Such, and such only, wherever they are to be found, are the ministers of God for good," and only such as these are to be obeyed and not resisted. Otherwise men are entitled to emulate the "primitive Christians, who refused to comply with the sinful commands of men in power; their answer in such cases being this, We ought to obey God rather than men." The result at length is then this: obedience is taught, as is the liberty of the subject, under *rightful* rule. *But*

it is also strongly implied, that when rulers become oppressive to the subject and injurious to the state, their authority, their respect, their maintenance, and the duty of submitting to them, must immediately cease; they are then to be considered as the ministers of Satan, and, as such, it becomes our indispensable duty to resist and oppose them. Thus we see that both reason and revelation perfectly agree in pointing out the nature, end, and design of government, *viz.*, that it is to promote the welfare and happiness of the community. . . . Reason and revelation . . . do both teach us that our obedience to rulers is not unlimited, but that resistance is not only allowable, but an indispensable duty in the case of intolerable tyranny and oppression.

It therefore must be concluded that Isaiah's great prophecy of millennial peace cannot yet be entered upon, for—to the contrary—we Americans now "must beat our ploughshares into swords, and our pruning-hooks into spears, and learn the art of self-defence against our enemies."[37]

From Rev. West's mighty jeremiad, we turn finally to the election sermon preached to the Massachusetts legislature in Boston in May 1778 by the Reverend Phillips Payson, who reminds us with Augustinian overtones of the differences between the heavenly and temporal city, the visible and invisible churches. These distinctions are as fundamental to the founders' thinking as to Christians of all ages. "It is common," Rev. Payson says,

for the inspired writers to speak of the gospel dispensation in terms applicable to the heavenly world, especially when they view it in comparison with the law of Moses. In this light they consider the church of God, and good men upon earth, as members of the church and family of God above, and

37. *Ibid.*, 259–327.

liken the liberty of Christians to that of the citizens of the heavenly Zion. We doubt not but the Jerusalem above, the heavenly society, possesses the noblest liberty to a degree of perfection of which the human mind can have no adequate conception in the present state. The want of that knowledge and rectitude they are endowed with above renders liberty and government so imperfect here below.

Having taken as his text for the occasion Galatians 4:26, 31 ("But Jerusalem, which is above, is free, which is the mother of us all. So then, brethren, we are not children of the bond woman, but of the free."), Rev. Payson continues.

Next to the liberty of heaven is that which the sons of God, the heirs of glory, possess in this life, in which they are freed from the bondage of corruption, the tyranny of evil lusts and passions, described by the apostles "by being made free from sin, and becoming the servants of God." These kinds of liberty are so nearly related, that the latter is considered as a sure pledge of the former; and therefore all good men, all true believers, in a special sense are children of the free woman, heirs of the promise. This religious or spiritual liberty must be accounted the greatest happiness of man, considered in a private capacity. But considering ourselves here as connected in civil society, and members one of another, we must in this view esteem civil liberty as the greatest of all human blessings. . . . A people formed upon the morals and principles of the gospel are capacitated to enjoy the highest degree of civil liberty, and will really enjoy it, unless prevented by force or fraud. . . . The voice of reason and the voice of God both teach us that the great end of government is the public good. Nor is there less certainty in determining that a free and righteous government originates from the people, and is under their direction and control; and therefore a free, popular model of government—of the republican kind—may be judged the most friendly to the rights and liberties of the people, and the most conducive to the public welfare.[38]

The founders' faith and rational schooling in things spiritual are intimated by these excerpts from sermons by some of the leading

38. *Ibid.*, 329–30. For the "Augustinianism" of the Congregational and other Protestant preachers in America, see Ralph Barton Perry's discussion of the "fallacy of difference" and his explanation of the inclusiveness of Puritan Christianity in Perry, *Puritanism and Democracy*, Chap. 5: "The main body of puritan doctrine . . . is medieval Christianity. In America, it was the chief link of continuity with the medieval past, being a traditional rather than an innovating doctrine . . . the Schoolmen were held in high respect. Puritanism was an offshoot from the main stem of Christian belief, and puritans, equally with Catholics, claimed descent from St. Paul and Augustine," p. 83. For a properly exuberant discussion of this material see the fine study by Nathan O. Hatch, *Sacred Cause of Liberty: Republican Thought and the Millennium in Revolutionary New England* (New Haven, 1977).

churchmen of the day. While our examples are from New England sermons, the message is almost the same throughout the country. The denominational differences are minimized partly as a result of the homogenizing and democratizing effects of decades of revivalism from the Great Awakening and its rumbling echoes and aftershocks. That the leading lights of the Revolutionary Congresses and the Federal Convention were generally men of faith can no longer be doubted. Subsequent scholarship shows that Robert C. Hartnett's essay considering the religion of six signers of the Constitution (George Washington, James Madison, James Wilson, Gouverneur Morris, Alexander Hamilton, and Benjamin Franklin) and two signers of the Declaration who soon rose to the presidency (John Adams and Thomas Jefferson) is essentially accurate, apart from the unbridled attack on Jefferson which is reminiscent of Timothy Dwight. Hartnett (a Jesuit) defines *religion* for the purposes of his analysis as "belief in the existence of a transcendent Being, endowed with intelligence and free will, Who created the universe, Who governs it by His Providence, and Who will reward and punish human beings according to whether they carry out His will as it is known to them. Such a belief involves, of course, belief in human intelligence capable of grasping with certitude suprasensible realities, in human freedom of choice, and in the immortality of the human spirit." His conclusion is that despite varying "shades of Christian orthodoxy," all the leading statesmen, except Jefferson, meet the test.[39] A substantial literature that cannot be explored here confirms Hartnett's conclusion and even restores Jefferson to religious respectability.[40]

Of course, Jefferson traditionally has been regarded as a Deist and rationalist comparable to Tom Paine in radicalism and antipathy to true religion. Had he not held such a special place in the minds and hearts of the country he might well have been included in Theodore Roosevelt's libel of the latter as "a dirty little atheist"—but all this has changed. When Jefferson was elected vice-president in 1796, the

39. Robert C. Hartnett, "The Religion of the Founding Fathers," in F. Ernest Johnson (ed.), *Wellsprings of the American Spirit* (New York, 1964), 50. The material published in this volume dates from 1948. *Ibid.,* 67–68.

40. A basic bibliography is supplied by Marty, *Pilgrims in Their Own Land,* 482–83. See also the general bibliography in George Armstrong Kelly, *Politics and Religious Consciousness in America* (New Brunswick, N.J., 1984), 281–300.

Reverend Judah Champion of Litchfield, Connecticut, prayed, "O Lord, wilt Thou bestow upon the Vice-President a double portion of Thy grace, for Thou knowest he needs it." Other Connecticut worthies reacted similarly. One minister called him "a debauchee, an infidel, and a liar." Another stated that "infidels in religion are apt to be Democrats." Samuel E. Morison and Henry S. Commager appear to have fresh illumination when they write of Jefferson in their textbook of American history, "Deeply religious without being a churchman, he had the serenity of one to whom now and then the Spirit has not disdained to speak."[41] After having been "praised and damned by contemporaries and later scholars as a Unitarian, a Deist, a rationalist, and an infidel," the true meaning of the Morison and Commager oracle was disclosed in 1983. Jefferson was a nontrinitarian Christian, a "demythologized Christian," or

one . . . who rejected all myth, all mystery, all miracles, and almost all supernaturalism in religion and sought instead to return to what he perceived to be the primitive purity and simplicity of Christianity. The cornerstone of Jefferson's religion was an unswerving commitment to monotheism. He firmly believed in the existence of one God, who was the creator and sustainer of the universe and the ultimate ground of being. . . . He lavishly praised Jesus for making the one true God worthy of human worship inasmuch as he took "for his type the best qualities of the human head and heart, wisdom, justice, goodness, and adding to them power, ascribed all of these, but in infinite perfection, to the supreme being."

The unity of God, the moral teachings of Jesus as the most sublime in the history of the world, and the expectation of personal immortality constitute the core of Jefferson's religion, his "Christianity," as disclosed through critical publication of all relevant materials from his papers.[42] It is impressive, indeed, that Jefferson assiduously concerned himself with the search for religious truth from the 1790s until the end of his life in 1826. He pursued this compelling concern through resolute study of the Bible, biblical scholarship, and mastery of theo-

41. Quoted from Charles R. Keller, *Second Great Awakening in Connecticut* (New Haven, 1942), 26. Samuel E. Morison and Henry S. Commager, *Growth of the American Republic*, (4th ed.; New York, 1950), I, 382.

42. D. W. Adams (ed.), *Jefferson's Extracts from the Gospels*, 39–41. The material in quotation marks is from Thomas Jefferson's letter to William Short, Aug. 4, 1820, included in the Appendix, *ibid.*, 391–94.

logical literature in Greek, Latin, French, and English. When urged, as a means of quieting sectarian bigotry, to publish his religious sentiments toward the end of his life, Jefferson replied with wonderful irony, "But have they not the Gospel? If they hear not that, and the charities it teacheth, neither will they be persuaded though one rose from the dead."[43]

V

With Jefferson now safely in the fold, our inspection of the religious setting of the Federal Convention can come to an end. If Thomas Jefferson was a believer, who disbelieved? The answer that is persuasively suggested is *nobody.* The founders were united in what John Adams long after called the general principles of Christianity, as we have seen, which for him meant especially the Ten Commandments and the Sermon on the Mount. Jefferson not only could agree that this was true of the country but also that he shared Adams' faith—although he did not *fully* inform his old friend of his convictions in their correspondence on religious matters but instead veiled the details in utter secrecy. Thus, only the printer who bound his devotional book *The Life and Morals of Jesus* even knew of its existence until it was found by the family after Jefferson's death.[44] How persuasive the claim will be that all the founders were men of faith remains to be seen, of course. Aristotle distinguishes between persuasion and coercion in argumentation, and the deep-seated skepticism in this matter may surpass the reach of persuasive evidence. As Representative William L. Hungate (Democrat from Missouri) remarked in a rare moment of levity toward the end of the impeachment proceedings against President Richard M. Nixon, even if an elephant strolled into the House Judiciary Committee room, some members would doubt its identity and surmise it might be a mouse with a glandular condition.

43. Thomas Jefferson to George Thatcher, Jan. 26, 1824, *ibid.,* 415.
44. The binder was Frederick A. Mayo of Richmond, *ibid.,* 38. See the letters of John Adams to Jefferson dated June 28, 1813, and Nov. 4, 1816, together with their responses in Cappon (ed.), *Adams-Jefferson Letters,* II, 338–40, 493–95.

The adduced evidence supports the conclusion that the founding was indeed a great feat of faith and reason. As one student summarizes the matter:

The core conviction of the Founders accommodated a nation that worshipped the Biblical Jehovah. This was essential to the ideology of their new creation and was, besides, heavily influenced by the vigorous participation of the American pulpits and congregations in the struggle for independence; since God was not, as it seemed to many of the French, a reactionary despot, there was no need for a profane Year One or a Cult of Reason. . . . Service of this God and service of the commonwealth were perceived as harmonious at the republic's moment of truth. . . . "Caesar's things" were recast in a way that could provoke no obvious conflicts with "God's things," while the latter, far more ethically than metaphysically interpreted, brought a sacred touch to the profane world. . . . Being in but not of the state (as patterned after the Virginia disestablishment of 1785), religion itself—not least because, until after the war, it had been everywhere, even in the liturgical churches, congregational in structure—could be seen as part of the realm of freedom. Precisely because it was "free," it could accommodate to the civil power without that fatal sense of moral conflict that had scarred Europe for centuries. If religion was "reasonable," so was the American constitutional experiment. If it was "revelatory," so was the American "garden in the wilderness." If it was pluralized, so were the areas of settlement and the economic interests.[45]

The question remains, however: what *difference* does this context of powerful conviction in things spiritual make in the Constitution, its framing and meaning? The short answer is, a very great difference in general, and some difference in the particulars. To begin with, as we have seen, the Constitution arises out of and revolves within a horizon of reality that is decisively structured by Judaeo-Christian revelation, itself a commanding edifice of faith and reason of enormous theoretical complexity and historical depth. We tend to be unduly provincial in our study of things American, to begin exploration of the founding with the Declaration of Independence, and seldom to look beyond the Puritans and Old Whigs in England. As J. G. A. Pocock and some others have been insisting, however, the subject is much wider and deeper. Ralph Barton Perry taught in the 1940s that puritanism was, at bottom, medieval Christianity, and I have to say

45. Kelly, *Politics and Religious Consciousness*, 44–45.

that the American founding partook of the whole amplitude of Western civilization's heritage and is not fully intelligible apart from a generous recognition of that fact and its implications.

In a sentence, the founding was the rearticulation of Western civilization in its Anglo-American mode. The founders were thoroughly educated in the Greek, Latin, and Hebrew sources of this civilization, often knowing the classic writings in the original tongues, in addition to French and English literature. While substantially influenced by the secularizing tendencies of the movement from Humanism to Enlightenment, the American Revolution was essentially restorative and retrospective, in the primary meaning of the term as a movement to re-establish truth and justice on a primordial foundation, one lost through corruption and rebellion by men motivated by the perversities of vaulting ambition and the lust for power engendered by selfishness, sin, and evil. This model of revolution as the "turning of a wheel" represents the primary—*not* exclusive!—tendency of the American and perhaps all earlier Western revolutions to be *restorations.*[46] We have seen some of the evidence for this interpretation in foregoing pages. The ransacking of historical sources by James Madison and others throughout the period of the revolutionary and constitutional crises is suggestive of the present point.

Exactly *what* is evoked when we refer to "Western civilization" is a question that will have to pass unanswered. And an even larger question must be mentioned and also set aside. As Arnold J. Toynbee discovered, a civilization is no intelligible field of historical study. His discovery came some twenty-five years after beginning his mammoth *A Study of History* and in the seventh volume. Rather, he found that civilizations are themselves generated out of multi-cultural move-

---

46. See Berman, *Law and Revolution,* 18–19 and *passim.* For education in this period see Lawrence A. Cremin, *American Education: The Colonial Experience, 1607–1783* (New York, 1970); for the generation of the founding as the "Golden Age of the Classics" see Gummere, *American Colonial Mind and the Classical Tradition;* and Meyer Reinhold, *Classica Americana: The Greek and Roman Heritage in the United States* (Detroit, 1984), esp. 1–203 and the bibliography, 352–64. Due to Reinhold's criticisms of Gummere, it should be said that the substantial influence of the Greek and Latin philosophers and other classical writers in America was not confined to those who were sufficiently fluent to read them in the original languages— any more than the enormous influence of the Bible was restricted to those who could read Greek and Hebrew. Nonetheless, the generalization stands that American education in the period 1760–1790 meant a solid grounding in classical languages and literature.

ments called religions and that the Western civilization is the creation of that "higher religion" called Christianity. While a dissertation on the philosophy of history need not now be attempted, the relationship discerned between spiritual aspects of human affairs and the others is indicative of present concerns.[47] The pertinent point, as we remind ourselves of the great existential and historical debt Americans owe to distant influences, including religion and ancient philosophy, is pungently stated by Northrop Frye.

Man lives, not directly or nakedly in nature like the animals, but within a mythological universe, a body of assumptions and beliefs developed from his existential concerns. Most of this is held unconsciously, which means that our imaginations may recognize elements of it, when presented in art or literature, without consciously understanding what it is we recognize. Practically all that we can see of this body of concern is socially conditioned and culturally inherited. Below the cultural inheritance there must be a common psychological inheritance, otherwise forms of culture and imagination outside our own traditions would not be intelligible to us. . . . The Bible is clearly a major element in our own imaginative tradition.[48]

It also is clearly a major element in our theoretical and political traditions. It is to a considerable degree in terms of its symbolic world that the founders comprehended themselves, contrived their great work, and grasped reality itself.

Perhaps it is not too much to say, and really not very surprising, that nearly all features of the constitutional system as it came from the hands of other founders bear the marks of the biblical-Christian symbolic world. This is not to deny the presence of other factors of even greater importance in the technical detail of political theory and legal structure. Yet biblical fingerprints are everywhere, and the commanding heights of meaning are heavily indebted to the controlling spiritual symbols and the experiences they mediate. The fact is evident from the proclamations and other sources quoted herein alone. Some of the major symbols can now be identified and characterized.

Love of liberty is the premier motif of the Revolution. It is juxtaposed to abhorrence of tyranny and a passionate insistence upon just rule, defined as dedication to the common good of all and conformity

47. Toynbee, *A Study of History*, VII, 381–544. *Cf.* Sandoz, *Voegelinian Revolution*, 127–32, 225–35.
48. Northrop Frye, *Great Code: The Bible and Literature* (San Diego, 1982), xvii.

to fundamental law. *Liberty* stands at the center of revelatory experience, not merely in terms of doctrine (with which I have little concern here) but in terms of the living faith from Abraham onward. Biblical religion is a drama of liberty. It is symbolized in the mystery of the free disclosure of a loving God who reveals himself and his truth to his creature, man, and who is met by the free response of the paradigmatic man of spirit, Abraham, whose sons we all are, Paul says (Galatians 3:6). Abraham sets out from Ur of the Chaldees for a land God will show him (Genesis 12:1). This is the pilgrimage of human faith, freely undertaken in response to the divine initiative and without which the revelation itself would be lost. The dynamic of grace and faith structures the whole questing dimension of the Christian adventure as exemplified in the Bible in the Exodus and as repeatedly reenacted thereafter in various settings and transformations. It is the *Pilgrim's Progress* of all spiritual men and women, individually and of universal mankind itself, tellingly represented by the English Baptist John Bunyan (1628–1688) in the famous book of that title. Life is a pilgrimage through time in partnership with God, a time for cooperatively and freely working out one's salvation in response to revealed truth. This dynamic lies at the core of the experience of divine transcendent Being as transmitted through biblical symbolism.

In New Testament revelation, the verses in John that underscore this point are especially those from Jesus' lips: "And ye shall know the truth and the truth shall make you free" (John 8:32); and "I am the way, the truth, and the life: no man cometh unto the Father, but by me" (John 14:32). They are set against a third in that Gospel: "Pilate saith unto him, What is truth?" (John 18:38). The understanding that *truth* is liberating, that it is not some abstract proposition but a living communion with the eternal God revealed in Christ who is Truth itself, and that salvation depends upon a free, personal acceptance of this truth and a spiritual rebirth are controlling elements in the Christianity of the Americans of the period under study. The thrust of the Great Awakening and the revival of true faith during and after that earthquake in Colonial America especially keyed on these elements. The insistence upon free, adult conversion and personal spiritual rebirth vivified religion. It was demanded of the ministry no less than of the congregations, and the experience itself gave powerful meaning to liberty as a formative force in the attainment of a mature Christian personality.

It is important to stress that we are not dealing with doctrines or creeds, but with the reality of immediate experiences as lived and consciously nurtured by the Protestant peoples in America with great perseverance throughout colonization and settlement from Plymouth onward, but particularly in our period when covenant progressed to revival. We have seen the appeal from form to the true spirit of the Gospel in President Langdon's sermon of 1775. The true *spirit* of the Gospel, of course, is not in the book itself but in the responsive heart of a faithful man or woman living in steady communion with the loving Father. Not merely more reading but better living is called for in all these appeals that go forth from Congress and the pulpits. Liberty and truth both are palpable *experiences* that radiate meaning into one's being and without which life in this world is slavish and hope for the next dashed. These experiences compose the radiating center of the Christian life and understanding of man and politics.

Liberty of conscience as a great desideratum arises in this experiential setting. It forms a major theme of the revolutionary ferment, especially when "sending a bishop to America" is in the air. It long antedated that crisis, however, which dated back to Plymouth. It is solidly built on the recollected atrocities committed during the wars of religious persecution as unflinchingly memorialized in John Foxe's *Book of Martyrs*, an illustrated sixteenth-century bestseller that ran 2,314 pages in the English version.[49] This book made a thoroughly convincing case for the proposition that Antichrist and the pope were one and the same, and it helped to make hating Roman Catholics a leading English national pastime. Liberty of conscience, as we noted earlier, was demanded when amendments to the Constitution were requested by the states during ratification. As James Lord Bryce explained matters about a century ago, there are both political and religious reasons for insisting on religious liberty. The political principle sets out from the principles of liberty and equality. It holds any attempt at compulsion by the civil power to be an infringement on liberty of thought, as well as on liberty of action, which could be justified only when a practice

49. Cf. Marty, *Pilgrims in Their Own Land*, 40, 44–46.

claiming to be religious is so obviously anti-social or immoral as to threaten the well-being of the community. . . . The second principle . . . starts from the conception of the church as a spiritual body existing for spiritual purposes, and moving along spiritual paths. It is an assemblage of men who are united by their devotion to an unseen Being, their memory of a divine life, their belief in the possibility of imitating that life, so far as human frailty allows, their hopes for an illimitable future. Compulsion of any kind is contrary to the nature of such a body, which lives by love and reverence, not by law. It desires no state help, feeling that its strength comes from above, and that its kingdom is not of this world. . . . Least of all can it submit to be controlled by the state, for the state, in such a world as the present, means persons many or most of whom are alien to its beliefs and cold to its emotions. The conclusion follows that the church as a spiritual entity will be happiest and strongest when it is left absolutely to itself, not patronized by the civil power, not restrained by law except when and in so far as it may attempt to quit its proper sphere and intermeddle in secular affairs.

Lord Bryce then concludes: "The former much more than the latter . . . has moved the American mind." As he later says, there are advantages to having no established church. "There are no quarrels of churches and sects. Judah does not vex Ephraim, nor Ephraim envy Judah."[50]

This evenhanded explanation is unexceptionable and reflects the kind of motivational synthesis that marked all the founders' work. Their sources of truth were experience, common sense, reason, and revelation, as they frequently said. Religion was no direct concern of the Convention because it had economic, political, and social problems to resolve. Their kind of urbane recognition of the layered structure of reality and the need for pluralistic approaches to a pluralistic reality is rooted in the mutually reinforcing foundations of Western thought: the Creation story in Genesis, with its layering of the cosmos and man, created between brute and angelic beings in the image and likeness of God, given dominion over all the earth; and the hierarchical structure of being of the Hellenic philosophers, for whom reality ranges from the material to the divine, man's composite nature being such as to participate in all layers and thus be their epitome. His essential being is Reason (*Nous*), which is mysteriously both hu-

50. James Lord Bryce, *American Commonwealth* (new ed.; New York, 1922), II, 767–69, 874. The first edition appeared in 1888.

man *and* divine.[51] The founders understood the hierarchical structure of being and acted as reasonable people would whose grasp of order is not deformed by fantasies of one kind or another.

My cautionary words at the beginning of this chapter were partly intended to recall the care we, who live in an ideological age, must take to attain the same high level of rationality so admirable in the founders and not impute to them our own idols of the mind, such as those intended by Perry Miller when he spoke of obtuse secularism. The differentiated structure of reality and of the human condition is a legacy of Western civilization and its symbolic world fully at the disposition of the leading lights of the founding. They do not commit the various reductionist and monocausal fallacies to which we are most susceptible from our deep imbibing of scientism, positivism, Marxism, and Freudianism. If we certainly cannot reduce the work of the founder to the Bible or Christianity, much less can we reduce it to economic determinism or a political ideology of one form or another. Rather, we are obliged to keep open minds and assume that these men and women were doing more or less what they said and thought they were doing, without imposing a master explanation as the key to history or silently suppressing evidence as irrelevant because of our prejudices and anachronisms. History and human affairs are woefully untidy, and neat explanations more apt to be wrong than right, unfortunately for grandiose academics who lust for fame. Most of all we must guard against mutilating the ample reality disclosed through our most precious experiential-symbolic sources, revelatory religion and noetic science and philosophy, by trivializing them into the substrata of being by this or that reductionism. From this perspective, it is cheering to read in 1982 that the enormous volume of scholarly work devoted to our subject lacks an orthodox interpretation. "The research of the last ten years, then, makes clear that it is no longer possible to see a single, monolithic political ideology characterizing American thought on the eve of the Revolution. While the new complexity adds depth to our understanding of republicanism, it also raises two important questions. First, what became of republican thought in the half century after the Revolution? Second, in light of

51. *Cf.* Gen. 1:1–27; Ps. 8; Aristotle *Nicomachean Ethics* Bk. I and Bk. X. 7.

the welter of new interpretations, how are historians to make sense of the role and function of republicanism in early American history?"[52]

There does seem to be nearly universal agreement, however, that James Madison is the leading light of the Convention. One writer even asserts that, "Had James Madison never lived, the Constitution would probably not have been written."[53] Madison went so far on one occasion as to write, "The people of the U.S. owe their Independence & their liberty, to the wisdom of descrying in the minute tax of 3 pence on tea, the magnitude of the evil comprised in the precedent." Whether knowledge of this sentence would have saved historians the long struggle with the economic interpretation of the founding from Charles Beard to Forrest McDonald ("economic interpretation of the Constitution does not work"), I do not know.[54] What is clearer from the same document containing Madison's sentence is that his concern for religious liberty is at least as strongly motivated by Bryce's "religious principle" as by political considerations. The "rights of conscience" are to be protected against both the "danger of silent accumulations & encroachments by Ecclesiastical Bodies" and their incipient establishment of religion and the pollution of true religion by accommodation to the political power. "Ye States of America," Madison urges, "which retain in your Constitution or Codes, any aberration from the sacred principle of religious liberty, by giving to Caesar what belongs to God, or joining together what God has put asunder, hasten to revise & purify your systems, and make the example of your Country as pure & compleat [*sic*], in what relates to the freedom of the mind and its allegiance to its maker, as in what belongs to the legitimate objects of political & civil institutions."[55]

The complementary structure to liberty in biblical religion is the absolute *sovereignty* of God. This is a matter of reason nearly as much as it is of power for Americans of this period. The fusion of

52. Robert E. Shalhope, "Republicanism and Early American Historiography," *William and Mary Quarterly*, 3rd ser., XXXIX (1982), 346.

53. Rakove, *Beginnings of National Politics*, 468.

54. Elizabeth Fleet (ed.), "Madison's 'Detached Memoranda,'" *William and Mary Quarterly*, 3rd ser., III (1946), 557. Forrest McDonald, *We the People: The Economic Origins of the Constitution* (Chicago, 1958), vii.

55. Fleet (ed.), "Madison's 'Detached Memoranda,'" 554–55.

the teachings of Deuteronomy with Newtonian science and classical Greek and Roman sources tends to produce a rational divinity and natural law. We have heard Samuel West affirm that "deity cannot make a law contrary to the law of nature" and that any pretended revelation that contradicts reason is "an imposture." While there is no suggestion that God's sovereignty and will are *wholly* explicable by the rationality accessible to the finite minds of men, there is very firm reliance upon an ultimate power who is rational, just, omnipotent, merciful, loving, *and* the personal deity revealed through Jesus Christ. The reiterated appeal to divine Providence in the material quoted earlier stresses the dependence of the creature upon the Creator as the Governor of the world and disposer of all events, the ineffable Sovereign.

That there *is a fundamental law* is the chief matter. That notion is imported into the Constitution in the "Supremacy Clause" and serves as the ultimate grounding of national power in the United States. Without attempting to resolve in detail the vexed dispute about the "kind" of natural law prevalent in the minds of the founding generation, we can simply point to the obvious debt owed the Christian or "traditional" idea of these matters. The key text for that is Sir Edward Coke, the universal tutor of lawyers before the Revolution and the emergence in the late 1760s of Blackstone as the legal authority of the English-speaking world. Coke's plain words may again be recalled.

The law of nature is that which God at the time of creation of the nature of man infused into his heart, for his preservation and direction; and this is the *Lex aeterna*, the moral law, called also the law of nature. And by this law, written with the finger of God in the heart of man, were the people of God a long time governed before the law was written by Moses, who was the first reporter of the law in the world. . . . And Aristotle, nature's secretary, in Book 5 of the *Ethics* saith that "natural justice is that which everywhere has the same force and does not exist by people's thinking this or that." And herewith doth agree Bracton . . . and Fortescue . . . and *Doctor and Student.*[56]

56. Sir Edward Coke as quoted in Edward S. Corwin, *"Higher Law" Background of American Constitutional Law,* 45–46. Coke's original Latin from Aristotle is replaced with Martin Ostwald's English. Blackstone echoed Coke's doctrine in powerful language but left it a dead letter by embracing parliamentary sovereignty; see Blackstone, *Commentaries on the Laws of England,* I, 40–41.

These notions were a living force in American minds in this period, as James Otis perhaps most eloquently demonstrates.[57]

The appeal to absolute Justice and to natural rights *as God-given* was pervasive and displays the conception of an order of being transcendent to merely mortal and earthly authority, effectively superior in obligation to it, and as rational as Newton found God's mind to be in ordering the cosmos. That the English constitution lacked such a dimension was a factor of consequence in the seventeenth-century struggles in which Whigs (Coke among them) and Puritans played crucial roles. The controverted notion is that arbitrary or "tyrannical" rule is inadmissible under terms of a "fundamental law": Magna Carta, custom, divine and natural law, or a combination of all of them composing the Ancient Constitution demand Reason and Justice. That such fundamental law is superior even to kings is the nub of the seventeenth-century struggle that eventually settled the issue in the Glorious Revolution of 1688, a settlement foreshadowed forty years before in the impeaching and executing of the Earl of Strafford and the trial and execution of King Charles I in 1649. Thus, Strafford was condemned as a traitor "on the ground that his many arbitrary acts furnished evidence of a settled purpose to place the king above the law, and that such a purpose was tantamount to treason." "Charles Stuart," for his part, the *Sentence of the High Court of Justice Upon the King* reads, "Being admitted King of England, and therein trusted with a limited power to govern by, and according to the law of the land, and not otherwise; and by his trust, oath, and office, being obliged to use the power committed to him for the good and benefit of the people, and for the preservation of their rights and liberties [is condemned to be beheaded for perverting his rule into a] tyrannical power to rule according to his will."[58]

Americans resolutely rejected absolute claims on the part of any government, whether by king or by Parliament. The eighteenth-century notion of the unlimited superior power of a sovereign parliament triggered much of the controversy leading to the Revolution. It

57. See Gordon S. Wood, *Creation of the American Republic. 1776–1787* (Chapel Hill, N.C., 1969), 262–64.
58. Quoted from Gardiner (ed.), *Constitutional Documents of the Puritan Revolution*, xxix–xxx, 377–80.

was this element in Blackstone's *Commentaries* (published in 1765–1769) that so aroused James Wilson, who knew arbitrary power and creeping tyranny when he saw them.[59] This sense of demanding a rule of law (in Aristotle's phrase) and not of men—hence, of absolute Justice as far as that is humanly attainable—is a higher law principle, however it may be disguised, and finds its experiential footing in the transcendental order of being in which men participate. Few statements in *Federalist* are so powerful as Madison's in *No. 51* where, as we have seen, he affirms this conviction. "Justice is the end of government. It is the end of civil society. It ever has been, and ever will be pursued, until it be obtained, or until liberty be lost in the pursuit."

The great frame of biblical symbolism is comprehended in Exodus, Covenant, and Canaan. That the American Israel understood itself as continuing this history through its pilgrimage to the American wilderness in analogy with the Mosaic adventures is well known but bears repeating. The fact that Americans organized themselves by covenants for civil as well as religious purposes and even in federations of covenants is clear; and that the Constitution itself is framed in the spirit of the covenant, compact, contract symbolism is evident. That this symbolism is indebted to Christian theory is also acknowledged, "Without the strong link that Augustine forged between consent and will, social contract theory would be unthinkable, since it defines consent in terms of will."[60] But then, the whole sequence of biblical covenants linking consent and will lay behind Augustine. That the symbolism of Exodus can be applied to the departure of America from the British Empire through independence also is clear and in keeping with the tenor of the religious literature of the period. That the Revolution was theorized as a just war is explicit in the resolutions of the Congress and even in Tom Paine's writings. That the fulfillment of time in the dawn of the millennium in America by establishment of *novus ordo seclorum* of Constitution and republic is a palpable hope of a faithful people and a theme that has played a

59. See James Wilson, "On Municipal Law," (Philadelphia, 1804), in Hyneman and Lutz (eds.), *American Political Writing*, II, 1264–98.

60. Patrick Riley, *Will and Political Legitimacy: A Critical Exposition of Social Contract Theory in Hobbes, Locke, Rousseau, Kant, and Hegel* (Cambridge, Eng., 1982), 5; see also Daniel J. Elazar and John Kincaid (eds.), *Covenant, Polity and Constitutionalism*, rpr. of *Publius: Journal of Federalism*, X (Fall 1980), no. 4 (Lanham, Md., 1980).

role in American consciousness into the present century. Who could doubt that America is a special and favored nation? Could this not be the beginning of time transfigured into the eternal Sabbath of the Eighth Day? Such apocalyptical enthusiasm, however, was generally kept in check by the robust good sense of the founders, and the watchful, hopeful waiting typified by President Ezra Stiles seems to be consonant with general sentiment.[61]

We dare not leave our subject without correcting the impression that Benjamin Franklin stood alone among his colleagues in Philadelphia on June 28, 1787, when the suggestion of prayer was turned aside. There is no reason to believe that they did not heartily share his sentiments on religious matters. Pragmatic considerations of timing, possible alarm to the country, and even economics seem decisive in their letting the matter drop. Franklin's sentiments, from all that I have seen, typify the settled views of most of the American community of the time. We can conclude by attending to the nation's favorite philosopher.

In the beginning of the Contest with G. Britain, when we were sensible of danger we had daily prayer in this room for the divine protection.—Our prayers, Sir, were heard, and they were graciously answered. All of us who were engaged in the struggle must have observed frequent instances of a Superintending providence in our favor. To that kind providence we owe this happy opportunity of consulting in peace on the means of establishing our future national felicity. And have we now forgotten that powerful friend? or do we imagine that we no longer need his assistance? I have lived, Sir, a long time, and the longer I live, the more convincing proofs I see of this truth— *that God governs in the affairs of men.* And if a sparrow cannot fall to the ground without his notice, is it probable that an empire can rise without his aid? We have been assured, Sir, in the sacred writings, that "except the Lord build the House they labour in vain that build it." I firmly believe this; and I also believe that without his concurring aid we shall succeed in this political building no better than the Builders of Babel.[62]

Even to the casual observer, the American passion for liberty in the period of Revolution and Constitution is a startling fact. Devotion to personal liberties and to what is rather mystifyingly called free gov-

---

61. For Ezra Stiles' election sermon of 1783 see Chap. 4 herein; the complete text is given in Thornton (ed.), *Pulpit of the American Revolution*, 397–520.

62. Farrand (ed.), *Records of the Federal Convention of 1787*, I, 451. *God* is underlined twice in Franklin's manuscript, Farrand observes.

ernment is easy enough to sustain in rebellion, but how are they to be reconciled and combined with government under a Constitution that announces itself to be the "supreme law of the land"? This difficult question was abruptly faced after the Convention ended and the ratification process began. The historical and theoretical answers that emerged next invite our attention.

CHAPTER 6 Liberty as Law:

The Constitution and Civil Rights

Love of liberty is the experiential core of the American founding, both with respect to the revolutionary rupture that brought independence and to the national community institutionalized in the Constitution. Liberty is the driving passion and controlling reason of America, the chief attribute of the nation then and now, and our own true self. The rhetoric of Patrick Henry, Sam Adams, Tom Paine, and other firebrands of revolution thought and spoke out of this common passion. The Liberty Boys were a force to be reckoned with by any who would foster the enslavement of America or do otherwise than defend against tyranny as relations with Britain worsened through the decade before Independence. Abraham Lincoln memorialized the root of American nationhood in the mighty phrase "conceived in liberty," uttered in the very midst of a tragic drama of liberty and deep travail. Devotion to liberty not only fomented revolution but nearly aborted the constitutional founding when ratification was jeopardized because the great rights of mankind were not expressly protected by the Constitution of 1787. In short, liberty is a holy thing in America.

Any discussion that wishes analytically to consider "liberty as law" and "the Constitution and civil rights" from the perspective of the founding generation must, I believe, begin from this experiential center of conviction and utmost resolve. Otherwise, we can only have an academic exercise in the properly pejorative meaning of that phrase.

Whatever it is, or turns out to be historically and analytically, reflection can best begin by recalling that liberty is an immediate presence for the founding Americans. They routinely speak of "the good old cause," of "the glorious cause," of "the sacred cause of liberty," of "the sacred rights of liberty," and so on. A twentieth-century historian, fired by his reading, wrote of "the contagion of liberty." He concluded that "rights obviously lay at the heart of the Anglo-American controversy."[1]

John Dickinson, writing as Fabius during the ratification debate, explains that "liberty is the sun of society. Rights are the beams."[2] With the Constitution and Bill of Rights as the focus of discussion, I shall follow the clue provided by Dickinson in considering the liberty embraced by Americans of the founding generation, the ways in which it is embodied in the Constitution, and close with some attention to the ratification controversy that ends in adoption of the Bill of Rights in 1791 as the articulation of liberty into civil rights.

I

It is customary to stress the essential continuity of American liberty, among much else, with English liberty. There is general validity in this practice, but there are complications, as we shall see. Edmund Burke's famous and still stirring words undoubtedly go to the heart of the matter before us. The Americans, he said to the House of Commons in March 1775,

are descendants of Englishmen. England, Sir, is a nation which still, I hope, respects, and formerly adored, her freedom. The colonists emigrated from you when this part of your character was predominant; and they took this bias and direction the moment they parted from your hands. They are therefore not only devoted to liberty, but to liberty according to English ideas and on English principles. Abstract liberty, like other mere abstractions, is not to be found. Liberty inheres in some sensible object; and every nation has

---

1. Bernard Bailyn (ed.), *Pamphlets of the American Revolution* (Cambridge, Mass., 1965), I, 139, 194; see also Levi Hart, *Liberty Described and Recommended: In a Sermon Preached to the Corporation of Freemen in Farmington* (Hartford, 1775), in Charles S. Hyneman and Donald S. Lutz (eds.), *American Political Writing During the Founding Era* (Indianapolis, 1983), I, 307.

2. John Dickinson, *Letters of Fabius* (1788), *Letter IV* in Schwartz (ed.), *Bill of Rights*, I, 549.

formed itself some favorite point, which by way of eminence becomes the criterion of their happiness. It happened . . . that the great contests for freedom in this country were from the earliest times chiefly upon the question of taxing.[3]

It is plainly true that *liberty* "for a century and a half in the Anglophone world . . . was a shibboleth of political thinking; one could not get into the game without it."[4] There also is merit in Burke's observation that the Americans' notions of liberty as they roared to the great crescendo of the 1770s found expression in the language of the prior century that had emerged in the contest with the Stuart kings. This Country, Old Whig, Commonwealthman English liberty was a far cry from the new whiggism of Burke's Britain, the aristocratic constitution of the Hanoverian monarchy, and the placid acquiescence in parliamentary sovereignty that called itself English liberty at Westminster.[5]

America and Britain had become two countries separated by a common constitution, and the incomprehension was greater then than the incomprehension of our common language to one another now is. James Madison's mentor at Princeton, John Witherspoon, keenly remarks that "the generous principles of universal liberty" are incomprehensible to the British, who think Parliament can do anything and who, therefore, "consider the liberty of their country itself as consisting in the dominion of the House of Commons." He states elsewhere that "there is not the least reason . . . to think that either the king, the parliament, or even the people of Great Britain have been able to enter into the great principles of universal liberty."[6]

3. Peter J. Stanlis (ed.), *Edmund Burke: Selected Writings and Speeches* (Chicago, 1963), 158.

4. J. H. Hexter, *On Historians: Reappraisals of Some of the Makers of Modern History* (Cambridge, Mass., 1979), 302.

5. See the account in Bailyn (ed.), *Pamphlets of the American Revolution*, "General Introduction," which is revised and expanded as Bailyn, *Ideological Origins of the American Revolution*; Pocock, *Machiavellian Moment*; J. G. A. Pocock, "*Machiavellian Moment* Revisited: A Study in History and Ideology," *Journal of Modern History*, LIII (1981), 49–72 and the literature cited therein; Caroline Robbins, *Eighteenth-Century Commonwealthman: Studies in the Transmission, Development and Circumstance of English Liberal Thought from the Restoration of Charles II until the War with the Thirteen Colonies* (1959; rpr. New York, 1968).

6. John Witherspoon, *On Conducting the American Controversy*, in *Works of The Reverend John Witherspoon* (Philadelphia, 1800–1801), IV, 210. Witherspoon, *Thoughts on Liberty, ibid.*, 214.

Because Witherspoon is both characteristic and uniquely influential, careful attention ought be given to his views of our subject. Thus, so far from conceding that an "act of Parliament is supreme and irresistible," as do the British, Witherspoon writes, "We esteem the claim of the British parliament to be illegal and unconstitutional. . . . We are firmly determined never to submit to it, and do deliberately prefer war with all its horrors, and even extermination itself to slavery, rivetted on us and our posterity."[7] Defiance and resolve are palpable in Witherspoon's powerful statement. He further explains that, whatever the great differences among the Americans, "they all agreed, that they considered themselves as bringing their liberty with them [when they left Britain for America], and as entitled to all the rights and privileges of freemen under the British constitution." Just as Burke had asserted in the House of Commons that liberty is no abstraction but inheres in some sensible object (such as taxing), so Witherspoon confirms the point. "The foundation stone of British liberty [is], that the freeholders or proprietors of the soil, should have exclusive right of granting money for public uses." The root grievance between the British and the Americans comes down to "raising a revenue without the consent of the American legislatures, to be directly carried to the British treasury." To insist on this is to demand "unconditional submission" to British power and that Americans acquiesce to tyranny. In a speech in the Continental Congress, Witherspoon states his conviction that the Revolution which was by then underway was a war "for the rights of mankind in general, . . . the prosperity and happiness of this continent in future times." The "cause of America at present [is] a matter of inexpressible moment. The state of the human race through a great part of the globe, for ages to come, depends upon it."[8] The contrast in the two English liberties is stark, as Witherspoon characterizes the matter, almost to the point of Hanoverian Newspeak where liberty means slavery, and slavery liberty, or so at least the American revolutionary leadership believed and persuaded the general public. "For Englishmen are no more to be slaves to Par-

---

7. Witherspoon, *Thoughts on Liberty, ibid.,* 215.
8. Witherspoon, *Memorial and Manifesto of the United States of North America, ibid.,* 219. Witherspoon, *Part of a Speech in Congress Upon the Confederation, ibid.,* 254. Witherspoon, *On Conducting the American Controversy, ibid.,* 212.

liaments, than to Kings," Daniel Defoe wrote already in 1701, and the American sentiments were the same in 1776.[9]

They were also the same in 1787 and 1791, even if new exigencies shifted critical concern from securing liberty to institutionalizing just and effective order in the new nation. The disintegrative and centrifugal forces threatening the country in the late 1780s were Bailyn's "contagion of liberty" run amok and verging on a fatal hemorrhage; and it was to stanch that hemorrhage that the leading lights of the country met in Philadelphia. As George Washington cried out in 1786: "There are combustibles in every state which a spark might set fire to. Good God! Who, but a Tory, could have foreseen, or a Briton predicted them?"[10] The closing of the county courts at Springfield during the upheaval in western Massachusettts called the Shays' Rebellion prompted Henry Lee to write Washington in September 1786, "The period seems to be fast approaching when the people of these U. States must determine to establish a permanent capable government or submit to the horrors of anarchy and licentiousness."[11] Liberty and license were poles apart to the founding generation, even if the distinction was lost on the distressed and dispossessed.

Such confusion among the general public was the ghost haunting the entire revolutionary enterprise down to its still shaky result in the framing of the Constitution of 1787. John Adams recounts the following episode from August 1775 in his *Autobiography:*

An Event of the most trifling nature in Appearance, and fit only to excite Laughter, in other Times, struck me into a profound Reverie, if not a fit of Melancholly. I met a Man who had sometimes been my Client, and sometimes I had been against him. He, though a common Horse Jockey, was sometimes in the right, and I had commonly been successfull in his favour in our Courts of Law. He was always in the Law, and had been sued in many Actions, at almost every Court. As soon as he saw me, he came up to me, and his first Salutation to me was "Oh! Mr. Adams what great Things have you and your Colleagues done for Us! We can never be grateful enough to you. There are no Courts of Justice now in this Province, and I hope there

9. E. Neville Williams, *Eighteenth-Century Constitution, 1688–1815: Documents and Commentary* (Cambridge, England, 1960), 386.

10. Quoted in John H. Hallowell, *Main Currents in Modern Political Thought* (New York, 1950), 156.

11. Quoted in Robert J. Taylor, *Western Massachusetts in the Revolution* (Providence, 1954), 168.

never will be another!" Is this the Object for which I have been contending? said I to myself, for I rode along without any Answer to this Wretch. Are these the Sentiments of such People? And how many of them are there in the Country? Half the Nation for what I know: for half the Nation are Debtors if not more, and these have been in all Countries, the Sentiments of Debtors. If the Power of the Country should get into such hands, and there is great danger that it will, to what purpose have We sacrificed our Time, health and every Thing else? Surely We must guard against this Spirit and these Principles or We shall repent of all our Conduct. However The good Sense and Integrity of the Majority of the great Body of the People, came to my thoughts for my relief, and the last resource was after all in a good Providence.—How much reason there was for these melancholly reflections, the subsequent times have too fully shewn.[12]

Liberty, freedom, and free government always have had obvious and unspeculative meaning to the Jack Cades, Wat Tylers, and Archie Bunkers of the world. The beginning of possibilities fully realized before our (if not John Adams') eyes followed in the 1780s and after when courts of law in America were urged to reject rules of law not suited to the spirit of free institutions.

Such reasoning produced challenges to a wide variety of traditional legal restraints. Thus one man charged with being a vagabond thought it appropriate to urge in his defense that America was "a free country," while another, who had been subjected to a form of preventive detention for uttering threats, argued that he had been placed in a "situation, in which no subject of a free government ought, or can, legally be placed, and which is equally forbidden by principles of humanity, as of justice." This contagion of liberty even led to claims of license for immorality, when one frequenter of "the Hill" in Boston "pretended he had a right to visit all Whore-houses."[13]

From the perspective of our present reflections, I think it pertinent to argue that the American revolutionary enterprise, as it came to a culmination in the Constitution and Bill of Rights, intended to secure *sacred liberty* in the American community from the perennial threats of *vulgar liberty* just glimpsed. This may be the most fruitful way of viewing the political theory of our founders. Two things, at least, are plain enough. The universal experience of human liberty is self-

12. Lyman H. Butterfield (ed.), *Diary and Autobiography of John Adams* (Cambridge, Mass., 1961), III, 326. This was written about thirty years after the episode described.
13. William E. Nelson, *Americanization of the Common Law: The Impact of Legal Change on Massachusetts Society, 1760–1830* (Cambridge, Mass., 1975), 89–90. Citations omitted.

evident in ordinary choosing and acting, and not dependent upon philosophical proof. Vulgar liberty, in choosing and rejecting physical satisfactions and means to them is as fundamental to the self-evidence of liberty as the delight in sensual perception is to Aristotle's self-evident desire to know, which is natural to all men. The founder of the Scottish common sense school of philosophy, Thomas Reid, pertinently states the matter in these words in 1788,

The arguments to prove that man is endowed with moral liberty, which have the greatest weight with me, are three: 1st, Because he has a natural conviction or belief, that, in many cases, he acts freely; 2dly, Because he is accountable; and, 3rdly, Because he is able to prosecute an end by long series of means adapted to it.

Reid then commences with the first argument on the next page, as follows:

We have, by our constitution, a natural conviction or belief that we act freely. A conviction so early, so universal, and so necessary in most of our rational operations, that it must be the result of our constitution, and the work of Him that made us.[14]

While the range of Reid's argument extends to the whole of human liberty, the immediate point to be stressed is this: by common sense and direct intuition, men universally believe in their natural liberty. This belief is itself philosophically significant as symbolizing the experiential ground of our insight into the structure of human nature.

The second point to mention is that the quest for decorum and order, together with what Henry Lee called "a permanent capable government," as the admitted task of the framers of the Constitution, was not an endeavor at odds with serving the sacred cause of liberty. To the contrary, no American founder was any less devoted to liberty in the best sense in 1787 than he had been in 1776, so to view the matter in terms of liberty versus order is to foster a false dichotomy. A direct line of consensus runs from the resolution adopted by the Concord, Massachusetts, town meeting on October 21, 1776, to James Madison's thinking in the Federal Convention over a decade later. As the Concord resolution states, "We conceive that a Constitu-

14. Thomas Reid, *Essays on the Active Powers of the Human Mind* [1788], intro. by Baruch A. Brody (1813; rpr. Cambridge, Mass., 1969), 303–304.

tion in its proper idea intends a system of principles established to secure the subjects in the possession and enjoyment of their rights and privileges against any encroachments of the governing part." [15] Madison's views are that "he should shrink from nothing which should be found essential to such a form of Govt. as would provide for the safety, liberty and happiness of the Community. This being the end of all our deliberations, all the necessary means for attaining it must . . . be submitted to." Madison subsequently speaks of the "necessary objects" essential to the national government and stresses "the necessity, of providing more effectually for the security of private rights, and the steady dispensation of justice. Interferences with these were evils which had more perhaps than any thing else, produced this convention. Was it to be supposed that republican liberty could long exist under the abuses of it practiced in some of the States." [16] He then proceeds to outline the theory of controlling faction along lines familiar from the later *Federalist No. 10.*

At the center of that famous statement of the principles of the Constitution is the sentence, "Liberty is to faction, what air is to fire, an aliment without which it instantly expires." And since the discussion at this point is of the cure for the factions (inevitable to "all civilized societies") that is woven into the new Constitution, Madison continues: "But it could not be a less folly to abolish liberty, which is essential to political life, because it nourishes faction, than it would be to wish the annihilation of air, which is essential to animal life, because it imparts to fire its destructive agency." [17] To what kind of *liberty* is Madison referring? The kind characteristic of all men considered to be fallible and imperfect beings—of himself and John Adams and other *aristoi* of the American founding no less than of the

15. Quoted from Samuel E. Morison (ed.), *Sources and Documents Illustrating the American Revolution* (Oxford, England, 1923), 177.

16. Farrand (ed.), *Records of the Federal Convention of 1787,* I, 53 (May 21); pp. 134–36 (June 6).

17. Cooke (ed.), *Federalist,* 58. Cf. Douglass Adair, "'That Politics May be Reduced to a Science'; David Hume, James Madison, and the Tenth Federalist," *Huntington Library Quarterly,* XX (1957), 343–60 (reprinted in Adair, *Fame and the Founding Fathers,* Chap. 4); David Hume, "Of Parties in General," in *Essays Moral, Political and Literary,* ed. Eugene F. Miller (Indianapolis, 1985), 58, 651. The phrase "all civilized societies" occurs in the background paper Madison prepared for the Philadelphia Convention in April 1787, *Vices of the Political System of the United States,* in Hutchinson, *et al.* (eds.), *Papers of James Madison,* IX, 345–58 at 355.

Horse Jockey and Daniel Shays' rebels. Fundamental human equality of the order affirmed in the Declaration of Independence remains self-evident truth in Publius' political theory.

Vulgar liberty and sacred liberty are not exclusive provinces of the depraved and virtuous respectively, considered as human types, the one to be condemned as wretches and scum, the other to be lauded as spotless paradigms, even if in concrete instances such condemnation and praise are warranted. Rather, it is recognized that human diversity as well as relative talent and goodness are attributes of heterogenous mankind and that the inclinations to vice and sin, and the aspirations to the noble and true are present in *every* human personality. The exercise of liberty by diverse, imperfect, and more often than not self-serving human beings will—even under the best of circumstances—produce the rival groupings called factions. Madison's language must be set forth and carefully considered.

As long as the reason of man continues fallible, and he is at liberty to exercise it, different opinions will be formed. As long as the connection subsists between his reason and his self-love, his opinions and passions will have a reciprocal influence on each other. . . . The diversity in the faculties of men from which the rights of property originate, is not less an insuperable obstacle to a uniformity of interests. The protection of these faculties is the first object of Government. From the protection of different and unequal faculties of acquiring property, the possession of different degrees and kinds of property immediately results: and from the influence of these on the sentiments and views of the respective proprietors, ensues a division of the society into different interests and parties.

The latent causes of faction are thus sown in the nature of man. . . . A zeal for different opinions concerning religion, concerning Government and many other points, as well of speculation as of practice; an attachment to different leaders ambitiously contending for pre-eminence and power; or to persons of other descriptions whose fortunes have been interesting to the human passions, have in turn divided mankind into parties, inflamed them with mutual animosity, and rendered them much more disposed to vex and oppress each other, than to cooperate for their common good. . . . The most common and durable source of factions, has been the various and unequal distribution of property. Those who hold, and those who are without property, have ever formed distinct interests in society. Those who are creditor, and those who are debtors, fall under a like discrimination. A landed interest, a manufacturing interest, a mercantile interest, a monied interest, with many lesser interests, grow up of necessity in civilized nations, and divide them into different classes, actuated by different sentiments and views. The regulation of these various and interfering interests forms the principal task of modern Legislation, and involves the spirit of party and faction in the necessary and ordinary operations of Government.

No man is allowed to be a judge in his own cause; because his interest would certainly bias his judgment, and, not improbably, corrupt his integrity.[18]

The context of Publius' discussion of liberty is the perennial philosophy of human affairs, as the last quoted sentence signals. Madison draws from the *Essays* of Hume, to be sure, but he draws from a great range of other sources in arriving at the remarkable synthesis before us, including the echo of Aristotle and of the Christian understanding of human reality just intimated. While an attempt to show the lines of connection in detail would derail the present discussion, some reminders of them are requisite for accurate understanding. Thus Aristotle: "Unjust action means to assign to oneself too much of things intrinsically good and too little of things intrinsically evil. That is why we do not allow the rule of a man but the rule of reason, because a man takes too large a share for himself and becomes a tyrant."[19] Thus Madison, in summarizing the rule of society by a faction gathered around "persons of distinguished character and extensive influence in the community" as essentially self-serving and judges in their own cases, writes: "The *passions* therefore not *the reason*, of the public, would sit in judgment. But it is the reason of the public alone that ought to controul and regulate the government. The passions ought to be controuled and regulated by the government." Madison does not disagree with the ancients that the *aristoi* or *spoudaioi*, the virtuous and true men among us, would do of their own volition what public and private good demand in the service of truth and justice. As Aristotle remarks, "A cultivated and free man, then, will have this kind of attitude, being, as it were, a law unto himself."[20]

18. Cooke (ed.), *Federalist*, 58–59.
19. Aristotle *Nicomachean Ethics* V. 6. 4–5. 1134A31–36; *cf.* Aristotle *Politics* III. 16. [III. 11. 4 in Loeb ed.] 1287A13–35.
20. Cooke (ed.), *Federalist*, 343 (No. 49), italics as in original; Aristotle *Nicomachean Ethics* IV. 8. 10. 1128A33.

The problems are the same for the founders as for the ancient Greek philosophers. On one hand, even the best of men are corrupted by the wild beast of passion and are thus unfit to judge in their own cases or to be safe repositories of just rule according to the demanding standard exacted by intelligence and right reason. On the other hand, except in extraordinary moments of unique and perhaps providential splendor, a community of virtue and reason guided by paradigmatic rulers is not normally available for human governance. In a letter to Madison, Washington reflects (in Hobbesian overtones) on essential repairs of the Articles needed to secure "good government" under current dire circumstances and writes: "I confess however that my opinion of public virtue is so far changed that I have doubts whether any system without the means of coercion in the Sovereign, will enforce obedience to the Ordinances of a Genl. Government; without which, every thing else fails." Laws unobeyed are worse than no laws at all.[21] Persuasion had reached its limits. Madison, for his part, is clear that in "a nation of philosophers . . . a reverence for the laws, would be sufficiently inculcated by the voice of an enlightened reason. But a nation of philosophers is as little to be expected as the philosophical race of kings wished for by Plato. And in every other nation, the most rational government will not find it a superfluous advantage, to have the prejudices of the community on its side."[22] That is to say, it is advantageous to rule with the consent of the people!

By Madison's analysis, the unique unity of the American community under pressure of the contest for sacred liberty during the Revolution was a splendid moment that had passed and given way to normal social and political circumstances. The assumption of extraordinary "virtue and intelligence of the people of America" that was grounded in the commonplaces of Revolutionary enthusiasm was basic to the "experiments" in the constitution-making of the newly independent states and of the nation. Thus, mutual dedication and danger "repressed the passions most unfriendly to order and concord," and gov-

21. George Washington to James Madison, Mar. 31, 1787, in Hutchinson, *et al.* (eds.), *Papers of James Madison*, IX, 343.
22. Cooke (ed.), *Federalist*, 340 (No. 49).

ernments were erected at a moment of "enthusiastic confidence of the people in their patriotic leaders, which stifled the ordinary diversity of opinions on great national questions," and "no spirit of party" affected the people's deliberations.[23] Normal conditions have returned and with them the diversity to be expected among free people.

Not *elimination* but merely "curing the mischiefs of faction" is the framers' hope. For Hume, however, factions are thoroughly bad, obnoxious "weeds" he wishes "to eradicate" from the political garden.[24] For the uniquely American theory of free government, this contrast is critically important. Factions are not without merit for Publius. To the contrary, a politics *without* factions "ought to be neither resumed nor desired; because an extinction of parties necessarily implies either a universal alarm for the public safety; or an absolute extinction of liberty." To repeat, the "diversity in the faculties of men" is both the ontological origin of "the rights of property" and *"the first object of Government"* in its protection of the people and every individual among them.[25] The ultimate requirement that free government secure the well-being of the people as the supreme law (*salus populi*) means justly ordering society to preserve natural liberty and the integrity of human beings who are created in the image and likeness of God and are God's property no less than merely their own.

Madison's initial analysis of the faction problem in his memorandum on the *Vices of the Political System* frames the discussion as a challenge to the fundamental principle of Republican Government, namely, that the majority who must rule in such a system "are the safest Guardians both of public Good and of private rights." Madison is concerned especially by "Injustice in the laws of States."[26] Tyrannical majorities express themselves (among other ways) through enactment of laws that are then enforced against hapless minorities to enslave them to injustice contrary to the principles of sacred liberty. One implication is that the least just among us has some justice in his cause, and this applied even to the celebrated Shays' Rebellion, which was manipulated to arouse the country to revise the Articles.

23. *Ibid.*, 341.
24. *Ibid.*, 58 (No. 10). Hume, *Essays*, ed. Miller, 55. *Cf.* Adair, "'That Politics May be Reduced to a Science,'" in Adair, *Fame and the Founding Fathers*, 104n.
25. Cooke (ed.), *Federalist*, 346 (No. 50). *Ibid.*, 58. Emphasis added.
26. Hutchinson, *et al.* (eds.), *Papers of James Madison*, IX, 354.

While Madison is circumspect on this specific instance, he plainly is horrified by the shoddiness and injustice of much state legislation and administration. In sum, the short shrift accorded the minority rights of debtors caught in the toils of the post-Revolution depression and at the mercy of the dominant creditor class of eastern Massachusetts smacked of abuse. Daniel Shays and other leaders were largely "solid, respectable men, many of them veterans who had been driven to desperation by the state's rigid financial policy."[27] General Henry Knox reported to a receptive and alarmed Washington of the rebels that "there [*sic*] creed is, that the property of the United States, has been protected from confiscation of Britain by the joint exertions of *all*, and therefore ought to be the *common property* of all. And he that attempts opposition to this creed is an enemy to equity & justice, & ought to be swept from off the face of the Earth." "They are determined to annihilate all debts public & private, and have Agrarian Laws, which are easily effected by the means of unfunded paper Money which shall be a tender in all cases whatever."[28] Thomas Jefferson from his vantage point in Paris was so little distraught by all this that he gave forth a famous utterance: "I hold it that a little rebellion now and then is a good thing, & as necessary in the political world as storms in the physical. Unsuccessful rebellions indeed generally establish the incroachments on the rights of the people which have produced them. . . . It is a medecine [*sic*] necessary for the sound health of government."[29]

Despite his eloquent apology for the Constitution through the press which we read as the *Federalist*, Madison was quite unsure that enough power had been vested by the Convention in the national government to attain the chief objects of his (and Alexander Hamilton's!) concern, the well-being of the country—justice through sound rule of law and protection of vital private rights and public (or "Republican") liberty. The failure of the Convention to include a federal veto power on state legislation was the main basis of uncertainty and

27. Robert Middlekauff, *Glorious Cause*, 600.
28. George Washington to James Madison, Nov. 5, 1786, quoting General Henry Knox, in Hutchinson, *et al.* (eds.), *Papers of James Madison*, IX, 161. Emphasis as in original. For use of the Shays affair as propaganda by such advocates of "energetic government" as Knox and Richard Lee see *ibid.*, 167n.
29. Thomas Jefferson to James Madison, Jan. 30, 1787, *ibid.*, IX, 248.

disappointment. Madison regarded this as vital to the cure of the most serious maladies afflicting the country, as he makes clear in the great letter to Jefferson written less than a month before *Federalist No. 10* was published.[30] The major source of injustice was in the states, Madison believed. When the Bill of Rights was drafted, he again failed when an amendment to secure basic liberties from state invasion was cut by the Senate. Madison regarded this amendment, prohibiting the states from infringing the freedom of conscience, speech, press, and jury trial, to be "the most valuable amendment in the whole lot."[31]

In sum, a new amalgam of distinctively American liberty emerged in the period and claimed a universal validity. From the perspective of individual persons, it was rooted in the vivid participation of every-man in transcendant divine Being in the modes of religious and philo-sophical experience noticed earlier. This expresses itself by expand-ing the sense of self-reliance and indestructible dignity of men in steady communion with a caring and loving Father. Formation of the experience of liberty by the cooperative venture of faith in commu-nion with highest reality effectively demolishes extravagant institu-tional claims to authority over such human beings. The experience liberates conscience and empowers reason so as to give new scope and meaning to the expression "free men." The judgment and reflec-tion of communities of such free men—in consonance with the con-gregational principle traditional in American religion and despite di-versities among various communities—forms powerfully to insist upon consent to public authority and binding laws, and to reject any-thing short of that as arbitrary, slavish rule.

Powerful conviction merging liberty, truth, and justice animates this vibrant center of American experience and the resilient social and institutional responses to successive crises during the period. The intensity of the Revolution behind them, however, the divisons of fal-lible men with differing interests appear with even greater force than earlier and in ways productive of factionalism *plainly presaging po-*

30. James Madison to Thomas Jefferson, Oct. 24, 1787, *ibid.*, X, 205–20. *Federalist No. 10* appeared on Nov. 22, 1787, in the *Daily Advertiser* in New York as Madison's first Publius essay.
31. Madison as quoted in Schwartz (ed.), *Bill of Rights*, II, 1145–46.

litical parties. Surely partisan political parties as those that emerged in the 1790s were less of a surprise to Madison and other astute analysts than our textbooks routinely tell us they were! In any event, persuasion reaches its limits, and effective representative government with artfully institutionalized coercive powers sufficient to maintain order and justice becomes the desideratum of the country and of the constitutional revisionists we call the framers. Pluralism in societies of free men is to be expected and even welcomed, as Madison explains, but this does not simplify the process of governing. The analyses sketched of human nature, politics, and what is truly precious in the legacies from the British constitution compose the groundwork of the endeavor and define the consensus reflected in the best thinking. The best thinking narrowly—and remarkably—carries the day, therewith opening an epoch in political history.

II

Alexander Hamilton, in the guise of Publius, wrote in the penultimate number of *The Federalist,* "The truth is . . . that the constitution is itself in every rational sense, and to every useful purpose, A BILL OF RIGHTS."[32] Some of his justification for this assertion has been seen in the foregoing discussion, even if it is admitted that this is debater's rhetoric and not entirely convincing either then or now. Nonetheless, there is more to Hamilton's claim than is usually supposed. Central purposes of the Constitution drafted in 1787 are the protection of rights of minorities against tyrannical majorities, the securing of just laws by limiting the scope of state authority and placing it under the constraints of the "supreme law of the land," and the fostering of the integrity of individual citizens by consciously protecting their natural liberty to live as free and rational beings according to their individual inclinations and talents. *The liberties most at issue in the Revolution are secured under the Constitution as it stood in September 1787.* Thus, the general powers of the national government are limited. The system of representation whereby policy is decided and laws enacted is closely designed to satisfy the demands of

32. Cooke (ed.), *Federalist,* 581 (No. 84).

the people and the states as constituents of the national community; and the taxing and impeachment powers are carefully lodged in the initiative of the House of Representatives, which alone can begin either revenue or removal measures. If the slogan "no taxation without representation" communicates the fundamental rights issue of the Revolution, then the members of the Federal Convention meticulously secured for the American public the broad spectrum of natural and constitutional rights contended for against British tyranny.

In sketching his likes and dislikes about the new Constitution to Madison, Jefferson writes in part: "I like the power given the Legislature to levy taxes, and for that reason solely approve of the greater house being chosen by the people directly. For tho' I think a house chosen by them will be very illy qualified to legislate for the Union . . . yet this evil does not weigh against the good of preserving inviolate the fundamental principle that the people are not to be taxed but by representatives chosen immediately by themselves. I am captivated by the compromise of the opposite claims of the great & little states of the latter to equal, the former to proportional influence."[33] What Jefferson principally dislikes about the Constitution in its original form is the absence of a Bill of Rights, a matter to which we return shortly.

The theories of human nature and of natural law and natural rights that underlie the Constitution demand some further clarification if American liberty as law is to be grasped. The theory of human nature is eclectic and broadly synthesizes classical, Christian, and Enlightenment elements. Publius provides the standard for the discussion when he (Hamilton in the first instance, then Madison) raises the question, "Why has government been instituted at all? Because the passions of men will not conform to the dictates of reason and justice, without constraint."[34] Vulgar liberty constantly threatens to overwhelm sacred liberty in human affairs because of the power of passions that seek to rule rather than to be ruled. To recall Madison's words again:

But what is government itself but the greatest of all reflections on human nature? If men were angels, no government would be necessary. If angels

33. Thomas Jefferson to James Madison, Dec. 20, 1787, in Hutchinson, *et al.* (eds.), *Papers of James Madison*, X, 336.
34. Cooke (ed.), *Federalist*, 96 (No. 15).

were to govern men, neither external nor internal controuls on government would be necessary. In framing a government which is to be administered by men over men, the great difficulty lies in this: You must first enable the government to controul the governed; and in the next place, oblige it to controul itself. A dependence on the people is no doubt the primary controul on the government; but experience has taught mankind the necessity of auxiliary precautions.[35]

These lines reflect the philosophers' and Christian notions of man's existence in the In-Between reality that is neither brute nor divine but properly human: that man is created a little lower than the angels and given dominion over the earth. The language itself is reminiscent of Pascal, whose writings became familiar to Madison during his Princeton years with John Witherspoon. As Pascal writes:

Man is neither angel nor brute, and the unfortunate thing is that he who would act the angel acts the brute. . . . We do not sustain ourselves in virtue by our own strength, but by the balancing of two opposed vices, just as we remain upright amidst two contrary gales. Remove one of the vices, and we fall into the other. . . . There is internal war in man between reason and the passions. If he had only reason without passions . . . If he had only passions without reason . . . But having both, he cannot be without strife, being unable to be at peace with the one without being at war with the other. Thus he is always divided against, and opposed to himself. . . . This internal war of reason against the passions has made a division of those who would have peace into two sects. The first would renounce their passions, and become gods; the others would renounce reason, and become brute beasts. . . . But neither can do so, and reason still remains, to condemn the vileness and injustice of the passions, and to trouble the repose of those who abandon themselves to them; and the passions keep always alive in those who would renounce them.[36]

With nine Princeton graduates in the Philadelphia Convention, the importance of John Witherspoon for our inquiry has been noticed. It has been asserted that "Witherspoon was probably the most influential teacher in the entire history of American education."[37] Madison and the other Witherspoon students learned Christian philosophy

---

35. *Ibid.*, 349 (No. 51).
36. Blaise Pascal, *Pensées and the Provincial Letters*, ed. Saxe Commins (New York, 1941), 118–31 (Nos. 358, 359, 412, 413). See James H. Smylie, "Madison and Witherspoon: Theological Roots of American Political Thought," *Princeton University Library Journal*, XXII (1961), 118–32 at 127n.
37. Garry Wills, *Explaining America: The Federalist* (Harmondsworth, England, 1981), 16.

and theology no less than Scottish Enlightenment literature at Princeton. Witherspoon's Evangelical Presbyterian faith felt no conflict between reason and revelation as modes of truth. As he states in the beginning of his *Lectures on Moral Philosophy,* "If the Scripture is true, the discoveries of reason cannot be contrary to it."[38] He found it easy to believe "both the certainty of God's purpose and the free agency of the creature," even if he could not fully comprehend it.[39]

Witherspoon's conception of man is essentially that reflected in the *Federalist* and is grounded in the biblical and philosophical views commonplace in America at the time, although some subtleties are observed. While men are sinful and depraved, their self-love is not so radically evil and egoistic as in Hobbes, Hume, or Augustine. For "man comes into the world in a state of impurity and moral defilement" as a result of the Fall. "What is the history of the world but the history of human guilt? and do not children from the first dawn of reason show, that they are wise to do evil; but to do good they have no knowledge?"[40] The *one true remedy* for this plight is the grace of God extended through Christ to the faithful to effect "the righteousness of Christ" among those bound together with Him through the "Covenant of Grace," for "salvation is of grace." Justice leads to perdition, Witherspoon stresses, so the "foundation of the whole" lies in the "free and unmerited mercy" of God disclosed in Scripture. From this leading idea follow the principles of the "freeness of salvation," what "faith alone brings us to it," and that faith means "renouncing all self-dependence" as it implies "daily pardon to the believer." Under all the divine covenants, including that of Grace through Christ, the Ten Commandments compose the "immutable law of righteousness" binding upon all creatures as duties and the very "moral law." Yet "nothing is more contrary to the spirit of the gospel than self-dependence," so the Christian's duty is to "abate pride" and "exalt the grace of God."[41]

With the central understanding of mankind's utter reliance upon

38. John Witherspoon, *Lectures on Moral Philosophy: An Annotated Edition,* ed. Jack Scott (Newark, N.J., 1982), 64 (Lec. I).

39. Witherspoon, *Lectures on Divinity: Introduction,* in *Works,* IV, 91.

40. *Ibid.,* 96–97.

41. *Ibid.,* 99–123.

divine grace for righteousness in the world and salvation in eternity as the abiding foundation, Witherspoon addresses the question of strengthening the government of the Union as a member of the Continental Congress.

I am none of those who either deny or conceal the depravity of human nature, till it is purified by the light of truth, and renewed by the Spirit of the living God. Yet I apprehend there is no force in that reasoning at all [under our present circumstances]. Shall we establish nothing good, because we know it cannot be eternal? Shall we live without government, because every constitution has its old age, and its period? Because we know that we shall die, shall we take no pains to preserve or lengthen out life? Far from it, sir; it only requires the more watchful attention, to settle government upon the best principles, and in the wisest manner, that it may last as long as the nature of things will admit.[42]

Witherspoon even confesses that some will think him "visionary and romantic," but he looks forward to "a progress, as in every other human art, so in the perfection of human society, greater than we have yet seen . . . human science and religion have kept company together, and greatly assisted each other's progress in the world." He refers to such "improvements in human nature" as the establishment of the "rights of conscience" as an instance of progress.[43]

The key to reconciling the depravity of man and the hope for a continuing improvement of society is divine *Providence*, writes Witherspoon in invoking the favorite symbolism of the times for the community's reciprocating participation in transcendent divine Being. Through the mercy of God and his favor, men are drawn to him and to righteousness, and thus to the keeping of the "great commandment" by the elect as the fruition of faith and grace: "Thou shalt love the Lord thy God with all thy heart, and with all thy soul, and with all thy mind."[44] In the single reference to Jonathan Edwards in *Lectures on Moral Philosophy*, Witherspoon concurs that "virtue consists in the love of being as such."[45] The "second" command-

42. Witherspoon, *Part of a Speech in Congress, ibid.*, 256. *Cf.* Smylie, "Madison and Witherspoon," 123–24.
43. Witherspoon, *Works*, IV, 257.
44. Matt. 22:37; *cf.* the *Shema* of Israel, Deut. 6:2.
45. Witherspoon, *Lectures on Moral Philosophy*, 85, 88 (Lec. IV). *Cf.* Sereno E. Dwight (ed.), *Works of President Edwards* (New York, 1830), III, 94.

ment of Jesus is "like unto" the first, "Thou shalt love thy neighbour as thyself." This is expressed by Witherspoon, following Frances Hutcheson and Adam Smith, as "benevolence," which is "the principle and sum of that branch of duty which regards others." "Love to others, sincere and active, is the sum of our duty" to man.[46] Yet it is not merely a duty *imposed* upon the mind and will by divine decree. Rather, the love of self of the second commandment, like the love of God of the first, presumes a natural *desire* of the creature for communion with the Creator and with fellow beings who also bear the divine image as part of their very selfhood. Hence, not mere duty or obligation alone but natural inclination or aspiration draws men to the love of the divine Good and to other goods proper to them. Both obligation and attraction structure the spiritual reality and community, even in the mutilated state of the fallen. God and the good remain the natural end of the beings created for communion with the divine Creator. In sum, *all* love—including self-love—is a love of God, even when it is most unaware of itself.[47]

The often neglected transcendental dimensions of our subject were significant for Witherspoon and his associates, including Madison, who was a "lay theologian" and in early life was strongly attracted to the ministry as a career.[48] Witherspoon especially commends study of the French writers, among whom Pascal is a favorite, and he makes a point of expressing admiration for their "popish divines."[49] He ex-

46. Matt. 22:39; *cf.* Lev. 19:18. Witherspoon, *Lectures on Moral Philosophy*, 109, 112 (Lec. VIII); Francis Hutcheson's *A System of Moral Philosophy*, (London, 1755) is the basis of Witherspoon's course of lectures; see Scott's introduction in *Lectures on Moral Philosophy*, 27–28 and *passim*.

47. *Cf.* Étienne Gilson, *Spirit of Medieval Philosophy*, trans. A. H. C. Downes (New York, 1940), 278, 269–303 generally; also see Aristotle *Nicomachean Ethics* IX. 4. 1. 1166a1 and 8. 1. 1168a27. Americans and Scots of the period were learned in the Greek and Latin classics. See Reinhold, *Classica Americana*, who characterizes the Revolutionary period as "the Golden Age of the classical tradition in America," p. 95. *Cf.* Chap. 3 herein.

48. Smylie, "Madison and Witherspoon," 125. That Madison seriously considered the ministry as his career is a conclusion of his editors in Hutchinson, *et al.* (eds.), *Papers of James Madison*, I, 97n; see also *ibid.*, 47n, for a comparison of Madison's faith with that of his friend and tutor at Princeton, Samuel Stanhope Smith, who succeeded Witherspoon as president in 1795. "The close and long friendship of JM and Smith, probably beginning when JM was at Princeton, may have helped to shape JM's religious views. Smith never wavered in his conviction that his Presbyterian faith squared with right and reason and hence was impregnable against any assault whose force depended upon a new philosophy or new scientific discoveries."

49. Witherspoon, *Works*, IV, 21.

horts his auditors to practice true religion, namely, "seek for inward, vital comfort, to know in whom you have believed, and endeavor after the greatest strictness and tenderness of practice." Dependence upon God is to be ever in mind, and one should "pray without ceasing." [50]

Adam Smith, at the beginning of *The Theory of Moral Sentiments*, writes: "How selfish soever man may be supposed, there are evidently some principles in his nature, which interest him in the fortune of others, and render their happiness necessary to him, though he derives nothing from it except the pleasure of seeing it." Benevolence is for Smith's teacher, Hutcheson, the summation of all virtue and a philosophical translation of Christian charity. To this Smith adds the virtue of Stoic self-command.

And hence it is, that to feel much for others and little for ourselves, that to restrain our selfish, and to indulge our benevolent affections, constitutes the perfection of human nature; and can alone produce among mankind that harmony of sentiments and passions in which consists their whole grace and propriety. As to love our neighbour as we love ourselves is the great law of Christianity, so it is the great precept of nature to love ourselves only as we love our neighbour, or what comes to the same thing, as our neighbour is capable of loving us. [51]

While the admiration of Stoicism was widespread in America, and the notions of self-command, nature as a cosmic harmony, and man himself as a citizen of the world all fitted with the law of nature and the system of natural liberty, they tended to be assimilated to the controlling Christian views of grace and divine Providence. Debates raged over the precise meaning of the conceptions just mentioned, not least of all over the question of a *general* Providence that accorded with the Deist and Stoic conceptions of the world machine and God as divine clockmaker versus a *special* Providence whereby divine interventions in His cosmic order and in human affairs generally occur, including such minor events as the creation of Man and the Exodus.

During his early years in Scotland, Witherspoon ridiculed the importation of Stoic and related philosophical notions into Christianity

50. *Ibid.*, 12–14.
51. Adam Smith, *Theory of Moral Sentiments*, ed. D. D. Raphael and A. L. Macfie (1979; rpr. Indianapolis, 1982), 9. *Ibid.*, 25; *cf.* Witherspoon, *Lectures on Moral Philosophy*, 84, 109.

and the controversy with the Moderates led by Frances Hutcheson. He dismissed as well the thesis of Bernard Mandeville that private vice results in public good.[52] Reliance upon Hutcheson's work for his own *Lectures on Moral Philosophy,* despite conducting a running debate on a great many points, blurs the issues and leads us to conclude that Witherspoon continued to ponder questions while he remained open to plausible arguments from all quarters. This is done, however, within the bounds of the basic convictions embracing faith in God and the validity of revealed truth. For Witherspoon, Providence in the forms of divine grace and concern for all of Creation and every human being, no less than for every sparrow, governs in human affairs and is the source of every good and virtuous action. Virtue and piety are inseparably connected. Evil is the result of sin, and human depravity is the condition of the world, so all *deserve* perdition by justice and can only be rescued through Christ's redemptive power of unmerited grace and ineffable mercy. This complex view of human reality leads to the obligations of living in faith, fulfilling all virtue commanded by divine will, and serving truth and justice in society. "The true nature of liberty is the prevalence of law and order, and the security of individuals," Witherspoon writes of life in society.

The human condition, however, is such that neither moral excellence nor civil virtue suffices to sustain a regime of liberty. The obligation to do good, even with the assistance of God, leaves the mystery of evil a present reality; by free will, all have sinned and fallen short of the glory of God. The temporal remedy for this unfortunate fact is effective government. This, Witherspoon taught young Madison and his classmates from 1770 to 1772 when they attended the College of New Jersey and the *Lectures on Moral Philosophy* were first delivered there, can only be a *mixed* and *balanced* form of government like that of Britain. All the simple forms—monarchy, aristocracy, democracy—are susceptible to vices that result in injustice and tyranny of one kind or another. "Hence it appears that every good form of government must be complex, so that the one principle may check the other. It is of consequence to have as much virtue among the particular members of a community as possible; *but it is folly to expect*

52. Witherspoon, *Lectures on Moral Philosophy,* 5–7, 35, 88, 89 (see Lec. IV).

that a state should be upheld by integrity in all who have a share in managing it. They must be so balanced, that when every one draws to his own interest or inclination, there may be an over poise upon the whole."[53] Witherspoon's view of man and government anticipates the central principle of the framers by fifteen years. As a standard element in the intellectual equipment of the times, this understanding of politics is well known from Polybius, Locke, Montesquieu, and Blackstone, as well as from the classical theory of the English constitution stated in Charles I's *Answer to the XIX Propositions* (1642).[54] Its strength here and as adapted and refined to American needs by John Adams and James Madison arises not from its literary ancestry, but from the subtle validity of the theory of human nature and political reality informing it.

Our concern for the moment is with the central place of Providence in the theory. From that perspective, human passion—whether the bad *eros* of Plato, the *superbia vitae* of First John 2:16 (and, by derivation, of Augustine, Calvin, and Witherspoon), the pride or egoism of Hobbes and Hume, or even the ameliorated self-love of Hutcheson and Smith—hinders righteousness, virtue, and the just rule of right Reason in human society. In the view of the founders, Providence alleviates this general problem in several identifiable ways, all of them expressive of the mystery of divine-human collaboration in the In-Between of participation in politics and history. (1) The collision of interested persons and groups tends to leave a tenable set of alternatives that serve the well-being of the community. This is the principle of "over poise," or balance that secures just rule in the British constitution and is adapted for the extended compound mixed republic by the framers. (2) The production of results that serve the common good of society somehow emerges even when only self-interest motivates individuals and groups. The "Invisible Hand" therewith appears, a metaphor favored by free market economists and coined by Adam Smith by blending the Christian notion of Providence and the

---

53. *Ibid.*, 144 (Lec. XII). Emphasis added.
54. Locke, *Second Treatise of Government*, Sec. 107; Montesquieu, *Spirit of Laws*, Bk. XI, Chap. 4; Weston, "Beginnings of the Classical Theory of the English Constitution," 133–44. See Pocock, *Machiavellian Moment*, Chap. 9, where the *Answer* is termed a "paradigmatic innovation," p. 361.

Stoic ideas of the cosmic rule of Reason and of universal harmony.[55] (3) The production of long-term good out of short-term or evident evil underscores the problem of theodicy.

The role of Providence in the affairs of the Revolution and founding is constantly acknowledged, often in the sense of "divine interposition,"[56] as in the various resolutions adopted by the Congress throughout the war. Such providential intervention is seen by Madison in the outcome of the Federal Convention, as he sums that up to Jefferson in the letter of October 24, 1787. "Each of these objects was pregnant with difficulties. The whole of them together formed a task more difficult than can be well concieved [*sic*] by those who were not concerned in the execution of it. Adding to these considerations the natural diversity of human opinions on all new and complicated subjects, it is impossible to consider the degree of concord which ultimately prevailed as *less than a miracle.*"[57]

The persuasive vanquishing of prejudice or self-interest by reason in deliberation, as in the Convention or other deliberative bodies, tends to blend the first and second manifestations of Providence. Madison shows his fondness for the symbolism of the invisible hand in the entertaining exchange he has with himself in first ghostwriting Washington's *First Inaugural Address* and then writing the response of the House of Representatives to it. Thus the pertinent passage in the *Inaugural Address* reads:

It would be peculiarly improper to omit in the first official Act, my fervent supplications to that Almighty Being who rules over the Universe, who presides in the Councils of Nations, and whose providential aids can supply every human defect, that his benediction may consecrate to the liberties and happiness of the people of the United States, a Government instituted by themselves for these essential purposes. . . . No people can be bound to acknowledge and adore the *invisible hand,* which conducts the Affairs of men more than the People of the United States. Every step, by which they have

55. Smith, *Theory of Moral Sentiments,* IV. 1. 10, p. 184; Smith, *Wealth of Nations,* IV. 2. 9. See Alec L. Macfie, "Invisible Hand of Jupiter," *Journal of the History of Ideas,* XXXII (1971), 595–99.

56. For example, the resolution adopted Aug. 3, 1784, proclaiming "a day of solemn prayer and thanksgiving to Almighty God" for the signing of the Paris peace treaty of 1783 formally ending the war. Ford *et al.* (eds.), *Journals of the Continental Congress,* XXVII, 627–28. Cf. Chap. 5 herein.

57. James Madison to Thomas Jefferson, Oct. 24, 1787, in Hutchinson, *et al.* (eds.), *Papers of James Madison,* X, 208. Emphasis added.

advanced to the character of an independent nation, seems to have been distinguished by some token of providential agency. And in the important revolution just accomplished in the system of their United Government, the tranquil deliberations and voluntary consent of so many distinct communities, from which the event has resulted, cannot be compared with the means by which most Governments have been established, without some return of pious gratitude along with an humble anticipation of the future blessings which the past seem to presage.[58]

The response to the President by the House of Representatives then includes these words.

You enjoy the highest, because the truest honor, of being the first Magistrate, by the unanimous choice, of the freest people on the face of the earth. . . . It is particularly suggested by the pious impressions under which you commence your administration, and the enlightened maxims by which you mean to conduct it. We feel with you the strongest Obligations to adore the INVISIBLE HAND which has led the American people through so many difficulties, to cherish a conscious responsibility for the destiny of Republican liberty, and to seek the only sure means of preserving and recommending the precious deposit, in a system of legislation, founded on the principles of an honest policy, and directed by the spirit of a diffusive patriotism.[59]

These words express the ritualistic formalities of the occasion, the momentous occasion when the specially favored community of America sets out for a destiny God will show them. The words are public words for public consumption, but the sentiments they express are authentic. The virtue of the community and leading of the invisible hand collaborate in fostering "Republican liberty" and the beginning of *novus ordo seclorum*. The mystery of such divine favor and human collaboration is a persistent theme of the period.

Witherspoon's famous sermon in May 1776 entitled *The Dominion of Providence Over the Passions of Men* reflects on the mysteries of theodicy, that the goodness of God yet permits evil and suffering from which may arise still greater good. These are matters that outrun rational comprehension. "There is an unsearchable depth in the divine counsels, which it is impossible for us to penetrate. It is the duty of every good man to place the most unlimited confidence in di-

---

58. *Address of the President to Congress*, April 30, 1789, *ibid.*, XII, 120–24 at 123. Emphasis added. On Madison's probable authorship of Washington's *Address* see *ibid.*, 120n.

59. *Address of the House of Representatives to the President*, May 5, 1789, in *ibid.*, XII, 132–34. Capitalization as in original.

vine wisdom, and to believe that those measures of providence that are most unintelligible to him, are yet planned with the same skill, and directed to the same great purposes as others, the reason and tendency of which he can explain in the clearest manner." [60]

Witherspoon is indebted to Leibniz, whose *Theodicy* is in his library and listed as recommended reading for students of moral philosophy. [61] He powerfully draws attention to an insufficiently noticed "distinction between the law of God and his purpose." The former enjoins love of God, neighbor, and purest righteousness; the latter orders all things for the greatest good. Thus, human wrath (the fruit of the passions), the "lust for domination," and entire depravity of men are "yet perfectly under the dominion of Jehovah." [62] Indeed, without sin there would be no suffering, no repentance of evil, no humility in the believer, or mercy and redemption through the Savior who came to heal the sick, not to call the righteous but sinners to repentance. Those (such as Thomas Paine) who deny the corruption of our nature also deny Christ. Thus, "the wrath of man in its most tempestuous rage, fulfills [God's] will, and finally promotes the good of his chosen." The greatest instance of this is the crucifixion itself,

that memorable event on which the salvation of believers in every age rests as its foundation, the death and sufferings of the Son of God. This the great adversary and all his agents and instruments prosecuted with unrelenting rage . . . when they scourged him with shame, when they had condemned him in judgment, and nailed him to the cross, how could they help esteeming their victory complete? But oh the unsearchable wisdom of God! They were perfecting the great design laid for the salvation of sinners. Our blessed Redeemer by his death finished his work, overcame principalities and powers, and made a shew [*sic*] of them openly, triumphing over them on the cross. [63]

As Leibniz argues in *Theodicy*, "the best plan is not always that which seeks to avoid evil, since it may happen that *the evil is accompanied by a greater good*." He cites Augustine and Thomas Aquinas, and remarks that "the ancients called Adam's fall *felix culpa*, a happy sin, because it had been retrieved with immense advantage by the Incar-

---

60. Witherspoon, *Works*, III, 20, 26.

61. Witherspoon, *Lectures on Moral Philosophy*, 187, 189 (Recapitulation and Appendix I).

62. Witherspoon, *Dominion of Providence*, in *Works*, III, 18. *Ibid.*, 18–22.

63. *Ibid.*, 26–28; see pp. 23–24 for the note attacking Paine's ridicule of original sin.

nation of the Son of God, who has given to the universe something nobler than anything that ever would have been among creatures except for it. . . . A world with evil might be better than a world without evil; but I have gone even farther . . . and have even proved that this universe must be in reality better than every other possible universe."[64]

III

The "great rights of mankind" for which Madison contends in the First Congress as the basis for the Bill of Rights are for a mankind and world conceived in the profound and complex ways limned in preceding pages. What divides Federalists from Anti-Federalists is far less significant than what unites them as Americans, namely, the sacred cause of liberty and the broad understanding of human purpose and the ultimate reality that form the shared common sense of those subjects. Differences between these rival parties arise primarily from uncertainties, distrust, and questions of means to acceptable ends. If it is right to say that Madison "made a mistake" in the Convention in not sponsoring a Bill of Rights in concert with George Mason, then it is a tactical and not a strategic or theoretical mistake. Accomplished politician that he is, Madison scarcely breaks stride in repairing the damage. As Edmund Pendleton states the matter: "There is no quarrel between government and liberty. The war is between government and licentiousness, faction, turbulence, and other violations of the rules of society, to preserve liberty."[65] The Anti-Federalists are *for* virtue and sacred liberty (not vulgar liberty) no less than the Federalists. If the "creed" attributed to Daniel Shays and his associates had been prevalent with any substantial number of reputable people in

64. Leibniz, "Theodicy: Abridgment of the Argument Reduced to Syllogistic Form" [1710], in Wiener (ed.), *Leibniz: Selections*, 510.
65. Edmund Pendleton quoted by Herbert J. Storing, "Constitution and the Bill of Rights," in *How Does the Constitution Secure Rights?*, ed. Robert A. Goldwin and William A. Schambra (Washington, D.C., 1985), 28. Edmund Pendleton was president of the Virginia Convention to ratify the Constitution. That Madison "made a mistake" is stated in the same volume by Robert A. Rutland, "How the Constitution Protects our Rights: A Look at the Seminal Years," *ibid.*, 1. See Jonathan Elliott (ed.), *Debates in the Several State Conventions on the Adoption of the Federal Constitution* (2nd ed.; 1836; rpr. New York, 1974), III, for the Virginia Convention's proceedings.

America at the time, then anti-property, anti-Christian, French-style Jacobin liberty might have emerged as a standard. Yet this was hardly the case, and John Pocock is plainly correct in reproving Judith Shklar on the point, as well as any others who may share the misconception. "English and American history [must] be studied in its own terms, which are Whig and not Jacobin."[66] American liberty is not French liberty.

Other misconceptions almost as misleading swirl around our subject. Among the most controverted is the meaning of "the Laws of Nature and Nature's God" in the Declaration and the liberties of Americans secured in descent from that phrase in the Constitution and Bill of Rights. Short of providential interposition, there is little hope that I can resolve the differences among contending parties in a few lines here—or even in many lines elsewhere. The spirit of sectarian strife is upon us, and the remarks of Benjamin Franklin in his conciliatory speech at the end of the Convention come to mind.

Most men indeed as well as most sects in Religion, think themselves in possession of all truth, and that whereever [*sic*] others differ from them it is so far error. Steele, a Protestant in a Dedication tells the Pope, that the only difference between our Churches in their opinions of the certainty of their doctrines is, the Church of Rome is infallible and the Church of England is never wrong. But though many private persons think almost as highly of their own infallibility as of that of their sect, few express it so naturally as a certain french [*sic*] lady, who in a dispute with her sister, said "I don't know how it happens, Sister but I meet with no body but myself, that's always in the right—*Il n'y a que moi qui a toujours raison.*"[67]

Without yielding to the temptation of declaring what is patently absurd and who is egregiously mistaken, I content myself with the following comments.

If we accept the standard of understanding the Americans of the period as they understood themselves, the meaning of the controverted phrase and the "unalienable Rights" connected with it harmonizes with the Christian religious and Whig political consensus that prevailed in the country at the time. We do not meet with any John

66. Pocock, "*Machiavellian Moment* Revisited," 72.
67. Benjamin Franklin on Sept. 17, 1787, in the Convention; Farrand (ed.), *Records of the Federal Convention of 1787,* II, 642.

Locke in sheep's clothes teaching the natural rights doctrine of the wolf Thomas Hobbes among influential American writers of the time. As far as we can usefully generalize about a consensus in an admittedly pluralistic community, Locke generally is read by Americans as a Christian Whig and an opponent of Hobbes no less than of Filmer. The remark Leo Strauss makes regarding Edmund Burke's natural law and natural rights teaching can properly be extended *at least* to the eighteenth-century Americans' reading of John Locke on those subjects. "He spoke of the state of nature, of the rights of nature or of the rights of man, and of the social compact or of the artificial character of the commonwealth. But he may be said to integrate these notions into a classical or Thomistic framework."[68]

I have stressed "at least" because recent scholarship has powerfully put before us the view that Locke's natural law and natural rights theory is *nothing less* than "the Thomist framework of positive natural law" itself and that this "constitutes the basis of his theory."[69] As was noticed in Chapter Two, Locke's ambiguity served both his conciliatory, pacifying purpose and his concealment of theoretical intentions. Thus, Locke *may* have been read quite accurately by Americans in the formative period as a spokesman for traditional Christian natural law and rights going back to Aquinas' and Jean Gerson's medieval theories.[70] In this guise, Locke was the conservative attempting to thwart the revolution of the Stuarts, whose absolutist divine right claims as advanced by Filmer were the true innovation. This general view of the Glorious Revolution was also that of Burke. Read in this way, the Ancient Constitution was preserved in 1688, although not very satisfactorily from Locke's perspective. In Burke's words, 1688 was a revolution "not made but prevented."[71]

In short, Americans of the founding generation relied especially

---

68. Strauss, *Natural Right and History,* 296. It should be stressed that a sharply different view of Locke's teaching is presented by Strauss than the one offered herein; see *ibid.,* 165–251.

69. James Tully, *A Discourse on Property: John Locke and His Adversaries* (Cambridge, England, 1980), 153; see also pp. 58, 64–65, 72, 111, 120, 157.

70. *Ibid.,* 65; also Tuck, *Natural Rights Theories,* 24–26, 50–56, 168. See John Dunn, *Political Thought of John Locke: An Historical Account of the Argument of the 'Two Treatises of Government'* (Cambridge, England, 1969); and John Dunn, *Political Obligation in its Historical Context: Essays in Political Theory* (Cambridge, England, 1980), Chap. 4.

71. Tully, *A Discourse on Property,* 157–58; Stanlis (ed.), *Edmund Burke,* 518.

upon the Bible, and a John Locke assimilated to it in holding that their sacred or Republican liberty derived from transcendence and a true higher law of the kind spoken of by Sir Edward Coke in *Calvin's Case* (1609).[72] On this widely embraced view, there *is* this higher law of God and nature intrinsic to man as the creature of the heavenly Creator and known to him through revelation, reason, and through experience of *his natural inclination to the good*. Even Blackstone, in the generation of the founders and despite acceptance of parliamentary sovereignty, affirms that this law is coeval with mankind, dictated by God himself, and that *no laws* are of any validity if contrary to it, since all their force derives directly or indirectly from the natural and divine order.[73] In so far as rights are "natural," they rest on claims that can be asserted consequent to the nature of man and of the creation in their dependence upon God. The divine and natural orders are logically prior and ontologically superior to the social and political orders. Hence, the rights that are natural as preserving the integrity of the creature in its participation in being are intrinsic to man as dimensions of his essence or humanity and are prior to political arrangements in their conventional aspects.

Leaving aside the details of a complicated congeries of theories intertwined in the political debate, the Cokean and Lockean presentation brings natural, eternal, and divine law together as higher law and natural—or unalienable or absolute—rights. As Edward Corwin writes, "The great constitutional struggle with the Stuarts . . . enabled Coke to build upon Fortescue, and it enabled Locke to build upon Coke."[74] This process was facilitated by a "fresh influx" of natural law influences from the Continent, including not least of all the revival of Thomism as that process culminated in the work of the Spanish Jesuit Francisco Suárez (1548–1617), whose writings were

72. Quoted in Chap. 5 on p. 158 herein. It should be noted that Coke is echoing Augustine *Confessions* II. 4. 9: "Theft is punished by Thy law, O Lord, and the law written in the hearts of men, which iniquity effaces not" (trans. E. B. Pusey); the same passage is quoted in Thomas Aquinas *Summa Theologica* I–II. q. 94, a. 6. Corwin's "higher law" argument is continued more recently by Thomas C. Grey, "Origins of the Unwritten Constitution: Fundamental Law in American Revolutionary Thought," *Stanford Law Review*, XXX (1982), 49–83 at 57.

73. Blackstone, *Commentaries*, I, 41; *cf.* the entire passage, *ibid.*, 38–44. I have herein used the abridged edition and cited standard pagination, *viz.*, *ibid.*, ed. George Chase (New York, 1882).

74. Corwin, *"Higher Law" Background of American Constitutional Law*, 46.

widely read and quoted in the House of Commons in the seventeenth century.[75] Americans were beneficiaries of these developments and built not *merely* on Locke but upon the broad Western political tradition rearticulated in his and countless others' work in memorable fashion by English Whigs.[76]

Due to the similarity of theoretical views, whatever their genealogy, it becomes important here to recall that for Thomas Aquinas himself the first principle of the practical reason and foundation of natural law is the *Good*. All things seek the good. From this arises the first precept of natural law (from which all others follow), that *"good is to be done and ensued, and evil is to be avoided."* This elementary natural inclination is perfected through reason as the form of man's being. The good so apprehended and perfected ascends in the order of man's natural inclinations, beginning with the *first* end or good all men seek, "preservation of [his] own being, according to its nature; and by reason of this inclination, whatever is a means of preserving human life and of warding off its obstacles belongs to the natural law." Other precepts of natural law stem from man's inclination to propagate and foster the well-being of his offspring, which belongs to his animal nature; and that which belongs to the reason which is proper to man as his distinction, the natural inclination "to know the truth about God and to live in society."[77]

Similarly in Locke, the center of the stage belongs to *"the Fundamental Law of Nature, Man being to be preserved,* as much as pos-

---

75. *Ibid.*; Tuck, *Natural Rights Theories*, 50–57; Tully, *A Discourse on Property*, 64–68 and citations therein. Francisco Suárez's writings figured, for example, in the impeachment of Roger Manwaring in John Pym's speech of May 1628; see Robert C. Johnson, Maija J. Cole, et al. (eds.), *Proceedings in Parliament, 1628* (New Haven, 1977–83), III, 408–13.

76. While it is doubtless true that the old notion of American thought as consisting almost exclusively of Locke and the Bible during the Revolution is untenable, both of these sources remain *centrally important* nonetheless. This is true despite the great flowering of scholarship in the field, one of whose effects is "a sophisticated understanding of eighteenth-century republicanism [that] has emerged in American historiography," in Robert H. Shalhope's words; see Adair, *Fame and the Founding Fathers*, xxv. See Pocock's excellent discussion in "*Machiavellian Moment* Revisited," 65–71, where he writes of "a double displacement of John Locke." *Cf.*, however, Donald S. Lutz, "Relative Influence of European Writers," 189–97, which demonstrates Locke to be *the* most cited political philosopher by American writers in the Revolutionary period. As for the Bible, a full one-third of *all* citations in political writing in America from 1760 to 1805 refers to it.

77. Quoted and summarized primarily from Thomas Aquinas *Summa Theologica* I–II. q. 94. a. 2. as given in Bigongiari (ed.), *Political Ideas of St. Thomas Aquinas*, 44–46.

sible." Through the sinuosities of his ambivalent account in the *Second Treatise of Government*, this fundamental natural law structures the formation of society and the creation of government as artifacts of liberty and reason for the "*chief end*" of uniting men "for the mutual *Preservation* of their Lives, Liberties and Estates, which I call by the general Name, *Property*."[78] The natural "*State of Liberty*" out of which these works of liberty and reason arise "is not a *State of Licence*," Locke writes,

> though Man in that State have an uncontroleable [*sic*] Liberty, to dispose of his Person or Possessions, yet he has not Liberty to destroy himself, or so much as any Creature in his Possession, but where some nobler use, than its bare preservation calls for it. The *State of Nature* has a Law of Nature to govern it, which obliges every one: And Reason, which is that Law, teaches all Mankind, who will but consult it, that being all equal and independent, no one ought to harm another in his Life, Health, Liberty, or Possessions. For Men being all the Workmanship of one Omnipotent, and infinitely wise Maker; All the Servants of one Sovereign Master, sent into the World by his order and about his business, they are his Property, whose Workmanship they are, made to last during his, not one anothers Pleasure. . . . Every one as he is *bound to preserve himself,* and not to quit his station wilfully; so by the like reason when his own Preservation comes not in competition, ought he, as much as he can, *to preserve the rest of Mankind,* and may not unless it be to do Justice on an Offender, take away, or impair the life, or what tends to the Preservation of the Life, the Liberty, Health, Limb or Goods of another.[79]

From the natural *law* to seek the good by acting rationally to preserve one's being, his fellow men and other creatures as far as practicable, and serving God's purposes in creating him, man derives the natural *rights* to life, liberty, and estate which Locke calls property. The law is the basis of the rights, and it limits their scope to *good* ends or those ends that serve one's own, and the community's, well-being. Natural law also limits the scope of human law and its execution to the preserving of the community and all its members. If these limits systematically are violated by the establishment of arbitrary government or perversion of a true government to the exploitation of the community and all its members, then resistance is not only men's

---

78. Locke, *Two Treatises of Government*, 296–97, 367–68; see *Second Treatise*, Secs. 17, 124, 123, respectively. Emphasis and capitalization as in original.
79. *Ibid.*, 288–89; *Second Treatise*, Sec. 6.

right but also their duty. Such destruction of men is contrary to the true grounds of social and political order, namely, the preservation of the people's well-being. It violates the terms of the trust and delegated power of the governors, so allegiance to them is *ipso facto* dissolved. But it is a violation of the obligation of natural law and of one's duty to God as well. For even though each man is his own property as a self and all that constitutes it (life, liberty, estate), he is not *sole* proprietor but is instead dependent upon God as his maker. He cannot surrender what he does not totally possess; and since he is dependent upon God as his Creator and (consequently) as God's property, he cannot completely surrender himself to the arbitrary or destructive will of another since he does not completely control his being. Thus, the right of resistance to tyrants, the "appeal to heaven" in Locke, emerges as a *duty* to serve higher law over positive human law, to serve God over man as the demand of reason and justice. The Lockean *self* participates in divine Being in that it would not be what it is (a nature) without God's gift and formation. Man participates in the hierarchy of being.

As Elisha Williams in eighteenth-century America summarizes matters, "*Reason* teaches Men to *join in Society,* to unite together into a Commonwealth under some Form or other, to make a Body of Law agreeable to the Law of Nature, and institute one common Power to see them observed."

The Fountain and Original of all civil Power is from the People, and is certainly instituted for their Sakes. . . . It is nothing but *their own Good* can be any rational Inducement to it: and to suppose they either should or would do it on any other, is to suppose rational Creatures ought to change their State with a Design to make it worse. And *that Good* which is such a State they find a need of, is no other than a *greater Security of Enjoyment of what belonged to them.* . . . *That greater Security* therefore of Life, Liberty, Money, Lands, Houses, Family, and the like, which may be all comprehended under that of *Person* and *Property,* is the *sole End* of all *civil Government.*

I mean not that all civil Governments (as so called) are thus constituted: (tho' the *British* and some few other Nations are through a merciful Providence so happy as to have such). There are too too many arbitrary Governments in the World, where the People don't make their own Laws. These are not properly speaking *Governments* but *Tyrannies;* and are absolutely against the *Law of* God and *Nature.* But I am considering Things as they be in their own Nature, what Reason teaches concerning them: and herein have given a *short Sketch* of what the celebrated Mr. *Locke* in *his Treatise of Government* has largely demonstrated; and in which it is justly to be presumed all are agreed who understand the Natural Rights of Mankind.[80]

IV

The natural and divine rights called "unalienable" by Jefferson in the Declaration had been called "absolute" by Sir William Blackstone a decade before when *Commentaries on the Laws of England* first began to appear (1765–1769). Perhaps there was something sinister in this terminology, and Thomas Jefferson and James Wilson thought so, especially since Blackstone upheld potential absolutism in the form of parliamentary sovereignty.[81] The root of the rather technical matter is that Blackstone follows Grotius and Pufendorf in attributing absolute natural rights to men. Yet (contrary to Locke) since they are absolute and are completely their property as human beings, they have absolute control over them and so can *relinquish* them absolutely to society and government. This smacks of a Hobbesian and Filmerian outcome to natural rights teaching, since there is no appeal to any higher law or rights derivative from it as a *limit* on human

---

80. Philathes [Elisha Williams?], *Essential Rights of Protestants: A Seasonable Plea for the Liberty of Conscience, and the Right of Private Judgment in Matters of Religion, Without any Control from Human Authority* (Boston, 1744), 4–5, rpr. in Sandoz (ed.), *Political Sermons of the American Founding*, 51–118. Emphasis, spelling, and capitalization as in original.

81. See James Wilson, *On Municipal Law*, in Hyneman and Lutz (eds.), *American Political Writing*, II, 1264–98; also Randolph G. Adams, *Political Ideas of the American Revolution: Britannic-American Contributions to the Problem of Imperial Organization, 1765–1775*, (3rd ed., with a commentary by Merrill Jensen; New York, 1958), Chaps. 7 and 8. In what may have been his last letter to James Madison, Thomas Jefferson wrote of the securing of faculty members for the University of Virginia. "In the selection of our Law Professor, we must be rigorously attentive to his political principles. You will recollect that before the Revolution, Coke Littleton was the universal elementary book of law students, and a sounder Whig never wrote, nor of profounder learning in the orthodox doctrines of the British constitution, or in what were called English liberties. You remember also that our lawyers were then all Whigs. But when his black-letter text, and uncouth but cunning learning got out of fashion, and the honeyed Mansfieldism of Blackstone became the students' hornbook, from that moment, that profession (the nursery of our Congress) began to slide into toryism, and nearly all the young brood of lawyers now are of that hue. They suppose themselves, indeed, to be Whigs, because they no longer know what Whigism or republicanism means. It is in our seminary that that vestal flame is to be kept alive; it is thence it is to spread anew over our own and the sister states." Thomas Jefferson to James Madison, Feb. 17, 1826, in Koch and Peden (eds.), *Life and Selected Writings of Thomas Jefferson*, 726–27. Jefferson died on July 4, 1826, as did John Adams.

positive law or administration. Locke's theory plausibly can be read as avoiding this by recurring to the traditional, medieval teaching at which we have just glanced, whereby man remains God's property and is therefore *bound* to observe the good, consequent to this unalterable ontological relationship. And the American founders read Locke in this way. By this circumstance, not only is all law subservient to higher law but rulers are also bound to adhere to the principle of *salus populi* and the good commanded by it. Gratian (*fl.* 1140), near the beginning of the revival of Roman law in the West, boiled all law down to one timeless principle. As quoted in Aquinas: "'The natural law is what is contained in the Law and the Gospel . . . by which everyone is commanded to do to others as he would be done by.'" And John Selden, during the Petition of Right debate in the House of Commons in 1628, elaborated the ancient maxim in a way the American founders would later approve when he asserted, "*Salus populi suprema lex, et libertas popula summa salus populi,*" the welfare of the people is the supreme law, and the liberty of the people the greatest welfare of the people.[82]

Despite rhetoric apparently leading toward an acceptance of higher law and natural rights as restraining government, Blackstone effectively negates any such limitation on sovereign power as Locke insists upon and leaves only a faint recollection of the notion of the directive power of higher law as formulated by Aquinas. Blackstone writes: "It is requisite to the very essence of a law, that it be made by the supreme power. Sovereignty and legislature are indeed controvertible terms: one cannot subsist without the other."[83] "In general, all mankind will agree that government should be reposed in such persons, in whom those qualities are most likely to be found, the perfection of which is among the attributes of him who is emphatically styled the Supreme Being; the three grand requisites, I mean of wisdom, of goodness, and of power: wisdom to discern the real interest of the

---

82. Thomas Aquinas *Summa Theologica* I–II. q. 94. a. 4. *ad* 1, in Bigongiari (ed.), *Political Ideas of St. Thomas Aquinas*, 50. This is to say that the Golden Rule is the foundation of *all* law, *i.e.*, Matt. 7:12. See Brian Tierney, *Religion, Law, and the Growth of Constitutional Thought, 1150–1650* (Cambridge, England, 1982), 13–19, 108. For John Selden's words see Johnson, Cole, *et al.* (eds.), *Proceedings in Parliament, 1628*, II, 183; *cf.* pp. 173–74. I am grateful to Professor Paul K. Christianson for this citation.

83. Blackstone, *Commentaries*, I, 46.

community; goodness, to endeavour always to pursue that real interest; and strength, or power, to carry this knowledge and intention into action. These are the natural foundations of sovereignty, and these are the requisites that ought to be found in every well constituted frame of government." Whatever the particulars of various forms of government, and however each began "or by what right soever they subsist, there is and must be in all of them a supreme, irresistible, absolute, uncontrolled authority, in which the *jura summi imperii,* or the rights of sovereignty reside." England's mixed constitution is then extolled and the virtues of the Almighty correlated with the three elements composing it: the people or Democracy and Commons with goodness, the aristocracy and Lords with wisdom, the monarchy and executive with power.[84]

In writing of the *leges scriptae,* or written laws of the kingdom, Blackstone comes at length to the rule (laid down by Coke) that "acts of parliament that are impossible to be performed are of no validity. . . . that acts of parliament contrary to reason are void. But if the parliament will positively enact a thing to be done which is unreasonable, I know of no power in the ordinary forms of the constitution that is vested with authority to control it; and the examples usually alleged in support of this sense of the rule do none of them prove, that, where the main object of a statute is unreasonable, the judges are at liberty to reject it; for that were to set the judicial power above that of the legislature, which would be subversive of all government."[85]

The admiration of Americans for British liberty as their shared birthright is a steady theme throughout the period of the founding, and Blackstone lucidly summarizes just what British liberty is in the opening chapter of the *Commentaries.* Despite the tension between liberty and authority that will be resolved in practice in favor of parliamentary supremacy in the final analysis, Blackstone affirms the centrality of "the *absolute* rights of individuals . . . which every man is entitled to enjoy, whether out of society or in it. . . . For the principal aim of society is to protect individuals in the enjoyment of those absolute rights, which were vested in them by the immutable laws of

84. *Ibid.,* 47–52.
85. *Ibid.,* 91.

nature; but which could not be preserved in peace without the mutual assistance and intercourse, which is gained by the institution of friendly and social communities. Hence it follows, that the first and primary end of human laws is to maintain and regulate these *absolute* rights of individuals."[86] These absolute rights are also known as the

natural liberty of mankind. This natural liberty consists properly in a power of acting as one thinks fit, without any restraint or control, unless by the law of nature; being a right inherent in us by birth, and one of the gifts of God to man at his creation, when he endued him with the faculty of freewill. But every man, when he enters society, gives up a part of his natural liberty, as the price of so valuable a purchase; and, in consideration of receiving the advantages of mutual commerce, obliges himself to conform to those laws, which the community has thought proper to establish.

This, then, results in the establishment of "political . . . or civil liberty, which is that of a member of society," and this is nothing "other than natural liberty, so far restrained by human laws (and no farther) as is necessary and expedient for the general advantage of the public."[87]

Liberty as law is embodied in the English constitution, common law, and statutes in the transition from absolute natural rights to the "absolute rights of every Englishman (which, taken in a political and extensive sense, are usually called their liberties), as they are founded on nature and reason, so they are coeval with our form of government."[88] In the phrase later adapted by Madison, Blackstone explains that these "rights of all mankind" formerly were universally enjoyed but had been corrupted almost everywhere else to remain only in force in the world as "the rights of the people of England." "And these may be reduced to three principal or primary articles; the right of personal security, the right of personal liberty, and the right of private property: because, as there is no other known method of compulsion or of abridging man's natural free will, but by infringement or diminution of one or other of these important rights, the preservation of these, inviolate, may justly be said to include the pres-

86. *Ibid.*, 123–24. Emphasis as in original.
87. *Ibid.*, 125.
88. *Ibid.*, 127.

ervation of our civil immunities in their largest and most extensive sense." [89]

These three primary rights are augmented by five other "subordinate" or "auxiliary rights" which serve to protect and maintain the subject's absolute rights: the constitution, powers and privileges of parliament; the limitations on the king's prerogative; the availability of courts and judicial remedies to redress injuries; the right to petition for redress in unusual cases; and finally, the right to have arms so as to meet emergency threats to self-preservation by exercising the natural right of resistance to oppression "when the sanctions of society and laws are found insufficient." "And all these rights and liberties it is our birthright to enjoy entire; unless where the laws of our country have laid them under necessary restraints. . . . For all of us have it in our choice to do every thing that a good man would desire to do; and are restrained from nothing but what would be pernicious either to ourselves or our fellow-citizens." Montesquieu is cited as rightly stating "that the English is the only nation in the world where political and civil liberty is the direct end of its constitution." [90]

V

In American eyes, the sun of liberty shooting its beams of rights through the pages of Blackstone is clouded o'er with the pale cast of corruption. His doctrine is better than the ministry's performance, but even the doctrine itself (especially when read with the words of the Declaratory Act drumming in their ears: "the power to bind in all cases whatsoever") becomes deeply subversive of true English liberty and the Ancient Constitution upon examination. Law as simply the *command* of the sovereign, whether proceeding on the basis of Stuart divine right claims or parliamentary sovereignty as outlined by Blackstone, especially absent respresentation of the affected community,

89. *Ibid.*, 129.
90. *Ibid.*, 141–45. Montesquieu, *Spirit of Laws*, XI. 5. and 6: "One nation there is also in the world that has for the direct end of its constitution political liberty." "The political liberty of the subject is a tranquility of mind arising from the opinion each person has of his safety. In order to have this liberty, it is requisite the government be so constituted as one man need not be afraid of another" (trans. Thomas Nugent). The Hobbesian cast of Montesquieu's definition may be noted.

stinks of tyranny. The divorce of human law from natural and divine law, which later comes to be called Positivism and is essentially the *will* of the sovereign, reduces politics to power and strips away the moral and ontological moorings of governance that Blackstone himself implicitly deprecates and explicitly sweeps aside as "airy metaphysical notions . . . started by fanciful writers."[91] Legal philosophy is on the road to John Austin's utility deity and the view that "to say that human laws which conflict with the Divine law are not binding, that is to say, are not laws, is to talk stark nonsense. The most pernicious laws, and therefore those which are most opposed to the will of God, have been and are continually enforced as laws by judicial tribunals. . . . The existence of law is one thing; its merit or demerit another."[92]

Perhaps this is the simple truth of the matter, but it is unacceptable truth to Americans of the founding generation. Rejection arises from multiple sources, not all of them consistent with one another but all fervent and determined not to embrace what all called the hateful principles of passive obedience and arbitrary government. In the Revolution, from the first thunderbolt of James Otis' mighty speech against the writs of assistance in the early 1760s down to the bitter quarrel over ratification of the Constitution and its merits, the Americans are clear that it is a *rule of law* and not of men they want, one wherein liberty is served and justice of the highest order institutionalized as the *real* criterion of positive law. The civil and religious leadership of the country set themselves against a declension of Truth in the world, whether civil or religious. In the rather amazing process, they managed to decry tyranny in a three-penny tax on tea (as Madison remarks in his old age) and trace its origins as policy not only to the ministry and George III but also to the Stuarts of the previous century, back through the centuries to the Normans who subverted the Ancient Constitution woven by the descendants of Brutus of Troy (as Coke thought) and the ancient Saxons (as Otis and Jefferson, not to mention Montesquieu believed). Thus, not only do Otis and those after him in the period quote Scripture and the classics but also the

91. Blackstone, *Commentaries*, II, 3.
92. John Austin, *Lectures on Jurisprudence*, ed. R. Campbell, (5th ed; London, 1885) I, 214–15.

historical argument. James Otis trumpeted these views with matchless power.

The law of nature was not of man's making, nor is it in his power to mend it or alter its course. He can only perform and keep or disobey and break it. The last is never done with impunity, even in this life, if it is any punishment for a man to feel himself depraved, to find himself degraded by his own folly and wickedness from the rank of a virtuous and good *man* to that of a brute, or to be transformed from the friend, perhaps father, of his country to a devouring lion or tiger.

Otis then continues as follows:

Few people have extended their inquiries after the foundation of any of their rights beyond a charter from the crown. There are others who think when they have got back to *Magna Carta* [A.D. 1215] that they are at the beginning of all things. They imagine themselves on the borders of chaos . . . and see creation rising out of the unformed mass or from nothing. Hence, say they, spring all the rights of men and of citizens. But liberty was better understood and more fully enjoyed by our ancestors before the coming in of the first Norman tyrants than ever after, till it was found necessary for the salvation of the kingdom to combat the arbitrary and wicked proceedings of the Stuarts.[93]

The commonplace of the British constitution that "in an Act of Parliament every Man's consent is included"[94] held no validity in American eyes on the impunged principle of virtual representation rooted in the electoral corruption derided by Old Whig writers as Robinarchy and now offered the colonials.[95] Consent has to be real and efficacious in linking the few with the many in all matters of policy, but most especially in matters of taxation if sacred liberty is to be preserved. The matter of taxing and property are not only the issues

93. James Otis, *Rights of British Colonies Asserted and Proved* (Boston, 1764), in Bailyn (ed.), *Pamphlets of the American Revolution*, I, 441. For the Old Saxon constitution see *ibid.*, 52–54 and the literature cited therein. Also Demophilus [George Bryan?], *Genuine Principles of the Ancient Saxon, or English Constitution* (Philadelphia, 1776), in Hyneman and Lutz (eds.), *American Political Writing*, I, 340–67: "That beautiful system, formed (as Montesquieu says,) in the German woods, was introduced into England about the year four hundred and fifty," p. 341. See Pocock, *Ancient Constitution*, 40–42, for Coke's Brutus of Troy and the origins of Parliament in King Arthur's Knights of the Roundtable.
94. Sir Francis Bacon, *New Abridgement of the Law*, I, 79; quoted in James H. Kettner, *Development of American Citizenship, 1608–1870* (Chapel Hill, N.C., 1978), 32n.
95. Bailyn, *Ideological Origins of the American Revolution*, 44–54 and *passim*. See Hatch, *Sacred Cause of Liberty*, Chap. 7, "Robinocracy."

of the Revolution but also the point of honor and test of constitutional right reason and true law in the British tradition, as Burke remarks.[96] While the Constitution of 1787 attends, as earlier said, to all the salient issues demanded in the name of liberty against England, both the provision for direct taxation and the scheme of representation are heated subjects of debate during the ratification controversy since they are seen to jeopardize the people's rights. It is not solely over the absence of a Bill of Rights that ratification is strongly contested. In fact, defusing the clamor of the Anti-Federalists by conceding a Bill of Rights is something of a sop and harmless concession to blunt an attack that threatens the entire scheme of effective national government, as Madison and his associates know. Everybody favors liberty and essential political rights, but not everyone favors a powerful national government at the expense of the states' autonomy.[97]

VI

To notice the pragmatic spirit of the Federalist decision to support a Bill of Rights in the First Congress is to be reminded that politics is a human affair and the art of the possible. It is not to denigrate motives, least of all those of James Madison. He led the drive for constitutional amendments in the new government by introducing the subject into Washington's *First Inaugural Address* as a legislative matter of vital importance to the country and by forcing the issue in a House of Representatives preoccupied with the urgent problems of inventing institutions and procedures to start the country operating under the Constitution. It is sometimes hard to remember that grandiose founding fathers such as Madison, Jefferson, and Washington are consummate politicians, too. To Madison's litany of objections to amending the Constitution and his doubt that any such "parchment barriers" to abuse of liberty will do significant good, for example, Jefferson crisply responds point by point in advocating such amendments. "Half a loaf is better than no bread. If we cannot secure all our rights, let us

96. Stanlis (ed.), *Edmund Burke*, 158–59, 170–75.
97. See Storing, "Constitution and the Bill of Rights," in Goldwin and Schambra (eds.), *How Does the Constitution Secure Rights?*, 19; see also Herbert J. Storing with Murray Dry, *What the Anti-Federalists Were For* (Chicago, 1981).

secure what we can. . . . A brace the more will often keep up the building which would have fallen with that brace the less." [98]

Madison, in the course of debate on the floor of the House, subtly reminds his colleagues what all know, and he and his Baptist supporters at home clearly appreciate, that "amending the Constitution" in the several ways pending before them is *"required by our constituents."* He continues: "Have not the people been told that the rights of conscience, the freedom of speech, the liberty of the press, and trial by jury, were in jeopardy; that they ought not to adopt the constitution until those important rights were secured to them. . . . as *a friend to what is attainable,* I would limit [our proposals] to the plain, simple, and important security that has been required." Shortly after he explains to a correspondent, "If amendts. had not been proposed from the federal side of the House, the proposition would have come within three days, from the adverse side. It is certainly best that they should appear to be the free gift of the friends of the Constitution rather than extorted by the address & weight of its enemies." By so proceeding, the Bill of Rights being thus offered "will kill the opposition every where . . . putting an end to the disaffection to the Govt." [99]

While eleven states have by this time ratified the Constitution, a number did so only because of a tacit understanding that suitable amendments would be forthcoming from the First Congress. Massachusetts ratified by a vote of 187 to 168 after the Federalists agreed to a proposal for a bill of rights. Maryland ratified in April of 1789 after proposing a bill of rights. South Carolina ratified and attached a list of proposed amendments to the Constitution. Virginia was among the last four states to ratify, and Patrick Henry led the opposition. Madison served in the ratification convention and was certain that Virginia only finally ratified because of the Federalist promise to seek amendments securing rights. Even so, the vote was eighty-nine for to seventy-nine against; a switch of six votes would have blocked ratification. New York at last ratified by a mere three-vote margin, de-

98. Thomas Jefferson to James Madison, Mar. 15, 1789, in Hutchinson, *et al.* (eds.), *Papers of James Madison,* XII, 14.

99. From the *Congressional Register* for Aug. 15, 1789, II, 215–16, *ibid.,* XII, 342. James Madison to Richard Peters, Aug. 19, 1789, *ibid.,* 347.

spite the mighty efforts of Publius. North Carolina and Rhode Island remained out of the Union, the former refusing to act until a bill of rights was proposed by Congress; the state convention adjourned until November, at which time it reconvened and ratified. Rhode Island finally called its convention and ratified in 1790.[100] In sum, eight states offered over two hundred amendments during ratification deliberations, including nearly one hundred different substantive provisions. Madison managed to incorporate into his initial proposal to the House of Representatives fourteen out of twenty-two amendments proposed by four or more states. He was more than a mere draftsman, however, and played a highly creative role in combining and refining concepts and language so that the Federal Bill of Rights would be "both an eloquent inventory of basic rights and a legally enforceable safeguard of those rights."[101]

The task of establishing liberty as law, in James Madison's eyes, is substantially achieved by the provisions of the Constitution as woven together with an institutional design that serves to ally human nature and the cause of good government. The theory of scientific government there in place, along with the necessary qualities in the country and the people, augur well for justice and liberty, not least of all because the Constitution and laws made pursuant to it are the supreme law of the land. Madison's distrust of the states as repositories of sound government leaves him unsure, however, that liberty and justice in government can be maintained without additional power in the national government, especially since the veto of state legislation had been rejected by the Federal Convention. Faced with the political necessity of a Federal Bill of Rights, he accepts from Jefferson ideas that promise to make such a set of additions to the Constitution substantively desirable after all.

The general reliance on jealousy and adversarial checking and balancing, Jefferson thinks, will be enhanced by a Bill of Rights when viewed from the division of powers between the state governments

100. See Howard, *Road From Runnymede*, 224–31. For Madison and his Baptist supporters see James Madison to George Eve, Jan. 2, 1789, in Hutchinson, *et al.* (eds.), *Papers of James Madison*, XI, 404–406; James Madison to George Washington, Nov. 20, 1789, *ibid.*, XII, 451–54.
101. Schwartz, *Great Rights of Mankind*, 156–59.

and the national government. It is true, Jefferson agrees with Madison, that the "limited powers of the federal government & jealousy of the subordinate governments afford a security which exists in no other instance. . . . The jealousy of the subordinate governments is a precious reliance. But observe that those governments are only agents. They must have principles furnished them whereon to found their opposition. The declaration of rights will be the text whereby they will try all the acts of the federal government. In this view it is necessary to the federal government also: as by the same text they may try the opposition of the subordinate governments." And Madison has overlooked a cardinal point:

In the arguments in favor of a declaration of rights, you omit one which has great weight with me, the legal check which it puts into the hands of the judiciary. This is a body, which if rendered independent, & kept strictly to their own department merits great confidence for their learning & integrity. In fact what degree of confidence would be too much for a body composed of such men as Wythe, Blair & Pendleton? On such characters like these the "civium ardor prava jubentium" would make no impression. [Horace: "The man tenacious of his purpose in a righteous cause is not shaken from his firm resolve by the frenzy of his fellow-citizens bidding what is wrong."] [102]

These arguments are not forgotten in Madison's speech of June 8, 1789, in the House of Representatives but in fact structure his presentation. What is important to notice is Madison's logic. The people expect the Congress to amend the Constitution so it will "expressly declare the great rights of mankind secured under this constitution." This is not unreasonable to do since "all power is subject to abuse." It is proper "to satisfy the public mind that their liberties will be perpetual, and this without endangering any part of the constitution, which is considered as essential to the existence of the government by those who promoted its adoption." After listing proposed amendments, Madison points to the misconceptions about protections of liberty under the British constitution. The principal defect is that only the executive is restrained and the legislature remains omnipotent.

Altho' I know whenever the great rights, the trial by jury, freedom of the press, or liberty of conscience, came in question in [Parliament], the invasion

102. Thomas Jefferson to James Madison, Mar. 15, 1789, in Hutchinson, *et al.* (eds.), *Papers of James Madison*, XII, 13–17; the translation in brackets is given *ibid.*, 17n.

of them is resisted by able advocates, yet their Magna Charta does not contain any one provision for the security of those rights, respecting which, the people of America are most alarmed. The freedom of the press and rights of conscience, those choicest privileges of the people, are unguarded in the British constitution. . . . It may not be thought necessary to provide limits for the legislative power in that country, yet a different opinion prevails in the United States.

Some of the key liberties are natural rights, others political rights. "Trial by jury cannot be considered as a natural right, but a right resulting from the social compact which regulates the action of the community, but is as essential to secure the liberty of the people as any one of the preexistent rights of nature." Whether embraced in statements of rights or protected by checks and balances of the constitutions in the several states, the universal purpose of the concern for liberty is to restrain government. "The great object in view is to limit and qualify the powers of the government, by excepting out of the grant of power those cases in which the government ought not to act, or to act only in a particular mode. They point these exceptions sometimes against the abuse of the executive power, sometimes against the legislative, and, in some cases, against the community itself; or, in other words, against the majority in favor of the minority."

Even considering that it is valid to say the Constitution is one of enumerated powers, and the "great residuum" of rights and powers not surrendered remains with the people, Madison continues, there is the "necessary and proper" clause that introduces discretion in the exercise of enumerated powers. This can lead to abuses of powers at the expense of liberty. On the other hand, the enumeration of some rights and silence about others can tend to disparage those rights retained but unmentioned, although a specific provision to guard against that ought to be included. It is also to be hoped that rights incorporated into the Constitution will be objects of special attention from "independent tribunals of justice" that "will consider themselves in a peculiar manner the guardians of those rights; they will be an impenetrable bulwark against every assumption of power in the legislative or executive; they will be naturally led to resist every encroachment upon rights expressly stipulated for in the constitution by the declaration of rights. . . . Beside this security, there is a great probability that such a declaration in the federal system would be enforced; because the state legislatures will jealously and closely watch the operations of this government . . . the greatest opponents to a federal government admit the state legislatures to be sure guardians of the people's liberty."

While there is some irony in Madison's last statement, we have noticed that he is a politician as well as a statesman. There is no doubting his intention to create legally enforceable rights, however, and it is his hope that all governments will face the prospect of a "general principle, that laws are unconstitutional which infringe the rights of the community." In a further echo of Jefferson's persuasive counsel sent from Paris, Madison holds out the hope that the mere "paper barriers" being proposed to secure rights will "have a tendency to impress some degree of respect for them, to establish the public opinion in their favor, and rouse the attention of the whole community, it may be one mean to controul the majority from those acts to which they might be otherwise inclined." [103]

VII

Gordon Wood speaks for a significant consensus among scholars in stating that "republicanism as the Americans expressed it in 1776 possessed a decidedly reactionary tone. It embodied the ideal of the good society as it had been set forth from antiquity through the eighteenth century." [104] Apart from the ideological swipe that *reactionary* makes at our subject, the liberty and rights to which the founders are devoted plainly bear out Wood's generalization and show it to remain true in 1789 and later, something not contended in his assertion. The movement from colonies in a limited monarchy, through a brief small republic phase during the Revolutionary War and Confederation, and into the extended compound mixed republic of the Constitution did little if anything to affect the fundamental convictions of Americans about liberty and rights. The self-evident truths of the Declaration are the common sense of the subject in 1789 as well as in 1776, as the evidence adduced here shows. The conviction of human equal-

103. Speech of Madison in House of Representatives, June 8, 1789, *ibid.*, XII, 197–210.
104. Wood, *Creation of the American Republic*, 59.

ity before God and the law persists; the self-evident truth that human beings who are created equal are endowed by their Creator with unalienable rights to life, liberty, and the pursuit of happiness persists; and so does the notion that governments exist primarily to secure these rights, rest upon the consent of the governed from whom all their powers arise, and can be altered or abolished if faith is not kept with the people.

The near horizon of liberty is articulated into the array of rights secured by laws in various jurisdictions, especially in the common law received by the states as the formal basis of their jurisprudence, more grandly in constitutions and bills of rights, and culminating in the Federal Bill of Rights and Constitution as the supreme law of the land. That the vast array of rights secured by law compose the texture of free government and emanate from the personalities of the individuals who collectively make up the *People* is a fundamental conviction in America. Civil rights may arise directly from natural rights *or* indirectly from them through the medium of a social and political order contrived out of the *consent* of the people given in constitutions, common law precedent, and statutes. Immemorial usage and natural liberties are not readily discriminated since both emanate from human nature and the rational order created by God. The achievement of James Madison and his colleagues during the Convention and First Congress is to devise a resourceful and substantially self-equilibrating set of processes and structures legally to enforce rights and supply standards of judgment for their realization in America. What these processes and structures consist of in detail is the subject matter of the constitutional theory of the country. The founders institutionalize rights in such a way as to make the amended Constitution itself a legally enforceable higher law, now brought down out of the clouds and firmly planted on the earth. We have seen that Madison and others viewed these developments as critical improvements over British constitutional arrangements and anticipated the eventual role of the judiciary through judicial review and guardianship of the fabric of fundamental rights.[105] Liberties thereby became the birthright of all Americans with citizenship dated from adoption of

---

105. Some attention is paid to the role of higher law in American jurisprudence in Sandoz, *Conceived in Liberty*, esp. Chaps. 1, 2, and 5.

the Declaration of Independence.[106] Whether comprising freedom *to* or freedom *from*, the thrust of rights is to protect the individual and limit intrusion into private life especially (but not exclusively) by government.

That the higher law perspective was intact at the end of the founding period is evident from the views of John Quincy Adams in 1791, a figure whose cardinal role in American statecraft continued long into the nineteenth century. He writes:

> This principle, that a whole nation has a right to do whatever it pleases, cannot in any sense whatever be admitted as true. The eternal and immutable laws of justice and morality are paramount to all human legislation. The violation of those laws is certainly within the power of a nation, but it is not among the rights of nations. The power of a nation is the collected power of all the individuals which compose it. . . . If, therefore, a majority . . . are bound by no law human or divine, and have no other rule but their sovereign will and pleasure to direct them, what possible security can any citizen . . . have for the protection of his inalienable rights? The principles of liberty must still be the sport of arbitrary power, and the hideous form of despotism must lay aside the diadem and the scepter, only to assume the party-colored garments of [ochlocracy].[107]

Sacred liberty encompasses constitutionally protected rights, but as natural law and natural rights it cannot be enforced in the country's courts. The emphatic legalizing of rights witnessed in the founding served both to give them practical effectiveness (especially after the process of absorption or incorporation began in 1925 in *Gitlow v. New York*)[108] and to reinforce the tendency remarked in Blackstone and matured in Austin of divorcing law from philosophical and ethical theories to make it an autonomous body of doctrine and knowledge. Because of the strength of the higher law tradition of American civilization, however, and the integral experience of reality that shapes the founding and subsequent history, this tendency to a pure theory

106. See Madison's memorandum entitled *Citizenship*, May 22, 1789, in Hutchinson, *et al.* (eds.), *Papers of James Madison*, XII, 178–82.

107. John Quincy Adams, "Letters of Publicola," in *Writings of John Quincy Adams*, ed. Worthington C. Ford (New York, 1913), I, 70; for discussion see also A. J. Beitzinger, *A History of American Political Thought* (New York, 1972), 258. The final word in the quotation is *democracy*, by which J. Q. Adams intended mob-rule, rather than our good term.

108. 268 U.S. 652. See Sandoz, *Conceived in Liberty*, 43–81; see also Berns, "The Constitution As Bill of Rights," in Goldwin and Schambra (eds.), *How Does the Constitution Secure Rights?*, 52.

of law (or legal positivism with a vengeance) never won a monopoly of American legal theory, but these are matters beside the point of the present discussion.[109]

The point deserving stress is that sacred liberty, as it emerges with such force in the formative period, is a philosophical and religious symbolism evoking the hierarchy of being and its order. Not merely political in meaning, it spills over the bounds of legal and constitutional categories as controlling fundamental Truth. Thus, sacred liberty is the freedom experienced by persons living in accordance with divine order. In one identifiable mode, it is the blissful life of no regrets of the Christ-filled man living in communion with God after the pattern announced by Jesus: "You shall know the truth and the truth shall make you free." This is the saintly life lived in process of redemption. In another identifiable mode, it is the philosopher's or the contemplative life of Plato and Aristotle, experienced as the best and happiest life for man *qua* man and the result of a conversion of the soul toward highest Good, such as is marked by the *periagoge* in the Parable of the Cave.[110]

When experiences of this order and volatility are melded through popularization with large-scale social movements, then one *possibility* is the kind of apocalyptical millenarianism and chiliasm that characterize the Civil War period in seventeenth-century England and remerge in America as potent social forces during the American Revolution. A significant number of people may then endow the tribulations of the time with eschatological meaning: the translation of time into eternity; the Second Coming of Christ in power and glory is at hand! As Pocock has shown, this is an ingredient of republicanism's modern career from the time of Machiavelli and Savonarola in Florence at the turn of the fifteenth century onward.[111] Thus, the "revolution of the saints" is the mark of Oliver Cromwell's enterprise and of the English Commonwealth. A former governor of Massachusetts, Sir Henry Vane, writes in *A Healing Question* (1656), one of the reputed classics of civil and religious liberty, that Godly union

109. For contrasting discussions see Hart, *Concept of Law*; and Berman, *Law and Revolution*; see also Ellis Sandoz, "H. Berman, *Law and Revolution*: A Review," *Louisiana Law Review*, XLV (1985), 1105–25.
110. John 8:32. Plato *Republic* 515C.
111. Pocock, *Machiavellian Moment*, 104–16, 294–95, 317–18.

must be perfected "by a spirit of meekness and fear of the Lord . . . to uphold and carry on this blessed cause . . . that is already come thus far onward in its progress to its desired and expected end of bringing in Christ, the desire of all nations, as the chief Ruler among us." The expectation is "the setting up of the Lord himself as chief judge and lawgiver among us." [112]

In the wake of the American Revolution, similar expectations had risen and fallen. The war ends and not the Lord but postwar depression and normalcy appear, thus dashing apocalyptic hopes. One writer has delineated the meaning of liberty for such Americans.

For evangelicals, liberty meant the total denial of the self and the obliteration of self-interest by the creation of a pure and perfectly united political community. Liberty thus was not thought of in terms of individuals but of the public collectively. For evangelical republicans, political liberty became synonymous with piety and true virtue, for only the moral reformation of the entire people could make possible the regeneration of the political world as well. Liberty thus became the freedom to be pure and virtuous, free from corruption and from sin. . . . Republicanism in 1776 involved nothing less than the attempt by many Americans to bring about the regeneration of American society and politics. . . . The Revolution of the American saints failed. By 1780, Samuel Adams, the arch-revolutionary of the country, had begun to despair even of Boston, since all the vices and sins of pre-revolutionary years had reappeared. [113]

The pathos is captured in Sam Adams' question to Richard Henry Lee in 1785. "Will the Lion ever associate with the Lamb or the Leopard with the Kid," asks the great republican Christian, "till our favorite principles shall be universally established?" [114] Such millennialist utopianism fades, and its epitaph as a dominant political movement is written in the Constitution, perhaps, whose political theory is not altogether removed from a modern skeptic's reaction to lions lying

---

112. Sir Henry Vane, *A Healing Question*, in *American Historical Documents*, ed. Charles W. Eliot (New York, 1910), *Harvard Classics*, XLIII, 141–43.

113. Philip J. Greven, Jr., *Protestant Temperament: Patterns of Child-Rearing, Religious Experience, and the Self in Early America* (1977; rpr. New York, 1979), 346–47, 354, 358. Basic to Greven is Alan Heimert, *Religion and the American Mind*. See Edmund S. Morgan's negative review of Heimert's book in *William and Mary Quarterly*, 3rd ser., XXIV (1967), 454–59.

114. Quoted from Hatch, *Sacred Cause of Liberty*, 182.

down with lambs: "That's O.K., son, so long as you add fresh lambs now and again."[115]

The word for the feverish zealotry that contributes so much to the country's unity in the Revolutionary War and subsequently becomes an obstacle to effective government on a continental scale is *enthusiasm*. The trouble with it, Publius says, is that "the noble enthusiasm of liberty is too apt to be infected with a spirit of narrow and illiberal distrust." This impedes rational deliberation, for "men . . . blinded by enthusiasm" cannot take account of matters that are being analyzed from a pragmatic perspective.[116] The consequence is that sacred liberty must be preserved against both vulgar liberty (the clamor of the base passions that urge us to do whatever we will) on one side, and from world-annihilating millennialism and related pneumatic eruptions and excesses on the other side. Apocalypticism permanently is a *possibility* of revelatory experience requiring delicate rational balancing, as in Augustine. Millennial hope, an essential feature of biblical faith and of the Christian vision more specifically, points eagerly toward the fulfillment of time in eternity, but it is, alas, not a program to be carried into effect on a knowable timetable.

It is crucial to grasp that Madison and his friends are not choosing between empire and virtue, for virtue remains *essential* to happiness and to the operation of the social and political order ordained by the Constitution. Rather, the framers are rejecting the temptation of God either by doing nothing and counting on divine deliverance or by building a Tower of Babel out of purely worldy means. Indeed, there is an Augustinian quality to their statesmanship, for the effect of their work is to purge apocalyptical excesses from faith through reason. The creation is intended to be lived in, and man's dominion over it is an augury of progress and the development of civilization, even of empire. The protection of property (*dominium*) is fundamental to a

115. Jack Crabb in Thomas Berger, *Little Big Man* (New York, 1964), quoted in James West Davidson, *Logic of Millennial Thought: Eighteenth-Century New England* (New Haven, 1977), 232.

116. Alexander Hamilton in Cooke (ed.), *Federalist*, 5 (No. 1). *Ibid.*, 565 (No. 83). The standard study is Ronald A. Knox, *Enthusiasm: A Chapter in the History of Religion, with Special Reference to the XVII and XVIII Centuries* (New York, 1961). See also Norman Cohn, *Pursuit of the Millennium*; and Voegelin, *New Science of Politics*, Chaps. 4–6.

reality in which mind and spirit are founded in physical bodies and are not imperceptible shades flitting about in ethereal existence. Life is given by God and meant to be lived, fostered, and enjoyed. In a sense, then, matter is spirit-bearing, and property is no mere impediment to man's existence in truth but is instead its necessary condition.

John Witherspoon's analysis is, once again, to the point. It provides an eclectic synthesis commanding wide assent and reflecting a balanced vision of faith and reason.

If we take tradition or Revelation for our guide, the matter is plain, that God made man lord of works of his hands, and puts under him all the other creatures. . . . Private property is every particular person's having a confessed and exclusive right to a certain portion of the goods which serve for the support and conveniency of life. . . . In civil society full formed, especially if the state is at all extensive or intended to be so, private property is essentially necessary, and founded upon the reason of things and public utility. The reasons are (1) without private property no laws would be sufficient to compel universal industry. There never was such a purity of manners and zeal for the public in the individuals of a great body, but that many would be idle and slothful and maintain themselves upon the labor of others. (2) There is no reason to expect in the present state of human nature, that there would be a just and equal distribution to every one according to his necessity, nor any room for distinction according to merit. (3) There would be no place for the exercise of some of the noblest affections of the human mind, as charity, compassion, beneficence, & c. (4) Little or no incitement to the active virtues, labor, ingenuity, bravery, patience, & c.[117]

The liberty of person and property are so intimately connected as to be inseparable, by this view. "There is not a single instance in history in which civil liberty was lost, and religious liberty preserved entire. If therefore we yield up our temporal property, we at the same time deliver the conscience into bondage."[118]

Consonant with this view is that the citizen, to be qualified to participate in politics as a voter or official, must possess an "independent will," a quality long measured in some kind of property qualification. This mark especially is valued in those who serve in offices of trust,

117. Witherspoon, *Lectures on Moral Philosophy*, 126–27 (Lec. X). For the problem in Augustine see Voegelin, *New Science of Politics*, 109, with reference to *City of God*, XX, 7–9. For discussion of apocalypse, transfiguration, and the problem of balance see Sandoz, *Voegelinian Revolution*, 233–43 and citations therein.
118. Witherspoon, *Works*, III, 37.

where the more propertied classes are generally prevalent in American assemblies, for the obvious reasons that such people have more leisure time to devote to public affairs, understand the complexities of business and government better, have a demonstrable stake in society, and evince "superior virtue by being able to amass and retain a certain amount of property. This presumably took discipline, sobriety, hard work, and a certain amount of intelligence—all of which are essential civil virtues."[119] The national regulation of commerce, assuring the validity of contracts, and maintaining uniform monetary and taxing policies as facets of the economic powers of the central government under the new Constitution all served to foster material well-being and prosperity as essential to the expansion of national power and prestige no less than to the happiness of the people.

The universal purpose of bills of rights is to place certain liberties beyond the reach of majorities on the premise that deprivation of certain rights diminishes the civil standing and very humanity of persons so affected. American government is conceived as a habitation fit for free men, as I have insisted. The pursuit of happiness of the Declaration is a goal fostered under the Constitution by maximizing security and protecting liberty so individuals and groups can seek their satisfactions with minimal interference from public entities. Whether *the* end of politics is happiness or justice is a puzzle as old as Aristotle's *Politics,* and that puzzle remains with the American founders. Perhaps the end of government is justice and the end of life happiness. Both entail the process of education whereby civic, moral, intellectual, and existential virtues form character, mind, and spirit to perfect the properly human in each person. It is evident that laws founded on justice can conduce to these ends. It is also evident that the achieving of sacred liberty in the lives of individuals and throughout the community involves living in accordance with truth and goodness as far as possible. That means as a starting point liberation from base passion (in contrast to Aristotle's slave by nature) and *desiring the truly good* in order to be a friend to oneself. The historic reason for the marriage of millenarianism and republicanism is, at least

119. Donald S. Lutz, *Popular Consent and Popular Control: Whig Political Theory in the Early State Constitutions* (Baton Rouge, 1980), 101–104, 205.

partly, the recognition that the rule of the many will normally be the rule of the largest part of the soul, which is the passions. Unless these are perfected through discipline and grace, the free rule of men by consent necessarily will degenerate into the disorders that beckon the demagogue and elevate the tyrant. The rule of the people reflects the order and disorders of their lives. Hence, cultivation of moral goodness and intellectual excellence is essential to the well-ordered society, especially where consent of the people is so thoroughly *the* fundamental of social and political operations as in a republic whose premise is majority rule.

We have seen the concern lavished by the founders on the solution of this set of problems. In the Bill of Rights, protection of what Madison calls the sacred rights of conscience occurs in the First Amendment and might have been secured in a comparable amendment proposed for the states had the Senate not declined it. Madison's entry into politics as a twenty-five-year-old delegate from Orange County to the Virginia Convention and General Assembly began in 1776, with a key revision of the liberty of conscience clause of Virginia's Declaration of Rights. From that beginning throughout a long career, he and Jefferson led the nation in advocating intellectual and religious liberty. By this leadership, including securing the provisions of the First Amendment as the supreme law of the land, it becomes an American principle that the pursuit of happiness and highest liberty as the goal of human existence primarily will be conducted *privately* under the protection of the Constitution. While that solution to the vexed problems of religion and politics is ambiguous and even paradoxical in a society formed by Christian civilization, it is theoretically acute and pragmatically sound. It reflects the general characteristic of the human condition that, neither beast nor divine, men live amidst the ambiguities of the In-Between reality, partaking of all levels of being. A politics that is purely secular perverts existence for such beings, no less than one which attempts to leap out of the human condition and proclaim the superman on a theistic or atheistic premise. To acknowledge every person and community only on condition of preserving peace and not infringing on others' rights is the founders' institutional solution to the vexing problem of the place of highest things in the American order. This is without doubt a great solution ventured under conditions of the time, one of the greatest achievements of the entire founding.

The sacred cause of liberty thereby finds a resting point in the new constitutional order where liberty is law. To borrow from Burke, "This kind of liberty is, indeed but another name for justice, ascertained by wise laws and secured by well-constructed institutions."[120] For Americans, whose rearticulation of Western civilization in the founding reasserted the classic and Christian experiences-symbols of transcendent reality in a way that runs directly counter to radical modernity by providing an ennobling alternative to it, the commonsense wisdom of Poor Richard is the philosopher's stone:

> Work as if you were to live 100 years,
> Pray as if you were to die To-morrow.[121]

120. Edmund Burke to Charles-Jean Francois Dupont, Nov., 1789, in Robert B. Dishman (ed.), *Burke and Paine: On Revolution and the Rights of Man* (New York, 1971), 74n.
121. From "Poor Richard Improved, 1757," in J. A. Leo Lemay (ed.), *Writings of Benjamin Franklin* (New York, 1987), 1290.

CHAPTER 7 The American Constitutional

Order After Two Centuries: Concluding Reflections

It is evident that the overt actions of the American founding cover at least the fifteen years from 1776 to 1791 and that, within that period, not one but four or five foundings—or at least phases within *the* founding—are readily identifiable: those associated with the adoption of the Declaration of Independence in 1776 and of the Articles of Confederation in 1781; with the framing of the Constitution in 1787; with the start-up of government in 1789 after nine states had ratified (as required by Article VII) and elections had been held; and lastly, with the ratification of the Bill of Rights along with the Constitution, which was realized by 1791. In completing the process, North Carolina (in 1789) and Rhode Island (in 1790) joined the Union by ratifying the Constitution. Maryland (in 1789) became the first state to ratify the Bill of Rights, and Virginia ratified on December 15, 1791, the tenth state to do so and thereby make the three-fourths majority required by Article V to put the new provisions of the Constitution into effect and end the ratification process. Connecticut, Georgia, and Massachusetts failed to ratify the amendments during the founding and only did so in a symbolic gesture made in 1939.[1]

I

Through the leadership of President George Washington and of Representative James Madison, as we have seen, the First Congress pro-

1. Schwartz, *Great Rights of Mankind*, 188–91.

posed twelve amendments to the Constitution for ratification, ten of which were approved to become the Bill of Rights. Its provisions had been gleaned from over two hundred recommendations for changes made by the states during the process of ratifying the Constitution.[2] Washington, Madison, and other Federalist leaders (as they soon were called) accepted the obligation of amending the original Constitution to meet the chief objections of the Anti-Federalists, who saw it as threatening individual liberties and unduly encroaching upon the rights of states viewed as (in some sense) sovereign entities. Fears ran to great intensity in many places in the country that a conspiracy was afoot among the Constitution's proponents to abolish both the liberties of the people and the existence of states. The Federalists responded, therefore, chiefly out of political necessity in order to conciliate opponents and appease public opinion. Many Americans had gone along with ratification with misgivings, persuaded to do so only on the basis of promises made (in Virginia and elsewhere) that, while prior amendment was not feasible, subsequent amendment to satisfy major dissatisfactions would be forthcoming after new government was launched. The political urgency of securing a Bill of Rights before adjourning Congress (and returning empty-handed to confront his Baptist constituents in Orange County) is discernible, as we have seen, in Madison's conduct in the summer of 1789 and in the correspondence of the period.[3]

All of this is offered as a reminder of the complexity of the American founding. It is also to notice the *political* dimension of the founding as of paramount importance. There is no sense in pretending with all the source materials now available to us that the Constitution of the United States, for example, was a blueprint for just government devised by a single brain or even a small elite of like-minded geniuses and then docilely accepted by a miraculously enlightened people. This is not to say that a just regime was not a conscious goal of American statesmen of the period, nor is it to denigrate the genius of those who deliberated or the enlightenment of the people in ratifying, nor is it to take away from the miracle in Philadelphia that even James Madison speaks of in his great letter to Thomas Jefferson of

2. *Ibid.*, and Schwartz, ed., *Bill of Rights*.
3. Hutchinson, *et al.* (eds.), *Papers of James Madison*, XII, *passim*.

October 24, 1787.[4] Rather, it is to pay heed to the political texture of preeminently political events. The Constitution was the work of a committee. Even if it is acknowledged that James Madison was the leading figure in the Convention, it remains to be said that some of his most cherished ideas were left out of the final version of the Constitution. A count of votes taken at the Convention shows that he lost forty out of seventy-one times when his specific proposals were at issue,[5] and the depth of Madison's disappointment as registered in the October 24 letter to Jefferson and elsewhere was profound, even though it was completely masked in public statements, including his first contribution to the *Federalist* (No. 10), published on November 22, 1787.[6]

Politics and prudence predominated both in the Convention and afterward. Success was won by concession, compromise, and persuasion, and then only by an eyelash, as John Adams and Benjamin Rush recalled with wonder in the correspondence of their old age.[7] Of the time of the events themselves, it is right to stress the principle articulated by John Dickinson in the Federal Convention on August 13: "Experience must be our only guide. Reason may mislead us."[8] Of course, Dickinson's *experience* is not merely the raw product of an uneducated existence in the highly literate world of the founders. Rather, it should be understood that such experience embraces political prudence informed by both education and action, and that it had been shaped by wide acquaintance not only with English traditions but also with indigenous American traditions, laws, and practices of self-government going back for more than a century and a half to Jamestown and Plymouth.[9] Through the famous salutary neglect of Britain, the Americans had independently and inadvertently rearticulated the British version of Western civilization in their own unique ways; the plural stresses the diversity within America itself and should be observed. Pre-revolutionary America is today described by social

4. *Ibid.*, X, 205–20.
5. Forrest McDonald, *Novus Ordo Seclorum: The Intellectual Origins of the Constitution* (Lawrence, Kan., 1985), 208–209.
6. Cooke (ed.), *Federalist*, 56.
7. Schutz and Adair (eds.), *Spur of Fame*, 222–26.
8. Farrand (ed.), *Records of the Federal Convention of 1787*, II, 278.
9. See Jack P. Greene, *Peripheries and Center: Constitutional Development in the Extended Polities of the British Empire and the United States, 1606–1788* (Athens, Ga., 1986), *passim.*

historians as a "crazy quilt" of "religious, political, and socioeconomic diversity" that demolishes the earlier picture of homogeneity and is further complicated by diverse patterns of experience and complex processes of development, with innovation and traditional patterns intertwined and coexisting side by side.[10]

Exactly when a properly "American" outlook was achieved can be debated, and even such a like-mindedness (or *homonoia*) of a community transcending the localities and states to constitute the people's self-identification, distinct from the English colonial ethos, obviously did not obliterate the diversity of the country intellectually and culturally. America was pluralistic from the beginning. It would seem to be conceded on all sides, however, that a new political culture came to startling maturity in the creative period we call the founding. This articulation of America as a society organized for action in history is proclaimed in the Declaration and realized in fact through the successive stages of founding previously noticed.[11] Nor, lastly, should it be forgotten that as politically spectacular as the Federal Convention with its assembly of demigods truly was, some of history's limelight should fall elsewhere. Americans living in the original thirteen states plus Vermont demonstrated astonishing political prowess during the last quarter of the eighteenth century, when they wrote, debated, and adopted no fewer than twenty-eight constitutions while rejecting a number of others along the way.[12] Nor should we neglect to say that constitution-making in America did not begin with the period of the founding but extends from the early seventeenth century onward, as Donald Lutz's collection of over seventy such "instruments of political foundation" demonstrates.[13]

II

What, then, can be identified as leading characteristics of the American founding?

10. James T. Kloppenberg, "The Virtues of Liberalism: Christianity, Republicanism, and Ethics in Early American Political Discourse," *Journal of American History*, LXXIV (1987), 9–33 at 20.

11. Voegelin, *New Science of Politics*, 27–51.

12. Lutz, *Popular Consent and Popular Control*, 44.

13. Donald S. Lutz (ed.), *Documents of Political Foundation Written by Colonial Americans: From Covenant to Constitution* (Philadelphia, 1986), *passim*.

First, there is the pragmatic spirit just noticed and given pungent statement by John Dickinson. Common sense rationality is characteristic, and it is exemplified nowhere better than in the period of constitutional framing and ratification. This is also to say that doctrinaire thinking—within the bounds of the Whig and later republican consensus that defined the patriots' convictions about political fundamentals in which everyone agreed, to remember Jefferson's claim—was subordinate to realistic political understanding of a sophisticated order, the kind reflected by the leading figures of the period and that found resonance through persuasion in the people themselves. American politics was (even then) non-ideological, to use a term coined in the last years of the eighteenth century. Dickinson's outlook is representative, and it bears affinity to Edmund Burke's notion of the prescriptive constitution as a product of the reason and wisdom of the ages rather than of the calculations of any given person or group of men, on the rationalistic pattern set by the French *philosophes.* Thus, the Dickinson remark of August 13 noted in Madison's *Debates* directly continues: "It was not reason that discovered the singular & admirable mechanism of the English Constitution. It was not Reason that discovered or ever could have discovered the odd & in the eye of those who are governed by reason, the absurd mode of trial by Jury. Accidents probably produced these discoveries, and experience has give [*sic*] sanction to them. This is then our guide. And has not experience verified the utility of restraining money bills to the immediate representatives of the people." [14]

The drift of the last sentence just quoted is noteworthy. It illustrates the turn of mind eloquently characterized by Burke in his March 1775 speech in the House of Commons urging conciliation with the Colonies for upholding true English political principles. [15] Liberty is no abstraction in English constitutional history, Burke argues. Rather, it inheres in the tangible, and more often than not it attaches to the matter of *taxing* in this tradition, as examples from Magna Carta onward amply illustrate. These are points well made for understanding the epochal events of our founding. After all, the motto of the Ameri-

14. Farrand (ed.), *Records of the Federal Convention of 1787,* II, 278.
15. Stanlis (ed.), *Edmund Burke,* 158–59, and partially quoted near the beginning of Chapter 6, pp. 164–65, herein.

can Revolution, if it had one, was "No taxation without representation!" Certainly this is a puny slogan when compared with the "Liberty, Equality, and Fraternity" of the French Revolution of 1789 and the "Bread, Peace, and Land" of the Bolshevik Revolution of 1917, with their grandiose rhetorical sweep. We have seen that Madison in old age wrote admiringly of the insight of his countrymen in discerning the hand of tyranny in a three-penny tax on tea. Dickinson, in the passage quoted, sees liberty protected by continuing the convention of money bills originating in the popular house of the future Congress, as they are by the same logic in the House of Commons. The concrete, the specific, the experiential predominate in this mode of political thinking.

Politics is itself a sort of mediocre thing, neither the noblest nor meanest realm but an in-between sphere; it is not the way to salvation, either in the beyond or in the world. By the time's ubiquitous symbolism of the Great Chain of Being, taught by Locke and Bolingbroke, Addison and Pope, a gloss on Plato, Aristotle, and Scripture alike, man is the "middle link" in the chain. Locke supposes he stands considerably closer to the lower creatures than to God from whom he is infinitely remote.[16] For Americans of the period, "the most popular source" for understanding man in this context is Alexander Pope's long poem *Essay on Man.*[17] A Roman Catholic, an accomplished classicist, and translator of a popular version of Homer's *Iliad* and *Odyssey*, Pope set out to express from the whole range of sources of Western civilization what he calls the "science of human nature," doing so in poetic form to make it more memorable and thereby "vindicate the ways of God to man."[18] Thus, he writes:

> Vast chain of being! which from God began,
> Natures aethereal, human, angel, man,
> Beast, bird, fish, insect, what no eye can see,
> No glass can reach; from Infinite to thee,
> From thee to nothing.

16. John Locke, *An Essay Concerning Human Understanding*, ed. John W. Yolton (rev. ed.; London, 1964), II, 50.

17. McDonald, *Novus Ordo Seclorum*, 164n.

18. Alexander Pope, *Essay on Man*, in Charles W. Eliot (ed.), *English Poetry, Vol. I: Chaucer to Gray* (New York, 1910), *Harvard Classics*, XL, 417–18.

Pope situates man in the In-Between reality (Plato's *Metaxy*) of God and the abyss out of which Creation emerged *ex nihilo* (to recall the imagery of Genesis), or alternatively, In-Between the philosophers' *Nous* (divine Reason) and *Apeiron*, (Boundless or Depth) first symbolized by Anaximander.[19] The imagery, in other words, represents the classical and Christian symbolizations of the hierarchy of being in which man tensionally participates as the substance of his existence. Thus, Pope further elaborates the plight of man to reveal the pathos of the being who partakes of things divine and yet is beset with all the corruptions of frailty and mortality. He writes:

> Plac'd in this isthmus of a middle state,
> A being darkly wise and rudely great,
> With too much knowledge for the sceptic side,
> With too much weakness for the stoic pride,
> He hangs between; in doubt to act or rest;
> In doubt to deem himself a god or beast;
> In doubt his Mind or Body to prefer;
> Born but to die, and reas'ning but to err; . . .
> Chaos of Thought and Passion all confus'd,
> Still by himself abus'd, or disabus'd;
> Created half to rise, and half to fall,
> Great lord of all things, yet a prey to all;
> Sole judge of Truth, in endless error hurl'd;
> The glory, jest and riddle of the world.[20]

Great as man's dignity and power are, his sphere is limited. He is "born but to die." He partakes of the image and likeness of God and holds dominion over all the earth, as Genesis teaches. He participates in all the levels of reality and his nature is their epitome, as Plato and Aristotle teach. Yet he is a potentiality to be actualized through habituation to the good and instruction in truth. The process of actualization involves among much else the search for immortality that is the ultimate common concern of the fallen Adam no less than of the Hellenic philosophers' paradigmatic man (or *spoudaios*) who pursues happiness (*eudaimonia, makarios*) in response to the pull or attraction of the divine to immortalize as the fulfillment of "each man's

19. See Sandoz, *Voegelinian Revolution*, 188–216.

20. Pope, *Essay on Man*, in Eliot (ed.), *English Poetry*, 424, 426; Arthur O. Lovejoy, *Great Chain of Being: A Study of the History of an Idea* (1936; rpr. Cambridge, Mass., 1964), 60, 199 and *passim*.

true self."[21] To make some of the technical terminology explicit here is to stress the point that the founders themselves were steeped in the classics and in the Bible as previously noticed. They, therefore, immediately grasped the poem's imagery and the associations of its symbolic world here briefly identified and directly communicated in other passages of Pope's poem itself, as common coin of the times.

The non-ideological, non-apocalyptical understanding of politics is distinctive and *ultimately* predominates in the work of the founders after the millenarian ardor of the Revolutionary period subsides and watchful waiting again is accepted as the lot of the faithful.[22] The Great Chain of Being and related symbolisms supply an enduring frame of reference for American attitudes during the late eighteenth and early nineteenth centuries. The pervasiveness of Protestant Christianity and of a knowledge of the Greek and Latin classics that made them second nature to educated members of American society conditioned all political thought in the period.[23] Political thinking also is heavily indebted to the intellectual configuration established in the great common law tradition and the English constitutionalism preserved there. In that horizon of thought, airy generalities do not carry the day and protect the substance of truth and justice in society. Rather, it is (for example) the common lawyers' insistence upon the details of procedure that make the protection of every free man by the law of the land (*per legem terrae*) affirmed in Magna Carta (Chapter 39 in the 1215 A.D. original; Chapter 29 in the 1225 version of Henry III that became authoritative) synonymous with due process of law by the mid-fourteenth century in England.[24] Sir Henry Maine's great aphorism may be recalled as a summary of this outlook. The liberties we enjoy, he writes, "are secreted in the interstices of procedure."[25]

21. Aristotle *Nicomachean Ethics* X. 7. 1. 1177a12–19.
22. Hatch, *Sacred Cause of Liberty*, passim; Greven, *Protestant Temperament*, 347–55.
23. See Gummere, *American Colonial Mind and the Classical Tradition*, passim; Reinhold, *Classica Americana*, and the literature cited therein; also Chap. 3 herein.
24. Sir Edward Coke, *Second Part of the Institutes of the Laws of England* (London, 1642), 46–50; William F. Swindler, *Magna Carta: Legend and Legacy* (Indianapolis, 1965), passim. See also Richard Thomson, *An Historical Essay on the Magna Charta of King John: To Which Are Added, the Great Charter in Latin and English.* . . . (London, 1829), 394–460.
25. Sir Henry Maine, *Dissertations on the Early Law and Custom* (London, 1883), 389; Sandoz, *Conceived in Liberty*, 25.

Second, a characteristic philosophical egalitarianism as articulated in the Declaration runs through the entire founding, reaching clear statement in the Federal Convention where, as Pierce Butler says, the task is not to devise the best plan of government they can conceive but (as Solon had done for Athens in antiquity) the best government the people will receive. A related sentiment is Gouverneur Morris' acknowledgment that in America "the people are the king."[26] This leading characteristic is exhibited also in the affirmation of the capacity of a free people to choose its form of government that Publius, on the very first page of the *Federalist,* announces as being put to the test for all time in the proposed ratification of the Constitution.

It has been frequently remarked that it seems to have been reserved to the people of this country, by their conduct and example, to decide whether societies of men are really capable or not of establishing good government from reflection and choice, or whether they are forever destined to depend for their political constitutions on accident and force. . . . The crisis at which we are arrived may with propriety be regarded as the era in which that decision is to be made; and a wrong election of the part we shall act may, in this view, deserve to be considered as the general misfortune of mankind.[27]

Publius' statement is both a clue to the meaning of the phrase *novus ordo seclorum* and an echo of the conception of the Declaration and of John Locke's *Second Treatise of Government* a century earlier that social and governmental structures and processes must (in some sense) be based on the *consent* of the people. That principle, however, is of great antiquity and long antedates the eighteenth or even seventeenth century as a mark of right rule. The American difference is that here it is consciously, explicitly, and repeatedly acted upon in covenant form during the colonial period and during the formation of the nation in establishing local, state, and national governments. The ratification of the Constitution poses as never before the challenge of responsible self-government by free men as the distinctive emblem of the American Era, with consequences for all mankind. This placement of sovereignty in the people ("popular sovereignty") rather than vesting it in the executive in the legislature (*e.g.,* king in parliament) is regarded by Pocock as "the most profound breach ever

26. Farrand (ed.), *Records of the Federal Convention of 1787,* I, 125; II, 69.
27. Cooke (ed.), *Federalist,* 3.

to have occurred in an anglophone political practice."[28] It is denominated "the revolutionary principle" by one of the chief architects of the Constitution, James Wilson of Pennsylvania, who fully appreciated its enormous significance in distancing the American from the British constitution, especially from Blackstone's version of it.[29] The founders may not have been democrats by and large, but the tendency of their work was inevitably democratizing.

Third, there is the characteristic controlling purpose of the framers, as they gather in Philadelphia in 1787 to establish energetic (or effective) government that would also secure liberty and preserve the people's well-being (*salus populi*). A favorite symbolism of the latter element is the verse from First Kings: "And Judah and Israel dwelt safely, every man under his vine and under his fig tree" (4:25).[30] The requirement of a powerful central government to remedy the deficiencies of the Articles had to be balanced with the preservation of liberties, including not least of all security in economic and property matters as fundamental to public and private happiness. To repeat, liberty was no abstract thing from this perspective; the material, intellectual, and spiritual all were bound together in a single texture of existence. The words of John Witherspoon at the beginning of the Revolution deserve reiteration. "There is not a single instance in history in which civil liberty was lost, and religious liberty preserved entire. If therefore we yield up our temporal property, we at the same time deliver the conscience into bondage."[31]

It was to control the uncertainties, inequities, and outright abuses of power, especially by the new state authorities, that a more powerful central government was widely regarded as imperative. The threat of wholesale civil insurrection became a credible possibility after the Shays' Rebellion in western Massachusetts so dramatized the problems that it alarmed even George Washington. The moral core that propelled the Revolution as a concerted resistance of tyranny in the

28. J. G. A. Pocock, "Radical Criticisms of the Whig Order in the Age Before the Revolution," in Margaret Jacob and James L. Jacob (eds.), *Origins of Anglo-American Radicalism* (London, 1984), 44.

29. James Wilson, *Lectures on Law* [1790–1791], in Robert G. McCloskey (ed.), *Works of James Wilson* (Cambridge, Mass., 1967), I, 79 and *passim*.

30. For example, quoted in John Dickinson, *Letters to Fabius, Letter III,* in Paul L. Ford (ed.), *Pamphlets on the Constitution of the United States* (1888; rpr. New York, 1968), 174–80.

31. Witherspoon, *Works,* III, 37.

name of sacred liberty and justice had not deteriorated by the time delegates gathered in Philadelphia in 1787. Powerful government was both needed and feared. The framers fully appreciated the delicacy of their task, and the anxiety that swirled around their activities has been suggested. While the Constitution addressed entirely different matters than had the Declaration, it effected no break with the latter's principles but remained fully consistent with them. The God who had created men equal and endowed them with the inalienable rights to life, liberty, and the pursuit of happiness had not lost his hold on the American mind in the decade since independence was declared. Consent of the people as the touchstone of political rule and the imperative of republican free government, proclaimed by Aristotle and Cicero no less than by Locke and Jefferson, lies at the center of the founders' conception of their handiwork.

III

The familiar notion that ours is a government of laws and not of men retains its validity as a fair statement of the intentions of the American founders. The journey of over two millennia of the principle from Aristotle's *Politics* (III. 16) to James Harrington's *Oceana* (1656) into the Massachusetts Constitution of 1780 and formal induction into American constitutional law in Chief Justice Marshall's famous opinion in *Marbury v. Madison* (1803) is familiar to all, but placing the notion in the context supplied by recent scholarship gives it new dimensions. Major correctives in this respect arise from the renewed recognition of the places of Christianity and of classical thought in the founding, not least of all in constitutional theory. There is also the matter of "which" British constitution was so admired by Americans during the period, which was asserted as the basis of liberties claimed early in the period and emulated (within the limits of ineluctable republicanism) during the framing and ratification phases.

It is of great importance to grasp that liberty and law are far from being polarities in the horizon of the founders. To the contrary, while the identity of the two does not exhaust meaning, it does constitute *primary* meaning as previously discussed. In classical Greek thought the person who is free is precisely one who lives in accordance with highest reason as the philosopher or mature man, and reason in the individual is equated with law in the society. The tyrant in Plato (*Republic*, Bk. VIII) and the slave by nature in Aristotle (*Politics*, Bk. I) are defective or deformed human beings by reason of their uncontrolled subservience to unsavory passions. They are quintessentially unfree because they pervert their humanity by allowing the naturally hegemonic part of their nature (reason, or *nous*) to become the servant of appetite. Liberty lies with reason and the life directed by it in the individual and with its social equivalent law, whose rule is that of "God and reason alone" (*Politics*, Bk. III, Chap. 16). A person is most truly free, on this understanding, when he lives in accordance with highest truth willingly and eagerly, prompted by his *love* of the good, beautiful, and divine, and corrected when he turns away from noble pursuits by his sense of shame for abandoning the greater for the lesser goods. Coercion takes its place in this horizon as the corrective needed by those incapable of living the philosophic life (which is to say most of mankind), and it is for this reason that laws carry enforceable sanctions to compel obedience. Cicero, a favorite author of the founders, typifies the viewpoint. He regards liberty as the end of law, so that living as we like means incorporation of justice as the rule of life by voluntary acceptance of laws and moral principles. He writes: "What, indeed, is freedom? It is the power of living as we wish. Who then lives as he wishes, except the man who follows the path of rectitude, who rejoices in the performance of his duty, and whose way of life is circumspect and deliberate?"[32] In the high Middle Ages these classical teachings were absorbed, with adaptations, by Christian political theory and woven into the institutions and practices of Western civilization.

Comparable meaning is directly found in the Bible, however, a point of importance since, while Americans knew the classics and were educated in medieval thought, reading the Bible was universal.[33]

32. Cicero *Paradoxa ad M. Brutum* V. 1. 34; *De officiis* I. 20. 70 (trans. George Sabine).

33. Perry, *Puritanism and Democracy, passim;* Nathan O. Hatch and Mark A. Noll (eds.), *Bible in America: Essays in Cultural History* (New York, 1982), esp. 39–58 (Noll, "The Image of the United States as a Biblical Nation"), and 59–78 (Hatch, "*Sola Scriptura* and *Novus Ordo Seclorum*"); John D. Woodbridge, Mark A. Noll, and Nathan O. Hatch, *Gospel in America: Themes in the Story of America's Evangelicals* (Grand Rapids, Mich., 1979), 21–45; Benjamin Hart, *Faith and Freedom: The Christian Roots of American Liberty* (Dallas, Tex., 1988); Sandoz (ed.), *Political Sermons of the American Founding.*

Life in Christ, the Gospels teach, is to "know the truth, and the truth shall make you free" (John 8:32). To keep the commandments of the New and Old Covenants is to "live by the law of liberty" (James 2:12). A favorite, if superficially unimpressive text of the preachers of the time was Galatians 4:26, 31, taken by Rev. Phillips Payson for the Massachusetts election sermon he preached in the troubled year of 1778. "But Jerusalem which is above is free, which is the mother of us all. So then, brethren, we are not children of the bondwoman, but of the free." We have seen that Payson then derives the whole economy of liberty and free government from his text.[34] These and numerous related expressions indicate the freeing through faith of men from the burden of sin and their participation in the soteriological drama of atonement and redemption. At the same time they also communicate the existential liberation of the person from the old life and his entry into the new life of blessedness and communion with the God of love and mercy that is the privilege of the regenerate in the here and now, in prefiguration of perfect union in the beyond. To live in *truth* is to experience perfect liberty in lives and in communities. Hence, there emerges the renewed emphasis from the Great Awakening of the 1730s onward of revivalists and those widely stirred by them in America of directly experienced conversion, of a converted ministry in the New Light, New Side congregations, of a living faith and communion with God, and of being born again (to use the currently fashionable phrase) by freely embracing liberating truth in a personal decision for Christ.

Since 1961, when Perry Miller hurled the epithet at Clinton Rossiter's *Seedtime of the Republic* as hopelessly wrong because of "obtuse secularism" in the portrayal of the American founding, a much clearer understanding of the place of religion in the period has begun to be developed by historians and by some social scientists.[35] Yet it is hard for a secular age to imagine, much less come to grips with the implications of the fact (to recall George Trevelyan's words) that "the

34. Thornton (ed.), *Pulpit of the American Revolution*, 329. See the discussion on pp. 145–146 herein.

35. *Cf.* Chaps. 4 and 5 herein, and the literature cited therein. Indispensable is Heimert, *Religion and the American Mind;* see also Harry S. Stout, *New England Soul: Preaching and Religious Culture in Colonial New England* (New York, 1986); Kelly, *Politics and Religious Consciousness;* Bruce Kuklick, *Churchmen and Philosophers: From Jonathan Edwards to John Dewey* (New Haven, 1985).

effect of the continual domestic study of [the Bible] upon the national character, imagination, and intelligence for three centuries—was greater than that of any literary movement in the annals, or any religious movement since St. Augustine."[36]

IV

The common law tradition and version of the British constitution most influential in America until the time of the Revolution was primarily the achievement of Sir Edward Coke. This is because it was embedded in the work of the reigning oracle of the common law down until the time of Blackstone and therefore held sway as authoritative among lawyers and students of legal and constitutional history. Coke's constitutional conceptions were reinforced by Montesquieu's *Spirit of the Laws,* which first appeared in 1748. Law as liberty is central in this tradition, as Coke directly says in the *Second Institute* in expounding Magna Charta when he comes to define *libertates.* The term has three meanings, and it first "signifieth the Laws of the Realme, in which respect this Charter is called, *Charta libertatum.*"[37] Sir John Fortescue, Coke's fifteenth-century master in constitutional law, stresses that an English king (unlike absolute monarchs ruling under Roman law with its provision of *lex regia,* in France and elsewhere) must rule according to the laws of England, which he has no power of himself to change. This is a liberty rather than a burden, Fortescue argues, since it better enables the kings of England to serve goodness and justice by curbing natural tendencies to succumb to selfish purposes. To do so would pervert kingship into tyranny, the slavery of coercion and passion symbolized in the Bible by the brutish rule of Nimrod the hunter who compelled beasts at natural liberty to obey him.[38]

Liberty is distinctive to the English constitution because the community must consent in order to give law legitimacy and rule effect.

36. George Trevelyan quoted in Niebuhr, "Idea of Covenant and American Democracy," 130. *Cf.* Henning Graf Reventlow, *Authority of the Bible and the Rise of the Modern World,* trans. John Bowden (Philadelphia, 1985), 211–14 and *passim.*
37. Coke, *Second Part of the Institutes,* 47.
38. Sir John Fortescue, *De laudibus legum Angliae,* ed. and trans. S. B. Chrimes (Cambridge, England, 1942), Chaps. 4, 9, 12, and 34. *Cf.* Gen. 10:8–9.

Under this mixed regime of "double majesty," which is both "political and regal dominion" (*dominium politicum et regale*), English laws "are made not only by the prince's will, but also by the assent of the whole realm, so they cannot be injurious to the people."[39] Such law is of great antiquity, reaching back to Brutus of Troy who first brought it to England.[40] This ancient constitution embodies divine and natural law, immemorial custom, and inculcates perfect justice. "Human laws are none other than rule by which perfect justice is manifested . . . the Justice which the laws disclose is itself the Perfect Virtue that is called by the name of Legal Justice. . . . This justice, indeed, is the object of all royal administration, because without it a king judges unjustly and is unable to fight rightfully."[41] Fortescue cites Aristotle, Augustine, and especially Thomas Aquinas to support his arguments.

It is this Lancastrian constitution that Coke embraces, revives, and elaborates in the seventeenth-century conflict with the Stuart kings, James I and Charles I. It descends to Americans in the subsequent century when he was, as Jefferson says late in life, the universal tutor "of law students[;] and a sounder Whig never wrote, nor of profounder learning in the orthodox doctrines of the British constitution, or in what are called English liberties."[42] For Coke, Fortescue's book is of "such weight and worthiness" that it should be "written in letters of gold."[43] In sum, medieval political and legal theory compose the substance of Coke's constitutional doctrine, as can hardly be better appreciated than from the quaint passage in his opinion in *Calvin's Case* (1609) quoted earlier.[44]

The supremacy of law, whose roots lie equally in the natural order of things as it comes from the hand of the Creator and in immemorial usage of the English common law, is Coke's great theme. It reaches a

---

39. Fortescue, *De laudibus*, 41; *cf.* Donald W. Hanson, *From Kingdom to Commonwealth: The Development of Civic Consciousness in English Thought* (Cambridge, Mass., 1970), 217–52.

40. *Cf.* Pocock, *Ancient Constitution*, "A Reissue with a Retrospect," esp. 30–55, 255–305.

41. Fortescue, *De laudibus*, 11–13.

42. Thomas Jefferson to James Madison, Feb. 17, 1826, in Koch and Peden (eds.), *Life and Selected Writings of Thomas Jefferson*, 726.

43. Quoted by Chrimes in the introduction to Fortescue, *De laudibus*, xlix.

44. See the quotation as given in Chap. 5, p. 158, herein.

climax in 1628 in the House of Commons debate over the Petition of Right and King Charles I's claim to sovereignty in expanding the Prerogative. Now acting as perhaps the leading member of the Commons, and with John Selden as the principal author of the Petition, Coke responds: "'Sovereign Power' is no parliamentary word. In my opinion it weakens Magna Charta, and all the statutes; for they are absolute without any saving of 'Sovereign Power'; and should we now add it, we shall weaken the foundation law, and then the building must needs fall. Take heed what we yield unto: Magna Charta is such a fellow, that he will have no 'Sovereign.'"[45]

Just how Coke might have comported himself on the occasion of the trial and conviction of Charles I in 1649 for murder, arbitrary rule, and tyranny is hard to guess since he died fifteen years earlier. Yet John Bradshaw in his peroration then concluded the prosecution before announcing the death sentence passed by the court by reading to the king the words of Bracton (d. 1268):

The king has a superior, namely, God. Also the law by which he is made king. Also his *curia*, namely, the earls and barons, because if he is without bridle, that is without law, they ought to put the bridle on him.

Bradshaw then continues in his own words:

This we learn: the end of having kings, or any other governors, it is for the enjoying of justice; that is the end. Now, Sir, if so be the king will go contrary to that end of his government, Sir, he must understand that he is but an officer in trust, and he ought to discharge that trust; and they are to take order for the punishment of such an offending governor. This is not law of yesterday, Sir, but it is law of old.[46]

The kind of whigism and republicanism the founders embrace is in substantial degree a lineal descendant of Coke's version of the British constitution and its implications. It preserves the medieval concep-

---

45. Coke quoted in Corwin, *"Higher Law" Background of American Constitutional Law*, 54; recent scholarship reads the famous, final sentence: "Magna Carta is such a fellow as he will have no saving," but meaning is unaltered. See Stephen D. White, *Sir Edward Coke and "The Grievances of the Commonwealth, 1621–1628"* (Chapel Hill, N.C., 1979), 267.

46. Henry de Bracton, *De legibus et consuetudinibus Angliae*, in Samuel E. Thorne (ed.), *Bracton on the Laws and Customs of England* (Cambridge, Mass., 1968), II, 110; *cf. ibid.*, 33, 305. *Trials of Charles the First, and of Some of the Regicides: With Biographies of Bradshaw, Ireton, Harrison, and others* [ed. anon.], (London, 1832), 81.

tion of the supremacy of law propounded by Coke during the tumultuous reigns of James I and Charles I, a dimension of whigism that informs the latter's *Answer to the XIX Propositions* in 1642 and concludes with words attributed to the Barons at the Merton Parliament of 1236, who cried *una voce: nolumus leges Angliae mutari.*[47] It is in the *Answer* that the paradigm first sees the light of the mixed and balanced British constitution of king, lords, and commons, with some identification given of a functional distribution of powers of government, an account more indebted to Aristotle, Polybius, and Aquinas, perhaps, than to the double majesty of the English constitution. In any event, this version of the admirably mixed and balanced constitution both antedates and shapes the Old Whig views of the Commonwealth period and remains highly influential (and controversial) in the Settlement following the Glorious Revolution of 1688 and afterward, a long and complicated story that cannot be retold here.[48]

Coke encountered the question of the nature of the British constitution in the context of the Stuart kings' assertion of absolute rule by divine right in the name of royal prerogative and sovereignty. The sovereignty of God and law is his response; the king is subordinate to both, however extensive his prerogative rightly is. So, far from being absolute, the English king's power is limited. Bracton had taught this, as had Fortescue, and with great fervor Coke carried this conviction into the seventeenth century. The tension between the supremacy of a law embodying liberty, "perfect justice," and the community's consent (Fortescue), and the omnipresent threat of injustice, abuse of power, arbitrary rule, and tyranny defined the debate become politi-

47. Weston, "Beginnings of the Classical Theory of the English Constitution," 144; Sir Edward Coke, *Reports of Sir Edward Coke, Knt., in English, In Thirteen Parts Complete,* ed. Serjeant George Wilson (London, 1776–1777), *Fourth Report,* vii–viii.

48. In addition to sources previously mentioned, indispensable for this story are: Corinne C. Weston, *English Constitutional Theory and the House of Lords, 1556–1832* (New York, 1965); Corinne Comstock Weston and Janelle R. Greenberg, *Subjects and Sovereigns: The Grand Controversy over Legal Sovereignty in Stuart England* (Cambridge, England, 1981); Paul K. Christianson, "Politics and Parliaments in England, 1604–1629," *Canadian Journal of History/Annales Canadiennes D'Histoire,* XVI (1981), 107–13; Paul K. Christianson, "Political Thought in Early Stuart England," *Historical Journal,* XXX (1987), 523–39; and Michael Mendle, *Dangerous Positions: Mixed Government, the Estates of the Realm, and the "Answer to the XIX Propositions,"* (Tuscaloosa, Ala., 1985).

cal and constitutional crisis. This tension forms the high ground of Coke's resolute assertion of law, parliamentary rights, and English liberties in his later career. It also defines the rudimentary meaning of free government in America in the crisis of the next century, when Burke believes the English may themselves have forgotten it. By a remarkable effort and utilizing all available means, Coke effectively reasserts, and through his personal persuasiveness and great historical authority helps make stick, the constitutional principles of law as limitations on the powers of human governors. Law is the enforcement of Justice in society directly protective of public interest and the people's liberties alike.

To the degree that such a government of laws and not of men stands at the center of American constitutional order, it is largely indebted to Coke and the ancient teaching he vivified. This is, however, to notice the remarkable fact that the United States Constitution is in considerable degree not merely a result of a Revolution that is the last act of the Renaissance, as Pocock convinces us, but an antimodernist embodiment of medieval principles of order. The great historian of English law, Sir William Holdsworth, writes, "Coke preserved the medieval idea of the supremacy of the law, at a time when political speculation was tending to assert the necessity of a sovereign person or body, which was above the law." "Coke's books are the great dividing line, and we are hardly out of the Middle Age till he has dogmatized its results," as Maitland tells Holdsworth.

The latter then continues. In the seventeenth century Parliament helped Coke to maintain the "medieval conception of the supremacy of law, and to apply it to the government of a modern state. In this matter also England became a model both to the framers of the Constitution of the United States and to the framers of the constitutions in continental states. The Supreme Court of the United States is a body which safeguards, more effectively than any other tribunal in the world, Coke's idea of the supremacy of the law."[49] And finally, Holdsworth writes, "It is largely owing to the influence of [Coke's] writings that these medieval conceptions have become part of our

49. Sir William Holdsworth, *Some Makers of English Law: Tagore Lectures of 1937–38* (Cambridge, England, 1938), 113, 126–32.

modern law. . . . *They preserved for England and the world the con-stitutional doctrine of the rule of law.*" [50]

V

The Constitution in Article VI's "Supremacy Clause" announces it-self and laws made in pursuance thereof to be the "supreme Law of the Land" in the United States, "and the Judges in every State shall be bound thereby, any Thing in the Constitution or Laws of any State to the Contrary notwithstanding." This is the root meaning of suprem-acy of law in the country, both then and now. As the basis of our government, it ought never be forgotten that the Constitution is more than a text, a historical document, or an expression of political phi-losophy. It is fundamental law, enforceable in courts in all its provi-sions as the law of the land superior to any other law, as almost five hundred volumes of *United States Reports* monumentally emphasize. All is lost if we forget that the Constitution is the Law, the monument to justice that is conjured in the phrase, a government of laws and not of men.

Yet nearly as much may be lost if we forget that the Constitution is more than merely law, even the supreme Law of the Land. The tri-umph of the framers was to see beyond the narrow vision of the "au-tonomy of the law" and recognize that dogmatic proclamation of the law is the law is the law—sovereign command based in will and de-manding obedience[51]—would not secure the blessings of liberty or establish justice as was their intention for America. Fortescue's and Coke's theory of the law as perfect justice and virtue was accepted as intellectually valid and spiritually necessary. The founding genera-tion's utterly determined resistance to tyranny from the British minis-try before Independence and from rapacious minorities or uncaring

50. Holdsworth, *History of English Law*, V, 493. See also Berman, *Law and Revolution*, 1–45; Tierney, *Religion, Law, and the Growth of Constitutional Thought*, esp. 80–108. The stature of Coke did not escape his parliamentary associates during the Petition of Right contro-versy, including the great John Selden, who praised him on the floor of the House of Commons as "that great *Monarcha Juris*, King of the Law, Sir Edward Coke." Quoted in Catherine Drinker Bowen, *The Lion and the Throne: The Life and Times of Sir Edward Coke (1552–1634)* (Boston, 1956), 487.

51. Cf. Hobbes, *Leviathan*, esp. Chaps. 17, 18, and 26; see Morton J. Horwitz, *Transfor-mation of American Law, 1780–1860* (Cambridge, Mass., 1977), 1–30.

majorities afterward is evident in the records as motivating the gathering of the Federal Convention and structuring the ratification debate and adoption of the Bill of Rights.

The range of problems that emerge at this point arise from the paradoxical status of human existence itself and from nothing less than that. The fruits of man's emphatic insistence that he is more than merely mortal and participates in things eternal, the realm of transcendent divine Being as philosophers say, are eagerly sought, yet only imperfectly realized in temporal existence. Neither God nor beast, neither merely mortal nor simply immortal, the human realm is the In-Between reality of perfections glimpsed but only fleetingly attained, of happiness interspersed with boredom, disappointment, and despair, redeemed by faith and hope—if it be redeemed at all. In short, we behold the human condition familiar to Everyman from all available sources of insight, as we are reminded by the poetry of Alexander Pope.

Confronted with such a picture of reality, what does the political realist do? With allowances for the unique features of time and place, he does just what the American founders did. An intrinsically paradoxical existence cannot be remedied by pretending it is less contradictory than it is without impaling oneself on the horns of existential dilemmas that produce the parade of reductionist ideologies, whose grotesque idolatries disfigure and torment modern mankind. The point is to erect and preserve a political order fit for habitation by human beings. Thus, Publius and his associates remember Fortescue's golden words that "the king is given for the sake of the kingdom, and not the kingdom for the sake of the king," and that "freedom was instilled into human nature by God,"[52] even as they write their own golden words.

Ambition must be made to counteract ambition. The interest of the man must be connected with the constitutional rights of the place. It may be a reflection on human nature that such devices should be necessary to control the abuses of government. But what is government itself but the greatest of all reflections on human nature? If men were angels, no government would be necessary. If angels were to govern men, neither external nor internal controls on government would be necessary. In framing a government which

52. Fortescue, *De laudibus*, 89–91, 105.

is to be administered by men over men, the great difficulty lies in this: you must first enable the government to control the governed; and in the next place oblige it to control itself. A dependence on the people is, no doubt, the primary control on the government; but experience has taught mankind the necessity of auxiliary precautions.

This policy of supplying, by opposite and rival interests, the defect of better motives, might be traced through the whole system of human affairs, private as well as public. We see it particularly displayed in all the subordinate distributions of power, where the constant aim is to divide and arrange the several offices in such a manner as that each may be a check on the other—that the private interest of every individual may be a sentinel over the public rights. These inventions of prudence cannot be less requisite in the distribution of the supreme powers of the State.[53]

While the virtue of the people is the *primary* guarantee of just government, the auxiliary precaution of checking and balancing within functionally separated (but overlapping) powers pits self-serving passion against passion, thereby to produce just and rational rule: Aristotle's rule of law, when God and reason alone rule, as far as this is possible in human governance. Through this three-way process of cancellation effected by the interaction of Congress, president, and courts, reason emerges as a noble residue of the ordinary operation of government when regulated by the central constitutional mechanism. This is the best we can do in an imperfect world. Nor is high purpose abandoned, for we have seen Publius insist that "Justice is the end of government. It is the end of civil society. It ever has been and ever will be pursued until it be obtained, or until liberty be lost in the pursuit."[54]

Plausible means to achieve noble ends thereby ingeniously structure American constitutional institutions rooted in a sound conception of human nature which remains sound today. Institutionally, the governmental structures as they operate become the means of utilizing the well-attested corruptions of human beings simultaneously to curb their worst tendencies and to drive the engine of a government dedicated to justice—reluctant assistants to reason and good intention in ordering human affairs.

This strategy, however, can only succeed as a supplementary means

53. Cooke (ed.), *Federalist*, 349 (No. 51).
54. *Ibid.*, 352.

of serving virtuous ends. The integrity and virtue of the people must remain the primary force shaping *civic consciousness* as the "first order of reliance."[55] Civic consciousness is highly differentiated in the founding period by reason of long self-government and attendant development of an indigenous common law and traditions of governance;[56] the sense of public spirit fostered by a pervasive congregationalist church polity; the sense of equality, dignity, and self-reliance generated by social and economic circumstance, and above all, by religious teachings of a Bible-centered faith premised on the priesthood of all believers;[57] and by decades of scrutiny of public policies and officials that engrossed while politically educating Americans as the quarrel with Britain intensified after 1760. In its operations, then, the American political order of separated, checked, and balanced central powers and divided powers throughout the federal system concretely compose an "invitation to struggle," as Edward Corwin aptly describes it. This is most especially true of relations between the president and the Congress regarding policy direction and control, as is verified every day in news reports.[58] The system works as the founders intended it would. Efficient government was not their first priority, Chief Justice Warren Burger once remarked.

The highest and noblest things can only indirectly concern government in this scheme. Life, liberty, and happiness self-evidently arise and are fulfilled in wider horizons than society and government reach. They relate to the natural and transcendental dimensions of human existence whose reality and truth, while superior and controlling in social and political affairs, still cannot finally be arbitrated politically; hence, the notion of rights protected by but not originating in the Constitution. Hence, also, is the great solution to the vexed problems of religion of the First Amendment and the exhortations throughout their lifetime of such stalwarts as Madison and Jefferson

55. Hanson, *From Kingdom to Commonwealth*, 33.
56. Greene, *Peripheries and Center, passim.*
57. Sanford Levinson, "'The Constitution' in American Civil Religion," *Supreme Court Review* (1979), 123–51 at 128.
58. Edward S. Corwin, *The President: Office and Powers* (rev. ed.; New York, 1984), 201; cf. Cecil V. Crabb, Jr., and Pat M. Holt, *Invitation to Struggle: Congress, the President, and Foreign Policy* (Washington, D.C., 1984), *passim.*

that churchmen stay out of politics and government keep out of religion and not intrude between the consciences of free men and their Maker.

To *pursue* happiness and the ultimate fulfillment of mind and spirit certain social, economic, and political institutions and processes are vital. These supply but the infrastructure, however, of fruitful and happy lives of individual men and women who are also citizens, for it is the individual person who stands at the center of public concerns in America. The attaining and enjoyment of happiness are subtle matters of personality in religion, no less than in other spheres of mind. Free government properly plays a role there that is no more than conducive and instrumental. Public and private spheres, neither coterminous nor perfectly discrete, ambiguously overlap. Hence, institutional representations of them will always be less than perfectly satisfactory. The political realm clearly is a modest one, by American lights. Politics not only does not exhaust reality, but—vital as it is for securing free existence—it is by far not the noblest or best part of reality.

This roughly summarizes the ground of the institutional solution achieved by a devout generation who yet favored separating church and state, men who (without exception among the founders, so far as I can see) like Benjamin Franklin deeply believed in Providence's blessing of America, "that God governs in the affairs of men."[59] They favored it in the name of liberty, religion, and peace in the society. It remains, on balance, a great solution, even in a rebellious age of ideological division. Descendants of the founders continue to revere liberty, justice, truth, and the noble vision of human and divine reality they mediated to posterity, a political order eminently fit for human habitation.

We still have a republic, if we can keep it, but now as it did then, that takes faith no less than intelligence.

59. Farrand (ed.), *Records of the Federal Convention of 1787*, I, 452; see p. 161 herein.

Bibliography

Aaron, Richard I. *John Locke*. 2nd ed. Oxford, England, 1965.

Aaron, Richard I., and J. Gibb, eds. *An Early Draft of Locke's Essay, Together with Excerpts from His Journals*. Oxford, England, 1936.

Adair, Douglass. *Fame and the Founding Fathers*. Edited by Trevor Colbourn. New York, 1974.

———. "'That Politics May be Reduced to a Science'; David Hume, James Madison, and the Tenth Federalist." *Huntington Library Quarterly*, XX (1957), 343–60.

Adams, Charles Francis, ed. *Letters and Other Writings of James Madison*. 4 vols. Philadelphia, 1865.

———, ed. *Letters of John Adams*. 2 vols. Boston, 1841.

———, ed. *Works of John Adams*. 10 vols. Boston, 1850–56.

Adams, Dixon W., ed. *Jefferson's Extracts from the Gospels: "The Philosophy of Jesus" and "The Life and Morals of Jesus."* Princeton, 1983.

Adams, Randolph G. *Political Ideas of the American Revolution: Britannic-American Contributions to the Problem of Imperial Organization, 1765–1775*. 3rd ed. With a commentary by Merrill Jensen. New York, 1958.

Ahlstrom, Sydney E. *A Religious History of the American People*. New Haven, 1972.

Anson, W. R. *Principles of the English Law of Contract*. Edited by J. C. Knowlton. 2nd American edition. Chicago, 1887.

Aristotle. *Politics*. Translated by T. A. Sinclair. Revised and re-presented by Trevor J. Saunders. Harmondsworth, England, 1981.

———. *Nicomachean Ethics*. Edited and translated by Martin Ostwald. Indianapolis, 1962.

Ashcraft, Richard. "Locke's State of Nature: Historical Fact or Moral Fiction." *American Political Science Review*, LXVII (1968), 898–915.

———. *Revolutionary Politics and Locke's Two Treatises of Government*. Princeton, 1986.

Austin, John. *Lectures on Jurisprudence*. Edited by R. Campbell. 5th ed. 2 vols. London, 1885.

Axtell, James L. *Educational Writings of John Locke: A Critical Edition with Introduction and Notes.* Cambridge, England, 1968.

Bagehot, Walter. *English Constitution and Other Political Essays.* Rev. ed. New York, 1877.

Bailyn, Bernard. *Ideological Origins of the American Revolution.* Cambridge, Mass., 1967.

———. *Origins of American Politics.* New York, 1969.

———, ed. *Pamphlets of the American Revolution, 1750–1776.* Cambridge, Mass., 1965.

Baldwin, Alice M. *New England Clergy and the American Revolution.* Durham, N.C., 1928.

———. "Sowers of Sedition: The Political Theories of the New Light Presbyterian Clergy of Virginia and North Carolina." *William and Mary Quarterly,* 3rd ser., V (1948), 52–76.

Beitzinger, A. J. *A History of American Political Thought.* New York, 1972.

Bergson, Henri. *Two Sources of Morality and Religion.* Translated by R. A. Audra and C. Brereton. New York, 1935.

Berman, Harold J. *Law and Revolution: The Formation of the Western Legal Tradition.* Cambridge, Mass., 1983.

Bigongiari, Dino, ed. *Political Ideas of St. Thomas Aquinas: Representative Selections.* New York, 1969.

Bluhm, William T. *Theories of the Political System: Classics of Political Thought and Modern Political Analysis.* Englewood Cliffs, N.J., 1965.

Bonomi, Patricia U., and Peter R. Eisenstadt. "Church Adherence in the Eighteenth-Century British American Colonies." *William and Mary Quarterly,* 3rd. ser., XXXIX (1982), 245–76.

Boorstin, Daniel J. *Mysterious Science of the Law.* 1941; rpr. Boston, 1958.

Bowen, Catherine Drinker. *The Lion and the Throne: The Life and Times of Sir Edward Coke (1552–1634).* Boston, 1956.

Boyd, J. P., ed. *Papers of Thomas Jefferson.* 52 vols. projected. Princeton, 1950–.

Brant, Irving. *James Madison.* 6 vols. Indianapolis, 1941–61.

Bridenbaugh, Carl. *Cities in Revolt: Urban Life in America, 1743–1776.* New York, 1955.

———. *Spirit of '76: The Growth of American Patriotism Before Independence, 1607–1776.* New York, 1975.

Brown, Richard D. "Founding Fathers of 1776 and 1787: A Collective View." *William and Mary Quarterly,* 3rd ser., XXXIII (1976), 465–80.

Brunner, Otto. *Land und Herrschaft: Grundfragen der territorialen Verfassungsgeschichte Oesterreichs im Mittelalter.* 4th ed. Wien-Wiesbaden, 1959.

Bryce, James [Lord Bryce.] *American Commonwealth.* New ed. 2 vols. New York, 1922.

Butterfield, Lyman H., ed. *Diary and Autobiography of John Adams.* 4 vols. Cambridge, Mass., 1961.

Camus, Albert. *The Rebel: An Essay on Man in Revolt.* Translated by Anthony Bower. New York, 1956.

Cappon, Lester J., ed. *Adams-Jefferson Letters: The Complete Correspondence Between Thomas Jefferson and Abigail and John Adams.* 2 vols. in 1. 1959; rpr. New York, 1971.

Cherry, Conrad, ed. *God's New Israel: Religious Interpretations of American Destiny.* Englewood Cliffs, N.J., 1971.

Christianson, Paul K. "Political Thought in Early Stuart England." *Historical Journal,* XXX (1987), 523–39.

———. "Politics and Parliaments in England, 1604–1629." *Canadian Journal of History/Annales Canadiennes D'Histoire,* XVI (1981), 107–13.

Cicero, Marcus Tullius. *On the Commonwealth.* Translated with an introduction by George H. Sabine and Stanley B. Smith. 1929; rpr. Indianapolis, 1976.

Cohn, Norman. *Pursuit of the Millennium: Revolutionary Messianism in Medieval and Reformation Europe and Its Bearing on Modern Totalitarian Movements.* 2nd ed. 1961; revised and expanded, New York, 1970.

Coke, Sir Edward. *Second Part of the Institutes of the Laws of England.* London, 1642.

Collins, Varnum Lansing. *President Witherspoon: A Biography.* 2 vols. in 1. 1925; rpr. New York, 1969.

Cooke, Jacob E., ed. *Federalist.* Middletown, Conn., 1961.

Corwin, Edward S. *"Higher Law" Background of American Constitutional Law.* 1928; rpr. Ithaca, N.Y., 1957.

———. *The President: Office and Powers.* Rev. ed. New York, 1984.

———, ed. *Constitution of the United States of America: Analysis and Interpretation.* Washington, D.C., 1953.

Cox, Richard. *Locke on War and Peace.* Oxford, England, 1960.

Crabb, Cecil V., Jr., and Pat M. Holt. *Invitation to Struggle: Congress, the President, and Foreign Policy.* Washington, D.C., 1984.

Cranston, Maurice. *John Locke: A Biography.* New York, 1957.

Craven, Wesley Frank. *Legend of the Founding Fathers.* 1956; rpr. Ithaca, N.Y., 1965.

Cremin, Lawrence A. *American Education: The Colonial Experience, 1607–1783.* New York, 1970.

Crick, Bernard. *American Science of Politics: Its Origins and Conditions.* Berkeley, 1967.

D'Elia, Donald J. "The Republican Theology of Benjamin Rush." *Pennsylvania History,* XXXIII (1966), 187–202.

d'Entreves, A. P. *Notion of the State: An Introduction to Political Theory.* Oxford, England, 1967.

Davidson, James West. *Logic of Millennial Thought: Eighteenth-Century New England.* New Haven, 1977.

Diels, Hermann, and Walter Kranz, *Die Fragmente der Vorsokratiker.* 7th ed. Berlin, 1954.

Dishman, Robert B., ed. *Burke and Paine: On Revolution and the Rights of Man.* New York, 1971.

Dunn, John. *John Locke.* Oxford, England, 1984.

———. *Political Obligation in its Historical Context: Essays in Political Theory.* Cambridge, England, 1980.

———. *Political Thought of John Locke: An Historical Account of the Argument of the 'Two Treatises of Government.'* Cambridge, England, 1969.

Dwight, Sereno E., ed. *Works of President Edwards.* 10 vols. New York, 1830.

Eckhardt, K. A., ed. *Sachsenspiegel.* Hanover, 1933.

Elazar, Daniel J., and John Kincaid, eds. *Covenant, Polity and Constitutionalism.*

Reprint of *Publius: Journal of Federalism,* X (Fall, 1980), no. 4. Lanham, Md., 1980.

Eliot, T. S. "Choruses from 'The Rock.'" In *Complete Poems and Plays, 1909–1950.* New York, 1971.

Elliot, Jonathan, ed. *Debates in the Several State Conventions on the Adoption of the Federal Constitution.* 2nd ed. 5 vols. 1830; rpr. New York, 1974.

Elton, G. R., ed. *Tudor Constitution: Documents and Commentary.* Cambridge, England, 1960.

Farrand, Max. *Framing of the Constitution of the United States.* New Haven, 1913.

——, ed. *Records of the Federal Convention of 1787.* 1911, rev. ed., 1937. 4 vols. New Haven, 1966.

Fleet, Elizabeth, ed. "Madison's 'Detached Memoranda.'" *William and Mary Quarterly,* 3rd ser., III (1946), 554–68.

Foner, Philip S., ed. *Complete Writings of Thomas Paine.* 2 vols. New York, 1945.

Ford, Paul L., ed. *Pamphlets on the Constitution of the United States.* 1888; rpr. New York, 1968.

Ford, Worthington C., ed. *Writings of John Quincy Adams.* 7 vols. New York, 1913.

——, ed. *Writings of Thomas Jefferson.* 10 vols. New York, 1892–99.

Ford, Worthington C., et al., eds. *Journals of the Continental Congress.* 34 vols. Washington, D.C., 1904–37.

Fortescue, Sir John. *De laudibus legum Angliae.* Edited and translated by S. B. Chrimes. Cambridge, England, 1942.

Friedrich, Carl J. *An Introduction to Political Theory: Twelve Lectures at Harvard.* New York, 1967.

Frye, Northrop. *Great Code: The Bible and Literature.* San Diego, 1982.

Gardiner, S. R., ed. *Constitutional Documents of the Puritan Revolution, 1625–1660.* 3rd ed., rev.; Oxford, England, 1906.

Gebhardt, Jürgen. *Die Krise des Amerikanismus: Revolutionäre Ordnung und gesselschaftliches Selbstverständnis in der amerikanischen Republik.* Stuttgart, 1976.

George, M. Dorothy. *London Life in the Eighteenth Century.* 1925; rpr. New York, 1964.

Germino, Dante. *Beyond Ideology: The Revival of Political Theory.* New York, 1967.

Gilmore, Myron P. *Argument from Roman Law.* Cambridge, Mass., 1941.

Gilson, Étienne. *Spirit of Medieval Philosophy.* Translated by A. H. C. Downes. New York, 1940.

——. *Unity of Philosophical Experience.* New York, 1937.

Goldwin, Robert A., and William A. Schambra, eds. *How Does the Constitution Secure Rights?* Washington, D.C., 1985.

Gough, J. W. *Fundamental Law in English Constitutional History.* Cor. ed. Oxford, 1961.

Green, T. H., and T. H. Grose, eds. *Philosophical Works,* by David Hume. 2 vols. 1886; rpr. Aalen, Germany, 1964.

Greene, Jack P. *A Bicentennial Bookshelf: Historians Analyze the Constitutional Era.* Philadelphia, 1986.

——. *Intellectual Heritage of the Constitutional Era: The Delegates' Library.* Philadelphia, 1986.

——. *Peripheries and Center: Constitutional Development in the Extended Polities of the British Empire and the United States, 1607–1788.* Athens, Ga., 1986.

Greven, Philip J., Jr. *Protestant Temperament: Patterns of Child-Rearing, Religious Experience, and the Self in Early America.* 1977; rpr. New York, 1979.

Grey, Thomas C. "Origins of the Unwritten Constitution: Fundamental Law in American Revolutionary Thought." *Stanford Law Review,* XXX (1982), 49–83.

Gummere, Richard M. *American Colonial Mind and the Classical Tradition: Essays in Comparative Culture.* Cambridge, Mass., 1963.

Hall, Verna May, ed. *Christian History of the American Revolution.* San Francisco, 1976.

Hall, Verna May, and Joseph A. Montgomery, eds. *Christian History of the Constitution of the United States of America.* Rev. ed. San Francisco, 1966.

Hallowell, John H. *Main Currents in Modern Political Thought.* New York, 1950.

———. *Moral Foundation of Democracy.* Chicago, 1954.

Hanson, Donald W. *From Kingdom to Commonwealth: The Development of Civic Consciousness in English Thought.* Cambridge, Mass., 1970.

Haraszti, Zoltan. *John Adams and the Prophets of Progress.* 1952; rpr. New York, 1964.

Hart, Benjamin. *Faith and Freedom: The Christian Roots of American Liberty.* Dallas, Tex., 1988.

Hart, H. L. A. *Concept of Law.* Oxford, 1961.

Hart, Levi. *Liberty Described and Recommended: In a Sermon Preached to the Corporation of Freemen in Farmington.* In *American Political Writing During the Founding Era, 1760–1805,* edited by Charles S. Hyneman and Donald S. Lutz. 2 vols. Indianapolis, 1983.

Hartnett, Robert C. "The Religion of the Founding Fathers." In *Wellsprings of the American Spirit,* edited by F. Ernest Johnson. New York, 1964.

Hartz, Louis. *Liberal Tradition in America: An Interpretation of American Political Thought Since the Revolution.* New York, 1955.

Hatch, Nathan O. *Sacred Cause of Liberty: Republican Thought and the Millennium in Revolutionary New England.* New Haven, 1977.

———, and Mark A. Noll, eds. *Bible in America: Essays in Cultural History.* New York, 1982.

Heimert, Alan. *Religion and the American Mind: From the Great Awakening to the Revolution.* Cambridge, Mass., 1966.

Hexter, J. H. *On Historians: Reappraisals of Some of the Makers of Modern History.* Cambridge, Mass., 1979.

Hobbes, Thomas. *Leviathan; or The Matter, Forme and Power of a Commonwealth Ecclesiastical and Civil.* Edited by Michael Oakeshott. Oxford, England, n. d.

Holdsworth, Sir William. *A History of English Law.* 13 vols. London, 1903–38.

———. *Some Makers of English Law: Tagore Lectures of 1937–38.* Cambridge, England, 1938.

Hooker, Richard. *Of the Laws of Ecclesiastical Polity.* 2 vols. Edited by Christopher Morris. New York, 1907.

Horwitz, Morton J. *Transformation of American Law, 1780–1860.* Cambridge, Mass., 1977.

Hosmer, James K., ed. *Winthrop's Journal: History of New England, 1630–1649.* 2 vols. New York, 1908.

Howard, A. E. Dick. *Road from Runnymede: Magna Carta and Constitutionalism in America.* Charlottesville, 1968.

Howe, John R., Jr. *Changing Political Thought of John Adams.* Princeton, 1966.

Hume, David. *Enquiries Concerning the Human Understanding and Concerning the Principles of Morals.* Edited by L. A. Selby-Bigge. 2nd ed. Oxford, 1902.

———. "Of Parties in General." In *Essays Moral, Political and Literary,* edited by Eugene F. Miller. Indianapolis, 1985.

———. *A Treatise of Human Nature.* 2 vols. 1740; rpr. London, 1911.

Hunt, Gaillard. *History of the Seal of the United States.* Washington, D.C., 1909.

Hutcheson, Francis. *A System of Moral Philosophy.* 2 vols. London, 1755.

Hutchinson, William T., *et al.* (eds.), *Papers of James Madison.* 17 vols. to date. Chicago, 1962–67; Charlottesville, 1968–.

Hutson, James H. "The Creation of the Constitution: The Integrity of the Documentary Record." *Texas Law Review,* LXV (1986), 1–39.

Hyneman, Charles, and Donald S. Lutz, eds. *American Political Writing During the Founding Era, 1760–1805.* 2 vols. Indianapolis, 1983.

Jaffa, Harry V. "Were the Founding Fathers Christians?" With a "reply" by Walter Berns. *This World,* VIII (Spring/Summer, 1984), 3–12.

James, William. *Essays in Radical Empiricism; A Pluralistic Universe.* Edited by Ralph Barton Perry. 2 vols. in 1. 1942; rpr. Gloucester, Mass., 1967.

Jaspers, Karl. *Vom Ursprung und Ziel der Geschichte.* Frankfurt-am-Main, 1955.

Johnson, Robert C., *et al.,* eds. *Proceedings in Parliament, 1628.* 6 vols. New Haven, 1977–83.

Kantorowicz, Ernst. *Frederick the Second, 1194–1250.* New York, 1957.

Keller, Charles R. *Second Great Awakening in Connecticut.* New Haven, 1942.

Kelly, George Armstrong. *Politics and Religious Consciousness in America.* New Brunswick, N.J., 1984.

Kettner, James H. *Development of American Citizenship, 1608–1870.* Chapel Hill, N.C., 1978.

King, Martin Luther, Jr. *Why We Can't Wait.* New York, 1964.

Kirk, G. S., and J. E. Raven. *Presocratic Philosophers: A Critical History with Selections of Texts.* Cambridge, England, 1960.

Kloppenberg, James T. "The Virtues of Liberalism: Christianity, Republicanism, and Ethics in Early American Political Discourse." *Journal of American History,* LXXIV (1987), 9–33.

Knox, Ronald A. *Enthusiasm: A Chapter in the History of Religion, with Special Reference to the XVII and XVIII Centuries.* New York, 1961.

Koch, Adrienne, and William Peden, eds. *Life and Selected Writings of Thomas Jefferson.* New York, 1944.

Kuklick, Bruce. *Churchmen and Philosophers: From Jonathan Edwards to John Dewey.* New Haven, 1985.

Lasky, Melvin J. "The Birth of a Metaphor: On the Origins of Utopia and Revolution (II)." *Encounter,* XXXIV (1970), 35–37.

Lasswell, Harold. *Politics: Who Gets What, When and How.* New York, n. d.

Lecky, W. E. H. *A History of England in the Eighteenth Century.* Cabinet ed. 7 vols. London, 1892.

Lemay, J. A. Leo, ed. *Writings of Benjamin Franklin.* New York, 1987.

Levinson, Sanford. "'The Constitution' in American Civil Religion." *Supreme Court Review* (1979), 123–51.

Lifton, Robert Jay. *History and Human Survival: Essays on the Young and the Old,*

Survivors and the Dead, Peace and War, and on Contemporary Psychohistory. 1961; rpr. New York, 1971.

Lipscomb, A. A., and A. E. Bergh, eds. *Writings of Thomas Jefferson.* 20 vols. in 10. Washington, D.C., 1905.

Locke, John. *An Essay Concerning Human Understanding.* Edited by John W. Yolton. Rev. ed. 2 vols. London, 1964.

———. *An Essay Concerning Human Understanding; Collated and Annotated, with Prolegomena, Biographical, Critical, and Historical.* Edited by A. C. Fraser. 2 vols. 1894; rpr. New York, 1959.

———. *Essays on the Law of Nature.* Edited by Wolfgang von Leyden. Oxford, 1954.

———. *Two Tracts of Government.* Edited with introduction, notes, and translation by Philip Abrams. Cambridge, England, 1967.

———. *Two Treatises of Government: A Critical Edition with an Introduction and Apparatus Criticus.* Edited by Peter Laslett. 1960; rpr. Cambridge, England, 1963.

———. *Works of John Locke.* New ed. corrected. 10 vols. 1823; rpr. Aalen, Germany, 1963.

Lovejoy, Arthur O. *Great Chain of Being: A Study of the History of an Idea.* 1936; rpr. Cambridge, Mass., 1964.

Lutz, Donald S. *Popular Consent and Popular Control: Whig Political Theory in the Early State Constitutions.* Baton Rouge, 1980.

———. "Relative Influence of European Writers on Late Eighteenth-Century American Political Thought." *American Political Science Review,* LXXVIII (1984), 189–97.

———, ed. *Documents of Political Foundation Written by Colonial Americans: From Covenant to Constitution.* Philadelphia, 1986.

Macfie, Alec L. "Invisible Hand of Jupiter." *Journal of the History of Ideas,* XXXII (1971), 595–99.

Macpherson, C. B. *Political Theory of Possessive Individualism: Hobbes to Locke.* Oxford, England, 1962.

Madison, James. "The Nature of the Union: A Final Reckoning." In *Mind of the Founder: Sources of the Political Thought of James Madison,* edited by Marvin Meyers. Indianapolis, 1973.

Maine, Sir Henry S. *Dissertations on the Early Law and Custom.* London, 1883.

Maitland, Frederic W. *English Law and the Renaissance.* Cambridge, England, 1901.

Mandeville, Bernard. *Fable of the Bees, or Private Vices, Publick Benefits.* Edited by Irwin Primer. New York, 1962.

Martin, James K. *Men in Rebellion: High Governmental Leaders and the Coming of the American Revolution.* New Brunswick, N.J., 1973.

Marty, Martin E. *Pilgrims in Their Own Land: 500 Years of Religion in America.* Boston, 1984.

Marx, Karl. *Die Frühschriften.* Edited by Siegfrid Landshut. Stuttgart, 1953.

———. *Economic and Philosophic Manuscripts of 1844.* Edited by Dirk J. Struik. Translated by Martin Milligan. New York, 1964.

May, Henry F. *Enlightenment in America.* New York, 1976.

Mayo, H. B. *An Introduction to Democratic Theory.* New York, 1960.

McCloskey, Richard G., ed. *Lectures on Law* [1790–1791]. In *Works of James Wilson.* 2 vols. Cambridge, Mass., 1967.

McDonald, Forrest. *Novus Ordo Seclorum: The Intellectual Origins of the Constitution.* Lawrence, Kan., 1985.

———. *We the People: The Economic Origins of the Constitution.* Chicago, 1958.

McDonald, Forrest, and Ellen Shapiro McDonald. "The Ethnic Origins of the American People, 1790." *William and Mary Quarterly,* 3rd ser., XXXVII (1980), 179–99.

McIlwain, Charles H. *American Revolution: A Constitutional Interpretation.* New York, 1923.

Mead, Sidney E. "The Nation with the Soul of a Church." *Church History,* XXXVI (1967), 262–83.

Mendle, Michael. *Dangerous Positions: Mixed Government, the Estates of the Realm, and the "Answer to the XIX Propositions."* Tuscaloosa, Ala., 1985.

Middlekauff, Robert. *Glorious Cause: The American Revolution, 1763–1789.* New York, 1982.

———. "Is America Still a Glorious Cause? A Conversation with Historian Robert Middlekauff." *Claremont Review of Books,* Dec. 1983, 10.

Miller, Eugene F. "On the American Founders' Defense of Liberal Education in a Republic." *Review of Politics,* XLVI (1984), 71–74.

Miller, Perry. "From the Covenant to the Revival." In *Religion in American Life,* edited by J. W. Smith and A. L. Jamison. 4 vols. Princeton, 1961.

———. "From the Covenant to the Revival." In *Religion in American History: Interpretive Essays,* edited by John M. Mulder and John F. Wilson. Englewood Cliffs, N.J., 1978.

Morey, William C. *Outlines of Roman Law, Comprising Its Historical Growth and General Principles.* 2nd ed., rev. New York, 1914.

Morison, Samuel E., and Henry S. Commager. *Growth of the American Republic.* 4th ed. 2 vols. New York, 1950.

Morison, Samuel E., ed. *Sources and Documents Illustrating the American Revolution.* Oxford, England, 1923.

Murrin, John M. "Great Inversion, or Court versus Country: A Comparison of the Revolution Settlements in England (1688–1721) and America (1776–1816)." In *Three British Revolutions: 1641, 1688, 1776.* Edited by J. G. A. Pocock. Princeton, 1980.

Needham, Joseph. *Science and Civilization in China.* 6 vols. Cambridge, England, 1954–75.

Nelson, William E. *Americanization of the Common Law: The Impact of Legal Change on Massachusetts Society, 1760–1830.* Cambridge, Mass., 1975.

Niebuhr, H. Richard. "The Idea of Covenant and American Democracy." *Church History,* XXIII (1954), 126–35.

Opitz, Peter J. "John Locke." In *Zwischen Revolution und Restauration: Politisches Denken in England im 17. Jahrhundert.* Edited by Eric Voegelin. List Hochschulreihe Geschichte des politischen Denkens. Munich, 1968.

Osgood, Herbert L. *American Colonies in the Eighteenth Century.* 4 vols. 1924; rpr. Gloucester, Mass., 1958.

Otis, James. *Rights of the British Colonies Asserted and Proved.* In *Pamphlets of the American Revolution, 1750–1776.* Edited by Bernard Bailyn. Cambridge, Mass., 1965.

Pascal, Blaise. *Pensées and the Provincial Letters*. Edited by Saxe Commins. New York, 1941.

Paton, G. W. *A Text-Book of Jurisprudence*. Oxford, England, 1946.

Pegis, A. C., ed. *Basic Writings of St. Thomas Aquinas*. 2 vols. New York, 1945.

Perry, Ralph Barton. *Characteristically American*. New York, 1949.

———. *Puritanism and Democracy*. New York, 1944.

Philathes [Elisha Williams?]. *Essential Rights of Protestants: A Seasonable Plea for the Liberty of Conscience, and the Right of Private Judgment in Matters of Religion, Without any Control from Human Authority*. Boston, 1744.

Pocock, J. G. A. *Ancient Constitution and the Feudal Law: A Study of English Historical Thought in the Seventeenth Century*. 1957; rpr. New York, 1967. Rev. ed. Cambridge, England, 1987.

———. *Machiavellian Moment: Florentine Political Thought and the Atlantic Republican Tradition*. Princeton, 1975.

———. "*Machiavellian Moment* Revisited: A Study in History and Ideology." *Journal of Modern History*, LIII (1981), 49–72.

———. "Radical Criticisms of the Whig Order in the Age Before the Revolution." In *Origins of Anglo-American Radicalism*. Edited by Margaret Jacob and James L. Jacob. London, 1984.

Pollock, Frederick, and Frederic W. Maitland. *History of English Law Before the Time of Edward I*. 2d ed. Reissued with a new introduction and select bibliography by S. F. C. Milsom. 2 vols. 1898; rpr. Cambridge, England, 1968.

Pope, Alexander. *Essay on Man*. In *English Poetry, Vol. I: Chaucer to Gray*, ed. Charles W. Eliot. New York, 1910. Vol. XL of Eliot (ed.), *Harvard Classics*. 50 vols.

Radin, Max. *Handbook of Anglo-American Legal History*. St. Paul, 1936.

———. *Handbook of Roman Law*. St. Paul, 1927.

Rakove, Jack N. *Beginnings of National Politics: An Interpretative History of the Continental Congress*. New York, 1979.

Reid, Thomas. *Essays on the Active Powers of the Human Mind*. Introduction by Baruch A. Brody. 1813; rpr. Cambridge, Mass., 1969.

Reinhold, Meyer. *Classica Americana: The Greek and Roman Heritage in the United States*. Detroit, 1984.

Reventlow, Henning Graf. *Authority of the Bible and the Rise of the Modern World*. Translated by John Bowden. Philadelphia, 1985.

Riley, Patrick. *Will and Political Legitimacy: A Critical Exposition of Social Contract Theory in Hobbes, Locke, Rousseau, Kant, and Hegel*. Cambridge, England, 1982.

Robbins, Caroline. *Eighteenth-Century Commonwealthman: Studies in the Transmission, Development and Circumstance of English Liberal Thought from the Restoration of Charles II until the War with the Thirteen Colonies*. 1959; rpr. New York, 1968.

Rodman, John R., ed. *Political Theory of T. H. Green*. New York, 1964.

Romanell, Patrick. *John Locke and Medicine: A New Key to Locke*. New York, 1984.

Rossiter, Clinton. *Federalist Papers*. New York, 1961.

———. *Seedtime of the Republic*. New York, 1953.

Rush, Benjamin. *A Plan for the Establishment of Schools . . . Thoughts Upon the*

Mode of Education Proper in a Republic. In *American Political Writing During the Founding Era, 1760–1805.* Edited by Charles S. Hyneman and Donald S. Lutz. 2 vols. Indianapolis, 1983.

Sabine, George H. *A History of Political Theory.* 3rd ed. New York, 1961.

Sandoz, Ellis. *Conceived in Liberty: American Individual Rights Today.* North Scituate, Mass., 1978.

———. "H. Berman, *Law and Revolution:* A Review," *Louisiana Law Review,* XLV (1985), 1105–25.

———. "Myth and Society in the Philosophy of Bergson." *Social Research,* XXX (1963), 171–202.

———. *Political Apocalypse: A Study of Dostoevsky's Grand Inquisitor.* Baton Rouge, 1971.

———. *Voegelinian Revolution: A Biographical Introduction.* Baton Rouge, 1981.

———, ed. *Political Sermons of the American Founding Era, 1730–1805.* Indianapolis, 1991.

Sanford, Charles B. *Thomas Jefferson and His Library.* Hamden, Conn., 1977.

Santayana, George. *Some Turns of Thought in Modern Philosophy: Five Essays.* Freeport, N.Y., 1933.

Schutz, John A., and Douglass Adair, eds. *Spur of Fame: Dialogues of John Adams and Benjamin Rush, 1805–1813.* 1966; rpr. San Marino, Calif., 1980.

Schwartz, Bernard, ed. *Bill of Rights: A Documentary History.* 2 vols. New York, 1971.

———. *Great Rights of Mankind: A History of the Bill of Rights.* New York, 1977.

Shalhope, Robert E. "Republicanism and Early American Historiography." *William and Mary Quarterly,* 3rd ser., XXXIX (1982), 334–56.

Smith, Adam. *Theory of Moral Sentiments.* Edited by D. D. Raphael and A. L. Macfie. 1979; rpr. Indianapolis, 1982.

Smylie, James H. "Madison and Witherspoon: Theological Roots of American Political Thought." *Princeton University Library Journal,* XXII (1961), 118–32.

Snell, Bruno. *Discovery of the Mind: The Greek Origins of European Thought.* Translated by T. G. Rosenmeyer. 1953; rpr. New York, 1960.

Solzhenitsyn, Aleksandr I. *First Circle.* Translated by Thomas P. Whitney. New York, 1969.

Spellman, W. M. *John Locke and the Problem of Depravity.* Oxford, England, 1988.

Spinoza, Benedict de. *Writings on Political Philosophy.* Edited by A. G. A. Balz. Translated by R. H. M. Elwes. New York, 1937.

Spragens, Thomas A., Jr. *Irony of Liberal Reason.* Chicago, 1981.

Stanlis, Peter J., ed. *Edmund Burke: Selected Writings and Speeches.* Chicago, 1963.

Stokes, Anson P. *Church and State in the United States.* 3 vols. New York, 1950.

Stone, Julius. *Social Dimensions of Law and Justice.* Stanford, 1966.

Storing, Herbert J., ed. *Essays on the Scientific Study of Politics.* New York, 1962.

Storing, Herbert J., with Murray Dry. *What the Anti-Federalists Were For.* Chicago, 1981.

Stout, Harry S. *New England Soul: Preaching and Religious Culture in Colonial New England.* New York, 1986.

Strauss, Leo. *Natural Right and History.* Chicago, 1953.

———. *Persecution and the Art of Writing.* Glencoe, Ill., 1952.

Sweet, Douglas H. "Church Vitality and the American Revolution: Historiographical Consensus and Thoughts Towards a New Perspective." *Church History*, XLV (1976), 341–57.

Swindler, William F. *Magna Carta: Legend and Legacy*. Indianapolis, 1965.

Syrett, Harold C., and Jacob E. Cooke, eds. *Papers of Alexander Hamilton*. 27 vols. New York, 1961–87.

Talmon, Jacob L. *Origins of Totalitarian Democracy*. New York, 1951.

———. *Political Messianism: The Romantic Phase*. New York, 1960.

Tansill, Charles C., ed. *Documents Illustrative of the Formation of the Union of American States*. 69th Cong., 1st Sess., House Doc. No. 398. Washington, D.C., 1927.

Taylor, Robert J. *Western Massachusetts in the Revolution*. Providence, 1954.

Thomson, Richard. *An Historical Essay on the Magna Charta of King John: To Which Are Added the Great Charter in Latin and English . . .* London, 1829.

Thoreau, Henry David. *Walden and Other Writings*. Edited by Brooks Atkinson. New York, 1937.

Thorne, Samuel E., ed. *Bracton on the Laws and Customs of England*. 4 vols. Cambridge, Mass., 1968.

Thornton, John Wingate, ed. *Pulpit of the American Revolution; or, the Political Sermons of the Period of 1776*. 1860; rpr. New York, 1970.

Tierney, Brian. *Religion, Law, and the Growth of Constitutional Thought, 1150–1650*. Cambridge, England, 1982.

Tocqueville, Alexis de. *Democracy in America*. Edited by Richard D. Heffner. New York, 1956.

———. *Democracy in America*. Edited by J. P. Mayer. Translated by George Lawrence. 2 vols. in 1. Garden City, N.Y., 1969.

———. *Old Regime and the French Revolution*. Translated by Stuart Gilbert. Garden City, N.Y., 1955.

Torrey, Bradford, and Francis H. Allen, eds. *Journal of Henry D. Thoreau*. 14 vols. in 2. 1906; rpr. New York, 1962.

Toynbee, Arnold J. *A Study of History*. 12 vols. Oxford, England, 1934–64.

Trenchard, John, and Thomas Gordon. *Cato's Letters: or, Essays on Liberty, Civil and Religious*. 6th ed. 4 vols. in 2. 1755; rpr. New York, 1971.

Trials of Charles the First, and of Some of the Regicides: With Biographies of Bradshaw, Ireton, Harrison, and Others. [Editor anon.] London, 1832.

Tuck, Richard. *Natural Rights Theories: Their Origin and Development*. Cambridge, England, 1979.

Tully, James. *A Discourse on Property: John Locke and His Adversaries*. Cambridge, England, 1980.

Tuveson, Ernest L. *Redeemer Nation: The Idea of America's Millennial Role*. Chicago, 1968.

van Tyne, C. H. "Influence of the Clergy, and of the Religious and Sectarian Forces, on the American Revolution." *American Historical Review*, XIX (1913/1914), 44–64.

Vane, Sir Henry. *A Healing Question*. In *American Historical Documents*. New York, 1910. Edited by Charles W. Eliot. Vol. XLIII of Eliot (ed.), *Harvard Classics*, 50 vols.

Vico, Giambattista. *New Science*. Edited and translated from 3rd ed. (1744) by T. G. Bergin and M. H. Fisch. Abr. and rev. ed. New York, 1961.

Voegelin, Eric. *Anamnesis: Zur Theorie der Geschichte und Politik.* Munich, 1966. English edition edited and translated by Gerhart Niemeyer. Notre Dame, 1978.

──. *From Enlightenment to Revolution.* Edited by John H. Hallowell. Durham, N.C., 1975.

──. "Industrial Society in Search of Reason." In *World Technology and Human Destiny.* Edited by Raymond Aron. Ann Arbor, Mich., 1963.

──. *New Science of Politics: An Introduction.* Chicago, 1952.

──. *Plato and Aristotle.* Vol. III of Voegelin, *Order and History.* 5 vols. Baton Rouge, 1957.

──. *Science, Politics, and Gnosticism.* Translated by William J. Fitzpatrick. Chicago, 1968.

Walsh, Correa M. *Political Science of John Adams: A Study in the Theory of Mixed Government and the Bicameral System.* New York, 1915.

Weber, Alfred, and Ralph Barton Perry. *History of Philosophy.* Translated by Frank Thilly. Rev. ed. New York, 1925.

Wector, Dixon. *Hero in America: A Chronicle of Hero Worship.* 1942; rpr. Ann Arbor, Mich., 1963.

Weston, Corinne Comstock. "Beginnings of the Classical Theory of the English Constitution." *Proceedings of the American Philosophical Society,* C (1956), 133–44.

──. *English Constitutional Theory and the House of Lords, 1556–1832.* New York, 1965.

Weston, Corinne Comstock, and Janelle R. Greenberg. *Subjects and Sovereigns: The Grand Controversy over Legal Sovereignty in Stuart England.* Cambridge, England, 1981.

White, Stephen D. *Sir Edward Coke and "The Grievances of the Commonwealth, 1621–1628."* Chapel Hill, N.C., 1979.

Whitehead, Alfred North. *Science and the Modern World: Lowell Lectures [of] 1925.* New York, 1967.

Wiener, Philip P., ed. *Leibniz: Selections.* New York, 1951.

Williams, E. Neville. *Eighteenth-Century Constitution, 1688–1815: Documents and Commentary.* Cambridge, England, 1960.

Wills, Garry. *Explaining America: The Federalist.* Harmondsworth, England, 1981.

──. *Inventing America: Jefferson's Declaration of Independence.* New York, 1979.

Wilson, Serjeant George, ed. *Reports of Sir Edward Coke, Knt., in English, In Thirteen Parts Complete.* 7 vols. London, 1776–1777.

Witherspoon, John. *Lectures on Moral Philosophy: An Annotated Edition.* Edited by Jack Scott. Newark, N.J., 1982.

──. *Works of the Reverend John Witherspoon.* [Editor anon.] 4 vols. Philadelphia, 1800–1801.

Wood, Gordon S. *Creation of the American Republic, 1776–1787.* Chapel Hill, N.C., 1969.

Woodbridge, John D., Mark A. Noll, and Nathan O. Hatch. *Gospel in America: Themes in the Story of America's Evangelicals.* Grand Rapids, Mich., 1979.

Yolton, John W. *Locke and the Compass of Human Understanding: A Selective Commentary on the "Essay."* Cambridge, England, 1970.

Zeller, Edward. *Stoics, Epicureans and Sceptics.* Translated by O. J. Reichel. New and rev. ed. New York, 1962.

Index